Risk in Academic Writing

NEW PERSPECTIVES ON LANGUAGE AND EDUCATION
Series Editor: Professor Viv Edwards, *University of Reading, Reading, Great Britain*

Two decades of research and development in language and literacy education have yielded a broad, multidisciplinary focus. Yet education systems face constant economic and technological change, with attendant issues of identity and power, community and culture. This series will feature critical and interpretive, disciplinary and multidisciplinary perspectives on teaching and learning, language and literacy in new times.

Full details of all the books in this series and of all our other publications can be found on http://www.multilingual-matters.com, or by writing to Multilingual Matters, St Nicholas House, 31–34 High Street, Bristol BS1 2AW, UK.

Risk in Academic Writing
Postgraduate Students, Their Teachers and the Making of Knowledge

Edited by
Lucia Thesen and Linda Cooper

MULTILINGUAL MATTERS
Bristol • Buffalo • Toronto

Library of Congress Cataloging in Publication Data
Risk in Academic Writing: Postgraduate Students, their Teachers and the Making of Knowledge/Edited by Lucia Thesen and Linda Cooper.
New Perspectives on Language and Education: 34
Includes bibliographical references and index.
1. Academic writing. 2. English language—Rhetoric. 3. Risk-taking (Psychology)
I. Thesen, Lucia, editor of compilation. II. Cooper, Linda, 1953- editor of compilation.
III. Series: New perspectives on language and education: 34.
PE1408.R5674 2013
808.02–dc23 2013032421

British Library Cataloguing in Publication Data
A catalogue entry for this book is available from the British Library.

ISBN-13: 978-1-78309-105-8 (hbk)
ISBN-13: 978-1-78309-104-1 (pbk)

Multilingual Matters
UK: St Nicholas House, 31–34 High Street, Bristol BS1 2AW, UK.
USA: UTP, 2250 Military Road, Tonawanda, NY 14150, USA.
Canada: UTP, 5201 Dufferin Street, North York, Ontario M3H 5T8, Canada.

Copyright © 2014 Lucia Thesen, Linda Cooper and the authors of individual chapters.

All rights reserved. No part of this work may be reproduced in any form or by any means without permission in writing from the publisher.

The policy of Multilingual Matters/Channel View Publications is to use papers that are natural, renewable and recyclable products, made from wood grown in sustainable forests. In the manufacturing process of our books, and to further support our policy, preference is given to printers that have FSC and PEFC Chain of Custody certification. The FSC and/or PEFC logos will appear on those books where full certification has been granted to the printer concerned.

Typeset by Techset Composition India (P) Ltd., Bangalore and Chennai, India.

Contents

Acknowledgements — vii
Acronyms and Abbreviations — ix
Contributors — xi

Introduction

Risk as Productive: Working with Dilemmas in the Writing of Research — 1
Lucia Thesen

Part 1: Deletion and Agency

1. 'Does My Experience Count?' The Role of Experiential Knowledge in the Research Writing of Postgraduate Adult Learners — 27
Linda Cooper

2. A Lovely Imposition: The Complexity of Writing a Thesis in isiXhosa — 48
Somikazi Deyi

Part 2: Strategies for Hybridity: Writing Together

3. Negotiating Alternative Discourses in Academic Writing and Publishing: Risks with Hybridity — 59
Suresh Canagarajah and Ena Lee

4. Academic Writing and Research at an Afropolitan University: An International Student Perspective — 100
Aditi Hunma and Emmanuel Sibomana

Part 3: Pedagogies that Invite the Edge

5 Rehearsing 'the Postgraduate Condition' in Writers' Circles 131
Clement Mapfumo Chihota and Lucia Thesen

6 Genre: A Pigeonhole or a Pigeon? Case Studies of the Dilemmas Posed by the Writing of Academic Research Proposals 148
Moragh Paxton

7 Of House and Home: Reflections on Knowing and Writing for a 'Southern' Postgraduate Pedagogy 166
Kate Cadman

Part 4: Reading the World in Students' Writing

8 'Error' or Ghost Text? Reading, Ethnopoetics and Knowledge Making 203
Mary Scott

9 'It Was Hardly about Writing': Translations of Experience on Entering Postgraduate Studies 219
Moeain Arend

Part 5: Peripheral Vision: Reflections from North and South

10 Resonances, Resistances and Relations: Reflecting on the Politics of Risk in Academic Knowledge Making 237
Theresa Lillis

11 Both Dead and Alive: Schrödinger's Cat in the Contact Zone 245
Brenda Cooper

Index 252

Acknowledgements

Where did this book begin? One answer is at the kitchen table in the warm winter sun, talking about students in postgraduate writers' circles. Were they likely to take the risk of trying out new forms in their writing? The word 'risk' hung in the air, and we decided to see where we could travel with it.

Many people have helped to make this book possible. First, we thank the Research Office at the University of Cape Town. Brenda Cooper encouraged us to write the initial research proposal for the Knowledge Project and led the workshop that brought all the authors together at Kalk Bay. She has remained interested in the project throughout. Robert Morrell continued with just the right mix of challenge and flexibility.

Shaheeda Jaffer, Robert Prince and Andrew Deacon were members of our lively Postgraduate Literacies research group in the Centre for Higher Education Development, where this project began. Heather Jacklin, Hilary Janks and Ann Johns gave useful comments in the early stages.

Special thanks to Anna Roderick and Tommi Grover at Multilingual Matters. Anna took a risk in accepting this manuscript and has eased our way at every step.

Mary Ralphs was a wise editor, writer's friend and sounding board. Tessa Botha generously read the manuscript with a careful eye.

We are grateful to the Carnegie Foundation for funding our part in the Knowledge Project, and to the Centre for Higher Education Development for supporting our Postgraduate Literacies initiative.

Finally as editors we thank the contributors to this book. Each one of you has turned risk into challenge and possibility. Surely this is a good sign for postgraduate students, their teachers and the making of knowledge.

Acronyms and Abbreviations

AAVE	African American vernacular English
ABET	Adult basic education and training
ANT	Actor network theory
NGO	Non-governmental organisation
RPL	Recognition of prior learning
UCT	University of Cape Town
Wits	University of the Witwatersrand

Contributors

Moeain Arend is a lecturer in the Language Development Unit in the Centre for Higher Education Development at the University of Cape Town. He currently teaches and convenes a first year academic literacy course in the Faculty of Humanities. His main research interests are in academic literacy, workplace literacy and ethnography, and the movement of written texts and literacy practices across institutional boundaries.

Kate Cadman is a consultant senior lecturer at the University of Adelaide in Australia where she specialises in English for academic and specific purposes, and transcultural research education in the humanities and social sciences. Kate has conducted international consultancies on the writing of theses and articles for international publication in many Asian countries, and currently reviews for several international journals including the *Journal of English for Academic Purposes* for which she is an editorial board member. Among her recent publications are a *TESOL Quarterly* article asking, 'TESOL and TESD in remote Aboriginal Australia – the true story?' (2011, with Jill Brown), and a co-edited book titled *Bridging Transcultural Divides: Asian Languages and Cultures in Higher Education* (2012, with Xianlin Song).

Suresh Canagarajah is Edwin Erle Sparks Professor of applied linguistics and English at Pennsylvania State University. He teaches postcolonial theory, composition and World Englishes. His latest publication is *Translingual Practice: Global Englishes and Cosmopolitan Relations* (Routledge, 2013).

Mapfumo Clement Chihota taught applied linguistics at the Zimbabwe Open University before joining the University of Cape Town (UCT) as a PhD student in English language and literature. Between 2003 and 2009, Mapfumo served in the UCT Centre for Higher Education Development as a writing centre consultant and a part-time lecturer on the Postgraduate Writing Project. Mapfumo currently lives with his family in New Zealand, where he works for the Ministry of Social Development. He previously published a reflection on the pedagogic space afforded by Writer Circles (*Journal of Applied Linguistics*, 2007).

Brenda Cooper was for many years the director of the Centre for African Studies and a professor in the English department at the University of Cape Town, where she is now an emeritus professor. In 2009 she moved to Salford, where she is an honorary research associate at the University of Manchester and runs *Burnish*, which organises workshops on academic writing. She has published widely on African fiction in English, postcolonial literary theory and African studies. Brenda is currently writing a cross-genre book that is a mixture of life writing, invention and diasporic African art and literary studies. It is titled *Floating in an Anti-bubble from South Africa to Salford: A Book about Art, Language, Diaspora and Personhood*.

Linda Cooper is associate professor in the Centre for Higher Education Development and teaches adult education at the University of Cape Town. She shares responsibility for widening access to adult learners and for implementing recognition of prior learning (RPL) within the institution. She has been involved over many years in supporting trade union education and is a member of the International Advisory Board of the Researching Work and Learning Conference. She has published on the history and contemporary practice of worker education; the impact of globalisation on workplace learning and knowledge; and on the theorization of different forms of knowledge.

Somikazi Deyi is currently a lecturer in the African Languages Department at the University of Cape Town and course convenor of isiXhosa in the Faculty of Health Sciences. Her love of expressing herself in writing started at an early age with poetry and short stories. Some of her poetry was published in 1993 by Buchu Books through a project known as the Omnibus Series for New Writers, and as an individual anthology of poetry titled *Praising God through Poetry*. She has also published the books, *Phila unikwe ubomi*; *Ndibonga iNkosi yam* (poetry) and *Umama* (collaborative work).

Aditi Hunma lectures at the University of Cape Town on a new foundational writing course called 'Working with texts in the Humanities,' offered by the Humanities Education Development Unit (EDU) for first year students in the extended degrees. Her involvement in the course design and teaching is aligned with her PhD research where she explores performative spaces and methods to nurture the writer identities of international students with English as an Additional Language (EAL). Over the years, she has also tutored on linguistics courses, offered one-on-one writing support at the UCT Writing Centre, taught English in two South African high schools and developed a writing module for international students at UCT. She is currently interested in the affordances of safe and dynamic online spaces to promote students' critical thinking in writing.

Ena Lee is a lecturer in the Faculty of Education at Simon Fraser University in Vancouver, British Columbia, Canada. She teaches EAL (English as an Additional Language) theory and methodology courses at both the undergraduate and graduate level as well as first-year foundational academic literacy courses. Her research interests include EAL teacher education, student and teacher identity and anti-racist education.

Theresa Lillis is professor in English language and applied linguistic at the Open University, UK. Motivated by an interest in the politics of access and participation, her research areas include the academic writing and literacy practices of students and professional scholars and writing across academic and non-academic domains, particularly in the area of social work. Her publications include *Student Writing: Access, Regulation, and Desire* (Routledge, 2001), *Academic Writing in a Global Context* (with Mary Jane Curry, Routledge, 2010) and *The Sociolinguistics of Writing* (Edinburgh University Press 2013).

Moragh Paxton is currently acting head of the Language Development Unit in the Centre for Higher Education at the University of Cape Town. She has nearly 30 years of experience teaching academic literacies at all levels of higher education and in many different disciplines. Her main research area is writing and she has used text-oriented ethnographic approaches to gain insights into the experiences and practices of a very diverse group of students at both undergraduate and postgraduate levels. She currently leads the *Integrated Literacies for Learning* in science research project, which explores a range of academic literacies, including the quantitative and digital.

Mary Scott has taught English literature and educational studies in universities in South and the United Kingdom. She has presented at international conferences in South Africa, the United States and China, and has published a number of peer-reviewed papers on postgraduate student writing, especially that of cross-national, cross-lingual students. She is the founding director of the Centre for Academic and Professional Literacy Studies at the

Institute of Education University of London and runs the Interuniversity Academic Literacies Research Group which has members on all five continents.

Emmanuel Sibomana taught English and French at different high schools in Rwanda, worked as a specialist for French examinations in the Rwanda National Examinations Council and lectured at Kigali Institute of Education (KIE) in the Department of Languages and Linguistics. Currently, he is a PhD candidate in Applied English Language Studies (AELS) at the University of the Witwatersrand (Wits). He is also a sessional lecturer of the following courses: New Literacies for Teachers in the Language in the Department of Literacies and Literatures (Wits School of Education), Communication and Learning Skills and Basic Research Skills at Wits Plus (Centre for Part-Time studies). His research interests are language pedagogy in ESL and EFL contexts and use of a foreign/additional language as a medium of instruction.

Lucia Thesen is a senior lecturer in the Centre for Higher Education Development at the University of Cape Town. Since the 1980s she has been working at the intersection of the politics of academic communicative practices and access for students on the margins of the university. From her current position as postgraduate literacies coordinator she is committed to teaching, debating and interrogating the current forms in which research is communicated in writing in the English language. She is co-editor (with Ermien van Pletzen) of *Academic Literacy and the Languages of Change* (Continuum 2006).

Risk as Productive: Working with Dilemmas in the Writing of Research

Lucia Thesen

Writing in the Contact Zone

The written product – thesis or journal article – has been central to the communication of research since the birth of the early modern university in the 18th century. As fleeting ideas and false starts slowly evolve into settled forms that give material expression to the outcomes of research processes, writing requires us to commit to *this* path, for *now*, and to leave other paths behind. Given the pressure to produce work that will pass through and travel safely on beyond academic gatekeepers, many student and novice researchers experience a sense of loss at the compromises made when developing a written account of their research. In the process of writing, various experiences and modes of expression are revised or erased along the way. In the contemporary higher education landscape, which is characterised by an unprecedented movement of people, texts and capital, this problem of erasures and silences is a deeply political issue. What forms and knowledges are being erased? Why? Who benefits, and who remains silent? The need to understand the dynamics and consequences of deletions and silencings, as well as to explore what is set aside as postgraduate researchers negotiate an unpredictable readership, is what brought the authors of this book together. The contributors approach these issues by means of a new reading of the idea of risk, one that emphasises risk taking as productive and by exploring what this means for the process and product of research writing.

The research project from which this book has grown began as a collaboration in Cape Town, South Africa, and then, as we saw that the writing-related challenges encountered by South African research students are not solely a local concern (albeit that they are amplified here by the legacy of apartheid), the circle widened to include colleagues in the United Kingdom, Australia, the United States and Canada. Clearly, the challenges involved in postgraduate writing are not a specifically 'African' or 'southern' concern; they are an expression of global phenomena related to changes taking place in higher education. The changes in question turn on policies and discourses of increasing participation and widening access to higher education, but are simultaneously constrained by a major shift in the nature of knowledge production in the direction of the 'knowledge economy', which, to quote Usher (2002: 144), 'replaces an epistemological with an economic definition of knowledge'. One of the effects of these changes is the significant increase in mobility for both 'international' students crossing national borders, and 'adult' students, entering university from the workplace (see Boud & Lee, 2009; Enders, 2004).

Mobility has complex effects. One is that the writing competencies students develop as graduates or professionals in countries on the margins of the world system may not translate successfully to new settings in which they may find themselves writing about their research. The pull of the centre also means that greater numbers of new researchers are writing in English, which is frequently neither their 'home' language nor their primary language of learning (Lillis & Curry, 2010). Research writing practices are not only skewed towards English – by no means a neutral language – but also realised in what Cadman (2003) calls 'divine discourse'. That is, the constraints on what counts as a relevant area of study, the criteria by which a thesis is assessed, and the fact that the styles that are conventional in the 'global university' are embedded in an intellectual worldview that 'does not recognise, and therefore cannot know, the limitations of its own taken for granted, almost sacred, understandings of what constitutes "knowledge" and its expression in the English language' (Cadman, 2003: 1).

There is a growing concern that this 'internationalisation' is reinforcing the historical dominance of 'northern' Anglophone knowledge production, rather than opening out new conversations and perspectives in a meaningful way (Connell, 2007; Keim, 2008). One expression of this dominance is the recycling of theory from the metropole. Theory, argues Connell, is typically 'made' in the global north, and applied or generalised to the south (2007), capturing the south as an ethnographic other.

As an alternative to starkly drawn north/south or centre–periphery geographical and conceptual divides, the metaphor of a contact zone permeates this study. For Mary Louise Pratt, who first coined the term, the contact zone refers to 'social spaces in which cultures meet, clash and grapple with each other, often in contexts of highly asymmetrical relations of power, such as colonialism, slavery and their aftermaths' (Pratt, 1999: 2). Pratt also uses the term as an imaginary – an 'attempt to invoke the spatial and temporal co-presence of subjects previously separated by geographic and historical disjuncture, and whose trajectories now intersect' (Pratt, 1992: 7). The contact zone offers a way of reading power as *relational* rather than binary. In our project, the concept offered a productive canvas for our exploration of the geographies of writing. The social spaces of the contact zone range from the writers' circles described later in this book to wider circles of geopolitical contact, including the relationships that have shaped the making of this book. It is no longer possible to imagine spaces in which the contact zone is an option, a matter of choice: rather, the contact zone is inevitable. This is felt particularly strongly among those writing and researching in the global south. The contact zone is the crucible in which we produce knowledge through writing. In contested spaces we need to understand the agency that informs the decisions that writers and gatekeepers make about what will go into texts, and what styles and languages are chosen. We can no longer ignore the many silences, stammers, whispers, deletions, or the bland pro-forma templates that offer the possibility of prefabricated meaning. Thus, in these contested spaces, risk is also not an optional, but rather an inevitable part of the condition of knowledge making, as writers and gatekeepers weigh up what can or cannot be said.

The remainder of this chapter has two sections. In the first, different approaches to writing pedagogy are briefly outlined, contrasting generic 'how to' guides with critical approaches to research writing. The concept of 'voice' is chosen as a way of tracking writer agency across spaces. The notion of voice also draws attention to the silences and erasures that occur if writers fail to make sense to their intended audiences. The section ends with the idea of writing one's way through what we call the 'postgraduate condition' – a sustained predicament over time – and the ways in which it leads writers to grapple with 'risky' decisions about both content and form. Having identified risk as an important element in the writing of research, a path is traced in the second section through the influential literature on risk in mainstream social theory. This scholarship tends to generalise across global spaces and feeds into a climate of 'risk management'. Arguing for an alternative and a more productive approach to risk and risk taking, our notion of risk is located in selected postcolonial writing that tends to foreground paradox rather than superficial coherence. The chapter ends with a return to risk and writing, and then introduces the chapters that follow, all of which are concerned with risk 'from below'.

Alternatives to the Template: Critical Approaches to the Writing of Research

One of the effects of increased mobility in higher education is the proliferation of 'how-to' books, such as *'Writing Your PhD Dissertation in Fifteen Minutes a Day'* or *Writing Your PhD: A Survivor's Guide*. These guides offer generic advice and a set process and structure for uncertain writers, and narrow the possibilities for what may be said, and in what way. Kamler and Thomson's (2006) analysis shows how these DIY texts over-generalise, over-simplify and, at the same time, deskill students by papering over real issues of power and knowledge, casting students as novices in need of rescue by the voice of experience. We share their view that this seemingly benign technical approach to writing further legitimises 'His Master's Voice'; in other words, these DIY guides implicitly and explicitly perpetuate a restricted and deficit model of student competence and language use. The guides tend to be instrumental in orientation, and tend to focus on how students can imitate *existing* conventions based on massively problematic assumptions about student homogeneity and the stability of disciplines.

In contrast to these templates, genre theory provides an example of a more generative resource for postgraduate writers and their teachers. Swales (2004) and Hyland (2006), among others, offer descriptions of the prevailing research genres in historical and disciplinary context. Other scholars are more concerned with developing pedagogies for teaching research writing. Here, a rich vein of work has developed in Australia (see Aitchison & Lee, 2006; Aitchison *et al.*, 2010; Kamler & Thomson, 2006). Kamler and Thomson (2006), for instance, outline the key genres relevant to research writing, and point out that the writing of research is related to the complex process of developing a research identity. They offer tools for both supervisors and students that highlight issues of power in postgraduate pedagogy. Increasingly, accounts of the dilemmas and vicissitudes of postgraduate writing and scholarly publication are welcomed (Bartlett & Mercer, 2000; Casanave & Li, 2008; Dixon & Janks, 2010). Of particular interest to us are writers who ask questions about the restrictive and formulaic styles available within academic writing, and about the consequences of these styles for how and what we know (Cadman, 2005; Schroeder *et al.*, 2002; Starfield & Ravelli, 2006).

As is probably clear to readers by now, this collection is broadly aligned to work that is interested in the critical and framed within the wider geopolitics of writing. The editors aim to engage in a global conversation, while being firmly located in the south. We are deeply interested in the effects of researcher mobility and in how research texts travel across physical and conceptual divides. Lillis and Curry's (2010) account of how the dominance of English is shaping academic publishing is exemplary here. They theorise the global movement of texts using a frame of academic *literacies* (Lillis & Scott, 2007). They use the plural form to denote an interest in locating reading and writing and other valued textual practices within wider contexts and ideologically inscribed contestations, rather than seeing writing as simply a matter of skill – as if skills are neutral competencies that are transferable across contexts. Academic texts from the margins seldom travel well, but the question of what constitutes the margins where, when and for whom, is perhaps more open than we have imagined. Arguments as diverse as those put forward by Comaroff and Comaroff (2012) in their provocatively titled, *Theory From the South: Or, How Euro-America is Evolving Towards Africa*, which reverses the narrative of a developing 'south' that is always struggling to catch up but can never do so, and The Royal Society's (2011) report on shifts in global patterns of publishing which shows that Sao Paulo in Brazil publishes more than Cambridge in the United Kingdom, represent seismic shifts in the higher education sector. We urgently need studies and theories that will help explore and explain these processes of translation across contexts. This is where the notion of 'voice' comes into play.

Between Voice and Silence

While we acknowledge the importance of the structural and material barriers to thesis completion and publication (see Canagarajah, 2002 for a powerful analysis of the global dynamics of academic publishing), our interest is in writer agency, the individual act of putting words on paper. This can be thought of as 'voice':[1] that is, 'the capacity for semiotic mobility' which is 'intrinsically creative, [but] is also oriented towards one or several centering institutions' in which meanings are organised and ranked through gatekeeping practices (Blommaert, 2005: 77). Through the practices of these centring institutions, real or imagined reductions of difference are created through norms, conventions and expectations, often resulting in difficult decisions for writers, as they grapple with questions such as: does this count as evidence; should I include it; how can I express it, does it sound scholarly enough, do I sound too much like the experts, will I be misunderstood? Gatekeepers and experts who make up the centring institutions experience similar dilemmas, often wondering if work they vet is good/ scholarly/ original enough.

Our understanding of voice can be taken back to Bakhtin's (1981) notion of language as heteroglossic, that is, always a site of struggle that forges a link between the individual and the social that exists at the point of articulation on the edge between the two. Individual voice, like language, is never neutral; it is always in tension between pulls towards convention (centripetal forces) and pushes away from the centre and towards more hybrid, experimental and open forms (centrifugal forces). Meanwhile, the pro forma 'how-to' guides and manuals referred to earlier present a smooth surface, a sort of paint-by-numbers approach that flattens and denies these struggles over meaning.

With writing, we are engaged in inscription, that is, in making marks that need to be able to cross various spaces without losing too much of their meaning. When voices do not carry as hoped, we must ask why. One response is to look at the completed product – the proposal, thesis or article that is formally submitted for assessment or peer critique, and is assessed as wanting in certain key aspects. Another approach is to ask what happened along the way. Did the meanings that the writer had in mind see the light of day, or were they filtered out during the writing process, either because the writer did not want to risk exposing an unusual style (perhaps more colloquial, or blended) or unusual subject matter (references to experience, to research designs that went wrong)? Or did the writer choose to hold back what might have been said and instead take the path of least resistance?

An important feature of this book is that we see voice as a two-sided phenomenon, inevitably involving both production and reception. We argue, therefore, that voice cannot be located only in a text. We are interested in voice, erasure and silence at the point of production *as well* as at the point of reception, where the judgements of centring institutions enter the picture. So we focus on the agency, dilemmas and risk taking of both writer and reader. All of the contributors to this volume have had experience of thesis writing; some are experienced gatekeepers who, as journal editors, reviewers and supervisors, routinely act as critical readers.

This brief exploration of critical approaches to writing, via the concept of voice, shows that voice is no simple matter. It cannot be read off the surface of a completed text. The next section looks at tensions and paradoxes inherent in postgraduate research writing, and how these bring risk to the forefront.

Writing Our Way through 'The Postgraduate Condition': Surfacing Risk

Several of the Cape Town-based contributors to the book have been involved in writers' circles, where we sought to create spaces in which postgraduate students could openly grapple with their research writing.

Many of the students who attended these circles had made geographical, professional, disciplinary or linguistic crossings. The stakes were high as they weighed up what they could or could not say and what their affiliations were to prior histories and future audiences. This engagement foregrounded the contradictions that permeate writing in the contact zone and stimulated our interest in the question of risk.

We named the state of being a research student 'the postgraduate condition' – a predicament, a pervasive state in which one lives with contradictions over time (see Chihota, 2007). Postgraduate writers are at once original yet scholarly; makers of new knowledge yet slaves to the old; anglicised yet not English; creative yet held by generic conventions; independent yet in need of supervision; assertive yet humble; at home as experienced writers yet estranged. This predicament over time has strong emotional content. In Frow's bleak words:

> The ordeal of [PhD] candidature is a *mad* process in its assignment of a structural role to insecurity. It challenges the candidate's sense of worth, provoking a trauma of loss as one of its central knowledge-producing mechanisms, one which is often cruelly prolonged or repeated. (quoted in Bartlett & Mercer, 2000: 197, emphasis in original)

While Bartlett and Mercer cite Frow's work as one example of the negative metaphors that prevail in postgraduate pedagogy, and attempt to substitute these with more positive ones, stories about research supervision and its written product always play into larger narratives of the contact zone. In response, writers' circles offer complementary and multidisciplinary spaces in which students can rehearse their postgraduate identities, and work out their attachment to various ideas before presenting these to more threatening audiences upstream – supervisors, journal editors, peers in their disciplines and so on. What we experienced is best described as a weighing up of risk against possible failure and censure. What is more, the danger of failure was not perceived to be located simply in the supervisory relationship. It was present also in exposing one's work to wider audiences (past, present and future), and in a pervasive uncertainty about whether one was 'in, out or colonized' as James Gee (1990) sharply summarises the literacy dilemmas for 'non-mainstream' students.

However, it is not good enough simply to approach the term risk intuitively: a key insight from social theory perspectives on risk is that it is as much about socially shaped meaning and perception as it is about external reality. The terms 'risk' and 'risky' are increasingly common in contemporary everyday and specialist discourse (Lupton, 1999). For example, a special issue of the journal *Critical Approaches to Discourse Analysis across Disciplines* is devoted to risk, using corpus linguistics to show how 'the risk semantic' has been on the rise across disciplines from medicine to media studies, as well as in public discourse since the Second World War (Zinn, 2010). A second reason why we cannot use the term risk intuitively is that there is a widespread scepticism about the audit culture which pervades contemporary universities, particularly in the United Kingdom and Australia, in which the assessment and management of risk plays an important part. This climate of risk management is uneven. In postcolonial settings, risk is experienced very directly as a pressure on peoples' lives – as 'living politics' (Chance, quoted in Comaroff & Comaroff, 2012) as people search for new forms of social action to access housing, schooling, health care and justice. It is clear that perceptions of risk are subject to meanings imposed by various layers of context, some of which are explored below. But before we look at risk as productive, we need to look at how it is defined from the centre, and this requires an excursion beyond writing into social theory.

Risk as Reductive: A View from the Centre

To understand contemporary meanings of risk, as defined from the centre, we need to see how the term has changed its meaning over time. The current obsession with risk is attributed to the modernist 'myth of calculability' (Reddy, quoted in Lupton, 1999: 7). Commentators link early uses of the word risk to mid-16th-century European maritime endeavours. Early meanings signified the possibility of external natural disaster or an 'act of God' beyond human control. Bernstein (1998: 1) for example sees the mastery of risk as the 'revolutionary idea that defines the boundary between modern times and the past', arguing that the emergence of modernity offered the possibility of taming uncertainty, fate and chaos – the Enlightenment's emphasis on objective, rational scientific knowledge was envisaged as harnessing people and institutions for progress and social order.

The end of the 20th century saw a number of influential publications (written initially without reference to one another) that placed a different meaning of risk at the centre of western experience. The key voices in this millennial angst were sociologists Giddens (1991), Beck (1992), Luhmann (1991) and anthropologist Douglas (1992). Beck and Giddens argue that late modern ways of being in the world (in what both have called 'the risk society') are characterised by a 'colonisation of the future'. They argue that the 'notion of risk becomes central in a society which is taking leave of the past, of traditional ways of doing things, and which is opening itself up to a problematic future' (Giddens, 1991: 111). Other features of this shift include the erosion of faith in the promise of science, and that risks have become more globalised, thus downplaying differences between countries, regions and even continents. Douglas, while identifying similar features, is more interested in risk as a western strategy for dealing with danger and otherness, and in why some dangers and not others, are identified as risks. With the exception of Douglas, these texts give the impression that risk is a western invention, and an engine of modernity.

A second wave of writing has emerged which sees risk as a critical concept in the social sciences.[2] These texts are also in a position to look back and identify various theoretical strands in the literature on risk. Lupton (1999: 17–35) sees a continuum of epistemological approaches to risk in the social sciences ranging from realist through weak constructionist to strong constructionist positions.

Briefly, the realist position holds that risk points to existing threats and dangers that are distorted by social interpretive frames. This 'techno-scientific' approach, which dominates disciplines such as engineering, psychology, statistics, epidemiology and economics, focuses on the relationship between science, technology and industry and its impact on the public, and often focuses on health and environmental hazards. However, as Lupton points out, it does not ask 'how risks are constructed as social facts' (Lupton, 1999: 18), yet lay people are often regarded as responding to risk 'unscientifically':

> Warm-blooded, passionate, inherently social beings though we think we are, humans are presented in this context as hedonic calculators calmly seeking to pursue private interests. We are said to be risk-aversive, but, alas, so inefficient in handling information that we are unintentional risk-takers; basically we are fools. (Douglas, quoted in Lupton, 1999: 22)

The weak constructionist position holds that objective threats are inevitably mediated by socio-cultural processes. This view includes a range of arguments – from the 'risk society' perspective of Giddens (1991) and Beck (1992), to Douglas's (1992) cultural/symbolic perspective – which ask how risk operates to establish boundaries between self and other.

The strong constructionist position, with its interest in governmentality, draws on Foucault's work. Here there are no risks in themselves; all are produced in and through historically, socially and politically contingent ways of seeing (discourse). Scholars in this grouping, with the exception of Caplan (2000), tend to endorse the work of the weak constructionists that was published in the early 1990s.

Caplan's *Risk Revisited* invites contributors to engage critically with the work of Giddens, Beck and Douglas. Caplan notes that while risk operates mainly as a hegemonic tool to discipline and regulate, it also involves agency at all levels – from personal relationships through to manoeuvring among layers of discourse. She argues strongly for research that can surface this agency (via the use of ethnographic tools that can engage with the specificity of contextual meanings), and she is interested in difference and inequality, rather than universality.[3]

One of the contributions to Caplan's collection, Vera-Sanso's analysis of gender and risk-talk in India, is worth singling out. Vera-Sanso sees risk-talk as a way of reading the moral and economic climate of particular settings. She strongly critiques Beck's eurocentric generalisations that concerns with health and environmental risk will not be experienced in the same way in the 'third world' because countries in this region can still be characterised as 'scarcity societies'. In her view, Beck perpetuates the stereotype that poor people are too involved with 'obvious material need, the "dictatorship of scarcity" rules the thoughts and actions' of people (Beck, 1992 quoted in Vera-Sanso, 2000: 109). Vera-Sanso sees these generalisations as both inadequate and offensive. She argues that Beck's theoretical concern with risk acts as a proxy for loss of power: 'technological risk becomes the stand-in for distant, unaccountable, often unidentifiable, shifting "centres" of power' (Vera-Sanso, 2000: 112). In her study of risk-talk related to women and health in low-income settlements in Chennai, she shows how risk is always political, and how women control risk-talk to enlarge their own spheres of influence.

Similar studies of risk-awareness, and its relationship to agency among young researchers (as well as among ourselves as teachers), can illuminate hidden dimensions of decision making, feeling and morality in relation to writing. Casanave's (2010) analysis of the experience of risk among Japanese writers in the United States shows a very different story to the stereotype of the uncritical Asian student who will readily assimilate to western Anglophone conventions.

All the texts on risk discussed above refer almost exclusively to Anglophone traditions. They are embedded in largely shared views of the ways in which what they unproblematically call post-traditional, predominantly secular societies work. However, three ideas can be taken forward from this literature.

- First, the notion of risk is always socio-culturally situated, whether one sees it as socially produced or socially mediated. As predicted by Luhmann (2002) and Douglas (1992), corpus linguistics shows that the term risk is supplanting the word danger in the English-speaking press in the United States and the United Kingdom (Zinn, 2010). It would be interesting to see whether similar trends are at work in the global south, in India and South Africa, for example.[4]

- Second, the gap between those who define risk just to manage people within institutions and those who move through institutions in less expert positions seems to be growing. Those who define risk tend to use numbers; those who undergo it (by definition) have little access to forms of capital, both economic and cultural. Those who define are entrenched; those who are defined are in movement, migrants, out of step.
- Third, risk often implies its other – a danger or hazard that lurks on the other side of where one is now, and it brings together the past and the future in a decision that needs to be taken in the present. As Luhmann notes, risk always 'protects an always precarious normality' (Luhmann, 2002: xxvii), and is thus interesting as a symbolic industry (Beck, 1992) in that 'demands are created by varying the definition of risk' (Beck, 1992: 56).

The next section reflects on the concept of risk within the domain of higher education in an attempt to move the implications of the above analysis closer to the writing of research.

Risk in Higher Education

Erica McWilliam draws on the social theory traditions above to explore how what she calls the 'cold' notion of risk increasingly permeates doctoral education in the 'First World'. This 'cold' notion is reductive, an expression of a climate of risk management, where, in the spirit of the modernist myth of calculability, universities seek to manage the dangers that may befall them in building their reputations. In a perceptive piece on doctoral education in 'risky times', she notes how the idea of risk contributes to the fraught dimensions of what we earlier called the postgraduate condition, arguing that risk is 'the condition in which we perform doctoral education, rather than the problem to be solved' (McWilliam, 2009: 198). McWilliam is interested in how doctoral studies play a vital role in how a university 'performs its achievements', that is, how it becomes visible and calculable to itself. She notes that, in late modernity, 'All social organizations, including universities, are now risk organizations. This is because all organizations need rational systems for calculating and managing threats to viability and reputation in whatever form they come' (McWilliam, 2009: 192). She argues that risk is further complicated in that the prevailing cold climate of risk with its negative logic of risk management – of 'what can go wrong and what systems are needed to guard against such possibilities' (McWilliam, 2009: 192) – is given a *positive* spin through being yoked to a aspirational logic of performance, with its elusive 'goods' of quality and excellence. This creates a contradiction that adds another dimension to the postgraduate condition.

We are interested in setting a 'warm' and productive notion of risk alongside this cold meaning. In its cold sense, risk plays a strong role in defining what is acceptable in the writing of research. The second meaning – which we hope to retrieve and describe in this book – is concerned with the experiential domain, the lived world of researchers weighing up what they will or will not say as they commit to writing. These represent two different but related responses to flux, uncertainty and volatility. The first attempts to manage, calibrate and fix risk; the second is interested in emergent meaning, and seeks instead to open up possibilities and trace meanings, both those realised and those that are lost.

Two aspects of research writing that receive much attention within universities (as well as in the media), and are possibly becoming 'risk objects', are plagiarism and ethics approval. Both can be read as symptoms of how an awareness of risk serves the forensic needs of universities in the context of a globalising higher education sector.

While an acknowledgement of one's sources lies at the heart of the research endeavour, it is also calculable, and thus lends itself perfectly to an audit culture. Promotion and research funding are increasingly tied directly to citation counts. And an impressive body of research shows just how citation practices lend themselves to gatekeeping in the contact zone (Angelil-Carter, 2000; Pennycook, 1996). In other words, as social movement escalates in higher education, so citations are increasingly caught up in policing the boundaries.

Similarly, the area of ethics is being drawn into risk management (see Rwomire & Nyamnjoh, 2006 on research ethics in Africa). In our view, ethics can be seen as a sensitive discursive and moral barometer, and its management as a risk object is likely to have consequences for that complex gatekeeping genre, the research proposal. The quasi-legal discourse of ethics-approval processes has the potential to restrict the exploratory functions of research proposals, and, in turn, have potentially limiting consequences for knowledge-making.

The 'At-Risk' Student

A brief look at the notion of the 'at-risk student' tells us much about how the term risk operates discursively in universities. The term 'at-risk student' is a recent arrival and can be seen as an index of changes in higher education that are broadly referred to as 'widening access'. In South Africa, the term first appeared after higher education was opened up to historically excluded students in the mid-1980s. From the perspective of historically 'white', English-speaking universities, the student who was seen as being at risk was typically 'black', working class, rural and spoke English as an additional language. In the United Kingdom such a student may well have been 'mature', female, studying at a distance, and/or dyslexic. What of the 'international' student? Do the fees they contribute offset the risk?

This suggests several features of how the term 'at-risk' functions discursively:

- It always implies its other against some norm, thus again demonstrating the pull of the centre.
- It always needs to be located historically and geographically.
- It is institutions that are most invested in conferring this label.
- Identifying someone as being 'at-risk' implies the need for a solution, for gathering arguments and resources to address a problem.

Of course, individuals may benefit from the policies that create space for at-risk students. But given the relational effects of power, how people actually experience these openings is contingent on many other factors. Several of the chapters in this collection explore the dilemmas and misrecognition of students who benefitted from policy spaces but experienced a marked erasure of voice during the writing process.

Risk as Productive: Working with Paradox

As mentioned earlier, the notion of risk as reductive cannot do justice to the dilemmas and contradictions that we have named 'the postgraduate condition'. And, anyway, as editors, our location in the south means that we experience risk differently because of a range of historical and social shifts.

Peripheral vision

The next section brings back into focus the dilemmas that attend writing in the contact zone. This involves an exploration of some arguments and concepts from traditions such as African literature and postcolonial theory, which developed in response to slavery, colonialism and apartheid. These negative histories load the meaning of Africa with a burden that aligns well with the pessimistic discourse around the postgraduate experience – the narratives of loss and the 'structural role' of insecurity that Frow refers to – as well as with the dilemmas of the postgraduate condition. This negativity needs to be countered with a more assertive, agency-focused approach, which may reveal the paradoxes more clearly.

Several writers have worked across languages and 'worlds' with a global vision that is acutely conscious of the old in the new, of the geopolitics of research and of how it is written and received. Interviews with two writers – Connell (2009) on the development of a 'peripheral vision', and Mbembe on his experience of the dilemmas in writing about Africa (Mbembe & Hofmeyr, 2008) – are instructive here. The two interviews illuminate what Bowker calls the 'trace' archive (Bowker, 2006, 2010), which is inextricably tied to, and yet often hidden by, the prevailing 'jussive' archive that shapes what we can or cannot say. The trace archive is sequential, grounded and embodied, rather than generalisable, and offers an often-untapped resource for exploring potential meaning. The interviews enable a dialogic form where fragments of the lived world of the writer in motion may be glimpsed, and express how Connell and Mbembe have honed theory in their own crossings and attempts to make sense.

Connell speaks of the influences on her development of 'peripheral visions' that originate in Australia, but can look in multiple directions, and work with contradictions and dilemmas, recognising that globalisation has a complex history that has grown out of bitter struggle over a long period. These peripheral visions provide openings for thinking about new theoretical syntheses and applications that have affinity with the production of voices that will travel. For Connell, it is not the theories themselves that are the problem, but how they are put to use. Peripheral vision suggests, too, that the more one looks at individuals' struggles with writing, the more one is forced to look beyond, wider and deeper.

Achille Mbembe addresses the challenges involved in writing from and about Africa. As a Camerounian who has studied and taught in the United States, and currently writes from South Africa, he too has had to use theory in a way that is refracted through a constantly shifting relocation. Much of the interview focuses on his experience of writing his book, *On the Postcolony* (2001). At about the same time that Giddens, Beck and Douglas were writing about risk in the north, Mbembe was grappling with the challenges of writing from and about Africa in ways that were not predetermined by what he calls 'the dogmas of developmentalism' (Mbembe & Hofmeyr, 2008: 249), that is, the imperial discourse, which renders the other incapable of agency, or the postcolonial refusal and inability to acknowledge a position outside of an insistence on difference and rejection.

Mbembe's interviewer, Isabel Hofmeyr, highlights the conclusion to Mbembe's book, in which he explores the difficulties of writing about Africa in a new way when 'our academic senses are so numbed by the existing formulaic discourses'. Mbembe proposes using a method that favours 'the glimpse', 'truths that flicker like fireflies' in 'a language that allows its pulse to be felt' through exploring the deconstituting force of language. He explains that this way of writing is 'intimately linked to a manner of reading, notably the reading of everyday life, that privileged site where the subject experiences her or his own history as present tense' (Mbembe & Hofmeyr, 2008: 254).

For Mbembe, as for writers such as VY Mudimbe (1994) and Olakunle George (2003), who used a notion of 'agency in motion' in African literary criticism, agency lies in being able to see, live with and work through a paradox. It is an ability to recognise that one can articulate difference that separates the west from what is African, but at the same time see that the tools we use are essentially borrowed from the very source of this difference. The agency lies less in the theory than in the awareness that one is working through an epistemological paradox.

Writing, Risk and Voice

Our concept of risk is that it is an analytical space for bringing into focus the tilting point between self and other, where the other refers to ideas, beliefs, places, relationships, audiences and forms. This tilting point is realised in writing through voice, or the erasure of voice. Risk lies on the cusp, unstable and volatile, between the production and reception of the written word.

This notion of risk is rooted in Bakhtinian understandings of the utterance as dialogic, always oriented towards competing heteroglot others. The act of writing involves decisions about which representations of the research world will prevail, which meanings will be invested, and find semiotic form capable of carrying meanings across contexts.

We are equally interested in what meanings are deleted, suppressed, crossed out – the meanings that do not see the light of day, that are shed along the way. Decisions about what will or will not be included will always be emotionally invested and cannot just be read off the surface of texts, but call for close attention to the grain of meanings with which writers invest their texts. Risk is about process; it is relational, seeking connections between what is brought along and what is achieved or realised; it is ontologically rich, inevitably indexing the writer's subjectivity and 'interest' (Kress, 2001: 72).

Thus, risk always points in (at least) two directions, both back to the past and forward to potential audiences and readers. It acknowledges dilemmas; and more than this, it actively seeks them out, interested in how dilemmas are lived in the writing of research.

The Chapters: Exploring Risk 'from Below'

Having made a case for seeing risk as productive in relation to the writing of research, we deliberately refrained from choosing a particular theoretical frame through which to view risk in this book, even though all the contributors perceive risk in broadly constructionist rather than 'technoscientific' terms. Instead, we invited the contributors to inflect the word risk, using the colours of their own situations and approaches to writing and knowing. Nevertheless, the theoretical choice we made was to explore how the notion of risk as productive – as a tilting point – could work across the contact zone, enabling us to find points of connection between our work.

When the authors met for the first time in Kalk Bay, Cape Town in 2010 the notion of risk had not yet fully come into focus. At that point we were working with a number of concepts including the postgraduate condition, voice and risk. As we shared our thoughts, risk began to move to the centre of our thinking. The other concepts are still present but risk became the organising construct. Whether experientially, metaphorically or theoretically, all of the contributors have embraced its central affordance, that is, they have brought into view the rough edges or tilting points that tend to be submerged in a research process, and which become invisible in the smooth surface of an end product.

In keeping with the theme, risk surfaced in all of our writing processes making us pause, reflect and weigh up as we lived through the tilting points that are described in the chapters. The focus on risk took writers into new territory and processes, which for most of us, raised unanticipated ethical and philosophical dilemmas. Introducing the risk lens to a project at times destabilised what had earlier seemed like relatively 'safe' work. Thus, the chapters give weight to the argument put forward in this introduction, and reveal how the contributors have engaged with the risks and tensions in situations they have identified.

The chapters have been grouped into five themes, as outlined below. Since we are all concerned with the postcolonial, we have deliberately mixed 'northern' and 'southern' voices. Similarly we have interspersed contributions from students and teachers, and some chapters were jointly written.

Part 1: Deletion and Agency

The first two chapters deal with the question of loss and are written retrospectively, to explore dimensions of experience. Linda Cooper's 'Does My Experience Count?' The Role of Experiential Knowledge in the Research Writing of Postgraduate Adult Learners,' comes from the observation that many of the adult educators and community development professionals she has taught arrive with a strong sense that *they have something they want to say* rather than (or in addition to) having pressing questions to which they are seeking answers. She revisits her supervision of these adult learners, and the ways in which they set aside experiential knowledge in the process of completing a thesis. She frames her analysis in a critique of both Experiential Learning theory and dualist notions of the need to keep academic knowledge separate from everyday knowledge. Tracking successive drafts of a thesis by one of her students, the chapter celebrates his achievements while naming losses experienced along the way.

Somikazi Deyi's 'A Lovely Imposition: The Complexity of Writing a Thesis in isiXhosa' reflects on her experience of writing her master's thesis on mathematics education in isiXhosa, an indigenous Nguni language of southern Africa. Deyi confronts the contradictions in multilingual language policy and practice in postcolonial settings as she describes the risks involved in her choice to write in isiXhosa. She describes how difficulties with supervision and examination were amplified, but also embraces her delight in the opportunity this gave her to validate her 'rich and creamy' home language as a language of scientific expression. The form of this chapter is innovative in that Somi is in conversation with Linda Cooper as they enact Bowker's (2010) 'dual archive' of both technological, official 'jussive' discourse of the academic thesis (here rendered from the isiXhosa thesis into English) with a 'trace' discourse that surfaces the experiential, experimental, resistant, sometimes playful 'what if?' possibilities of engaging in this 'lovely imposition'.

Issues of loss and deletion have a particular resonance in South Africa. As shown in Cooper's chapter, many adult learners were denied access to education under apartheid, and their contributions were shaped by their oppositional politics – expressed through trade unions, civic movements and non-governmental organisations. For those voices now to be denied in their writing feels like a double violence. Deyi's chapter shows that writing a thesis in isiXhosa is still a highly political statement given the way indigenous languages have been caught up alongside European languages through colonialism and apartheid. Interestingly both Cooper and Deyi's explorations of loss yield unexpected forms of agency. While Deyi's decision to write in isiXhosa was to some extent imposed, she also embraced the opportunity to take her language into new scientific domains. Similarly, the main informant in Cooper's research explains how one path might have seemed to be blocked, but another opened up. And in the process of conducting her research, Cooper, too, found ways of surfacing hidden knowledge forms within the supervision process.

Part 2: Strategies for Hybridity: Writing Together

In contrast to the first two chapters which revisit moments of loss, the next two chapters explore a different strategy to express voice(s) in difficult processes. Both chapters are written dialogically, where two authors write together but from different positionalities in order to find similarities and differences in writing-related experience.

Suresh Canagarajah and Ena Lee's 'Negotiating Alternative Discourses in Academic Writing and Publishing: Risks with Hybridity' is an account of an unsuccessful mentorship related to publishing a journal article. The chapter explores the dilemmas that confront authors and gatekeepers when they aim to broaden academic conventions and publish new forms of research and writing in scholarly journals. Although there is a general readiness to accommodate broader identities and hybrid discourses in academic publishing, the terms of negotiation, and the extent of the compromises that are seen as acceptable, remain unclear. Through their correspondence, drafts of articles, reviewer comments and subsequent interviews, the authors reconstruct their negotiation process, and illuminate how the dominant discourses of the profession and the journal exerted a passive pressure on the editor and the referees to request the author to move towards a hybrid text that meshed the academic and the personal. But as an emerging scholar, who was new to publishing, Lee experienced these requests as an imposition on her preferred voice and objectives. This chapter also makes a strong theoretical contribution as it engages the notion of risk to challenge the pervasive yet vague use of the concept hybridity in the literature on writing.

Aditi Hunma and Emmanuel Sibomana are doctoral students from Mauritius and Rwanda, respectively, who are studying in South Africa. In their chapter, 'Academic Writing and Research at an Afropolitan University: An International Student Perspective' they are in conversation about how their research relates to the idea of an 'Afropolitan' university – a term adopted by the university where Hunma is studying. The two authors explore their respective writing-related risk moments, as well as those experienced by the students involved in their research projects. The two authors provide another perspective on 'internationalisation', exploring what it means to be at 'the centre of the periphery' as international students at South African universities. They raise important issues such as how international students are deemed to be 'uncritical' in their approach to academic discourse, and how subcultures form around national identity. In exploring the process of writing together, and bringing the lens of risk into their thinking, the contributors to this section open up new theoretical insights.

Part 3: Pedagogies that Invite the Edge

The authors of the next three chapters are all interested in pedagogy and risk taking. They focus on dilemmas faced by teachers of writing who work outside of established disciplines. While they are often expected to make the conventions of academic writing explicit, they show how difficult this is, and ask fundamental questions about the value of uncritically inducting postgraduate students into valued western norms of scientific writing in English.

First is Mapfumo Clement Chihota and Lucia Thesen's 'Rehearsing "the Postgraduate Condition" in Writers' Circles.' In this chapter, the authors describe their own experiences of facilitating writers' circles. These circles are an emerging peer-based pedagogy, mainly accessed by students on the margins of the university, which aim to complement the supervisory relationship and provide support for students in various high-stakes situations. Using the concept of 'the postgraduate condition' as a way of encapsulating the postgraduate experience in postcolonial settings, Chihota and Thesen describe some of the tensions and dilemmas at the heart of facilitating these multidisciplinary groups. By conceiving of writers' circles as rehearsal spaces, the authors draw on performative approaches to writing to illuminate the pedagogy used in these circles, and their relationship to postgraduate practices.

Next, Moragh Paxton's chapter looks at the complex gatekeeping genre of the research proposal. 'Genre: A Pigeonhole or a Pigeon? Case Studies of the Dilemmas Posed by the Writing of Academic Research Proposals' focuses on the genre of the research proposal as a contested site, and extends genre theorists (such as Bazerman), who argue that genres are 'familiar places to which we go'. Her case study of two researchers in a 'mixed mode' master's programme in the health sciences shows this genre to be anything but familiar. Of particular interest is her role as mediator between students and supervisor – we see how her role, as a writing specialist outside of the discipline, was used to afford a 'third space' in which two experienced midwives could try out their writing voices. Paxton explores risk both in the contested site of the proposal and in her professional engagement as mediator, and highlights the positive effects that this mediating role may play in giving both student and supervisor an outside sounding board during a research process.

Kate Cadman's 'Of House and Home: Reflections on Knowing and Writing for a "Southern" Postgraduate Pedagogy' is a searching account of her changing awareness of how her teaching might lead to some of the forms of symbolic violence enacted in the name of the 'divine discourse', which are encapsulated in an unexamined Anglocentric approach to the teaching of research writing. Cadman locates risk in her role as gatekeeper and in the need to interrogate one's own privilege having 'made it' as a writer. She engages the paradox that the more skilled she becomes as a writer of scholarly texts, the more she loses confidence in what this writing can do in the global university. While she does not advocate the risk taking that she seeks in her own writing for her students – 'international' students in Australia – she argues that this kind of self-interrogation is necessary to change practices in the academy. Her chapter does more than deconstruct: it also offers resources for a transformative pedagogy as well as a realisation of these in a range of genres. Her chapter also forms a bridge to the next section.

Part 4: Reading the World in Students' Writing

The chapters in this section provide new lenses for reading the dynamics and paradoxes of risk. In '"Error" or Ghost Text? Reading, Ethnopoetics and Knowledge Making,' Mary Scott's ethnopoetic analysis of stylistic 'errors' in the writing of international students studying in London demonstrates an acute awareness of how students' prior literacy practices may shape their writing voices. Scott is interested in what supervisors and teachers of 'advanced academic literacy' for 'international' students bring to their students' writing. Scott's chapter offers a powerful yet subtle method for reading through the lens of ethnopoetics. She invites an engagement with writers' intentions at the tilting point of risk, where students may be looking back at previous genres as well as forward to new forms in academic prose in English. Ethnopoetics invites readings that encompass national and international histories and inter-relations.

Moeain Arend's chapter '"It Was Hardly about Writing": Translations of Experience on Entering Postgraduate Studies' is also about a theoretical reading – one that offers new ways of understanding the journey of a political activist who made use of a policy shift towards the recognition of prior learning to enter university. Arend demonstrates that all storytelling can be seen as a form of social ordering, and notes that some theoretical approaches are more attuned to risk – and its unexpected consequences – than others. He introduces actor network theory to take us behind the scenes, and into the agency of Sadia as she charts a path opened up by the policy shift. Arend shows actor network theory to be robust at making the contradictions visible.

Part 5: Peripheral Vision: Reflections from North and South

Two scholars reflect on the significance of this project from their different geopolitical and disciplinary standpoints. Both writers have been invited to find 'hooks' in the text, to link to their respective research interests. Theresa Lillis of the Open University comments from the field of academic literacies. In 'Resonances, Resistances and Relations: Reflecting on the Politics of Risk in Academic Knowledge Making,' she finds *resonance* with her experience and research as a professional, underlining the international aspect of the project of this book; in a powerful shift of voice, she *resists* the potential essentialising of her own location as 'northern', drawing attention to other social geographies, particularly to class. There are other 'norths' not least the north of England, that have shaped her, and that index a different, inverse, class-sensitive north–south divide. Lillis ends with a focus on *relations* as a core strength of this book, and a plea for us all to take up 'the risk of reconfiguring the global relationship around academic knowledge production, sharing and exchange'. The final piece is written by Brenda Cooper, former director of the Centre for African Studies at the University of Cape Town, who was involved in the early stages of this project. Cooper also picks up on the relational, against-the-binaries emphasis of this book, as expressed in the idea of the contact zone. In 'Both Dead and Alive: Schrodinger's Cat in the Contact Zone' she makes a series of imaginative links between postcolonial fiction, theory building and scientific method to conclude with the need for us to 'metamorphose risk into challenge' as we 'wrestle with a turnpike to pull an opening just wide enough' for new possibilities and practices to emerge. Invited to offer generative commentaries, they have both read deeply and generously, challenging us to continue with this kind of risky work.

Notes

(1) Voice is a contested term. For those of us with backgrounds in adult education, where discourses of voice have been promoted and supported, questions have been asked as to whether knowledge can simply be reduced to the knower's standpoints

and interests (see Young, 2008). For those with histories in applied linguistics, the romantic notion of voice as inherent (rather than achieved through struggle) is problematic (see Maybin, 2001).
(2) Texts such as Lupton (1999) published in Routledge's Key Ideas series, Caplan's collection *Risk Revisited*, and Arnoldi (2009) in Polity's Key Concepts series, show how influential the concept is in the social sciences.
(3) A discussion on the views of Connell and Mbembe later in this chapter offers a more nuanced approach to difference in relation to research and representations of Africa.
(4) In the collection of stories, *At Risk: Writing On and Over the Edge of South Africa*, McGregor and Nuttall (2007: 12) suggest that perceptions of risk are heightened in post-apartheid South Africa: 'to live in South Africa is to be subliminally primed for major loss'. Here the epochal event is the end of apartheid, not the Second World War, as is the case for many of the scholars writing from the centre.

References

Aitchison, C., Kamler, B. and Lee, A. (eds) (2010) *Publishing Pedagogies for the Doctorate and Beyond*. Abingdon: Routledge.
Aitchison, C. and Lee, A. (2006) Research writing: Problems and possibilities. *Teaching in Higher Education* 11 (3), 265–278.
Angelil-Carter, S. (2000) *Stolen Language? Plagiarism in Writing*. Harlow: Pearson.
Arnoldi, J. (2009) *Risk*. Cambridge: Polity.
Bakhtin, M. (1981) *The Dialogic Imagination: Four Essays*. Austin: University of Texas Press.
Bartlett, A. and Mercer, G. (2000) Reconceptualising discourses of power in postgraduate supervision. *Teaching in Higher Education* 5 (2), 195–204.
Beck, U. (1992) *Risk Society: Towards a New Modernity*. London: Sage.
Bernstein, P.L. (1998) *Against the Gods: The Remarkable Story of Risk*. New York: John Wiley.
Blommaert, J. (2005) *Discourse: A Critical Introduction*. Cambridge: Cambridge University Press.
Boud, D. and Lee, A. (eds) (2009) *Changing Practices in Doctoral Education*. Abingdon: Routledge.
Bowker, G. (2006) *Memory Practices in the Sciences*. Cambridge, MA: MIT Press.
Bowker, G. (2010) The archive. *Communication and Critical/Cultural Studies* 7 (2), 212–214.
Cadman, K. (2003) Divine discourse: Plagiarism, hybridity and epistemological racism. In S. May, M. Franken and R. Barnard (eds) *LED 2003, 1st International Conference on Language, Education and Diversity: Refereed Proceedings and Keynotes*. Hamilton: University of Waikato Press.
Cadman, K. (2005) Towards a 'pedagogy of connection' in critical research education: A REAL story. *Journal of English for Academic Purposes* 4 (4), 353–367.
Canagarajah, S. (2002) *The Geopolitics of Academic Writing*. Pittsburgh, PA: University of Pittsburgh Press.
Caplan, P. (ed.) (2000) *Risk Revisited*. London: Pluto Press.
Casanave, C.P. (2010) Taking risks? A case study of three doctoral students writing qualitative dissertations at an American university in Japan. *Journal of Second Language Writing* 19, 1–16.
Casanave, C.P. and Li, X. (2008) *Learning the Literacy Practices of Graduate School: Insider's Reflections on Academic Enculturation*. Ann Arbor, MI: University of Michigan Press.

Chihota, C. (2007) 'The games people play': Taking on postgraduate identities in the context of writer circles. *Journal of Applied Linguistics* 4 (1), 131–136.
Comaroff, J. and Comaroff, J.L. (2012) *Theory from the South: Or, How Euro-America is Evolving Towards Africa*. Boulder, CO: Paradigm.
Connell, R. (2007) *Southern Theory: The Global Dynamics of Knowledge in the Social Sciences*. Sydney: Allen and Unwin.
Connell, R. (2009) Peripheral vision: Beyond the metropole. In J. Kenway and J. Fahey (eds) *Globalizing the Research Imagination*. Abingdon: Routledge.
Dixon, K. and Janks, H. (2010) From poster to PhD: The evolution of a literature review. In M. Walker and P. Thomson (eds) *The Routledge Doctoral Supervisor's Companion: Supporting Effective Research in Education and the Social Sciences*. Abingdon: Routledge.
Douglas, M. (1992) *Purity and Danger: An Analysis of the Concepts of Pollution and Taboo*. London: Routledge.
Enders, J. (2004) Research training and careers in transition: A European perspective on the many faces of the PhD. *Studies in Continuing Education* 26 (3), 419–429.
Gee, J.P. (1990) *Social Linguistics and Literacies: Ideology in Discourses*. London: Falmer.
Giddens, A. (1991) *Modernity and Self-identity: Self and Society in the Late Modern Age*. Cambridge: Polity.
George, O. (2003) *Relocating Agency: Modernity and African Letters*. New York: SUNY Press.
Hyland, K. (2006) Disciplinary differences: Language variation in academic discourses. In K. Hyland and M. Bondi (eds) *Academic Discourse Across Disciplines*. Frankfort: Peter Lang.
Kamler, B. and Thomson, P. (2006) *Helping Doctoral Students Write: Pedagogies for Supervision*. Abingdon: Routledge.
Keim, W. (2008) Distorted universality: Internationalization and its implications for the epistemological foundations of the discipline. *Canadian Journal of Sociology* 33 (3), 555–574.
Kress, G. (2001) Sociolinguistics and social semiotics. In P. Cobley (ed.) *The Routledge Companion to Semiotics and Linguistics*. London: Routledge.
Lillis, T. and Curry, M.J. (2010) *Academic Writing in a Global Context: The Politics and Practices of Publishing in English*. Abingdon: Routledge.
Lillis, T. and Scott, M. (2007) Defining academic literacies research: Issues of epistemology, ideology and strategy. *Journal of Applied Linguistics* 4 (1), 5–32.
Luhmann, N. (1991/2002) *Risk: A Sociological Theory*. New Jersey: Aldine Transaction.
Lupton, D. (1999) *Risk*. London: Routledge.
Maybin, J. (2001) Language, struggle and voice: The Bakhtin/Volosinov writings. In M. Wetherell, S. Taylor and S.J. Yates (eds) *Discourse Theory and Practice: A Reader*. London: Sage.
Mbembe, A. (2001) *On the Postcolony*. Berkeley: University of California Press.
Mbembe, A. and Hofmeyr, I. (2008) Writing Africa: Achille Mbembe in conversation with Isabel Hofmeyr. In N. Shepherd and S. Robins (eds) *New South African Keywords*. Johannesburg and Athens, OH: Jacana Media and Ohio University Press.
McGregor, L. and Nuttall, S. (eds) (2007) *At Risk: Writing On and Over the Edge of South Africa*. Cape Town: Jonathan Ball.
McWilliam, E. (2009) Doctoral education in risky times. In D. Boud and A. Lee (eds) *Changing Practices of Doctoral Education*. Abingdon: Routledge.
Mudimbe, V.Y. (1994) *The Idea of Africa*. Bloomington, IN: Indiana University Press.

Pennycook, A. (1996) Borrowing other people's words: Ownership, memory and plagiarism. *TESOL Quarterly* 30 (2), 201–230.
Pratt, M.L. (1992) *Imperial Eyes: Studies in Travel Writing and Transculturation*. London: Routledge.
Pratt, M.L. (1999) Arts of the contact zone. In D. Bartholomae and A. Petrosky (eds) *Ways of Reading: An Anthology for Writers* (5th edn). New York: Bedford/St Martins.
Royal Society (2011) Knowledge, networks and nations: Global scientific collaboration in the 21st century, accessed December 2012. http://royalsociety.org/policy/projects/knowledge-networks-nations/report/
Rwomire, A. and Nyamnjoh, F. (2006) *Challenges and Responsibilities of Social Research in Africa: Ethical Issues*. Addis Ababa: OSSREA.
Schroeder, C., Fox, H. and Bizzell, P. (eds) (2002) *ALT DIS: Alternative Discourses and the Academy*. Portsmouth, NH: Heinemann.
Starfield, S. and Ravelli, L.J. (2006) 'The writing of this thesis was a process that I could not explore with the positivistic detachment of the classical sociologist': Self and structure in new humanities research theses. *Journal of English for Academic Purposes* 5 (3), 222–243.
Swales, J. (2004) *Research Genres: Explorations and Applications*. Cambridge: Cambridge University Press.
Usher, R. (2002) A diversity of doctorates: Fitness for the knowledge economy. *Higher Education Research and Development* 21 (2), 143–153.
Vera-Sanso, P. (2000) Risk-talk: The politics of risk and its representation. In P. Caplan (ed.) *Risk Revisited*. London: Pluto.
Young, M. (2008) *Bringing Knowledge Back In: From Social Constructivism to Social Realism in the Sociology of Education*. London and New York: Routledge.
Zinn, J.O. (2010) Risk as discourse: Interdisciplinary perspectives. *Critical Analysis of Discourse across Disciplines* 42 (2), 106–124.

Part 1
Deletion and Agency

1 'Does My Experience Count?' The Role of Experiential Knowledge in the Research Writing of Postgraduate Adult Learners

Linda Cooper

> *Who will be given social agency is both an epistemological and political question. Whose experience of the past and whose vision of the future will be considered credible? Whose modest testimony will be allowed to contribute to a shared understanding of the nature of the world?*
>
> Michelson, 2004: 27

In this chapter, I explore the dissertation-writing experiences of a selection of adult learners completing a master's degree in adult education at a South African university. The master's programme, on which I taught, includes a coursework component followed by a research dissertation of 25,000 words. The majority of learners entering the programme have many years of practitioner experience in the field of adult education and allied fields such as community development. Since a significant proportion of students have had few opportunities for formal study, many access the programme via a process in which their 'prior learning' is recognised; they bring rich practitioner expertise and skills, having occupied positions of considerable authority within their organisations, and having developed impressive conceptual repertoires and social understanding. As Casanave (2002: 82) has argued of professionals who enrol on graduate master's programmes: 'Years of work experience may in fact provide masters degree students with more real, as opposed to symbolic knowledge and expertise than could ever be provided in a (formal) program of study.'

It has become clear to me, over 10 years of supervising postgraduate thesis writing, that many adult learners enter this master's programme because they have a powerful desire to make their voices heard. In other words, they *have something they want to say,* and start the programme with a 'ready-made' thesis or argument, rather than (or in addition to) having pressing questions to which they are seeking answers. As Casanave notes, such master's students are 'positioned precariously between the status of novice and specialist' (Casanave, 2002: 84). The questions that these students and their supervisors must grapple with are the following: What role can adult learners' working knowledge or professional experience play in their postgraduate research? What status should be accorded their prior experience and what risks are involved in drawing on professional experience as a source of new knowledge? What role can this experience legitimately play in the writing of the research? How should it be viewed or treated by the supervisor in terms of postgraduate pedagogy?

Questions about the role of workplace or experiential knowledge in the writing of research are not peculiar to the South African context. Internationally, trends towards lifelong learning, and pressures to widen access and increase participation in higher education, have led to increasing numbers of working adults entering postgraduate study after having gained a number of years of professional and life experience. In South Africa however, given its apartheid history, these questions hold particular significance for those adults who were previously excluded on the basis of 'race', class or gender, and who are currently entering postgraduate study in increasing numbers. For this reason, post-apartheid higher-education policy has foregrounded the recognition of prior learning (RPL) as a mechanism for widening access to those previously excluded, who have amassed considerable experiential knowledge.

For more radical theorists, RPL is viewed not only as a mechanism of addressing past discrimination and disadvantage, but also as a vehicle for the recognition of 'knowledge from below' (Grossman, 1999; Michelson, 1998). It has been argued that when brought into dialogue with academic knowledge, experiential, work-based or professional knowledge has the potential to enrich the curricular, pedagogical and critical practices of the academy (Ralphs, 2009). However, little has been written about what this conversation or dialogue between prior experiential knowledge and academic knowledge involves. In this chapter, I seek to contribute to an understanding of 'what happens' when experiential knowledge is brought into dialogue with established academic knowledge. I do this by drawing on illustrative examples of the research-writing practices of a selection of adult learners, all of whom entered postgraduate study via RPL. First, however, I explore the following two questions: How should the relationship between adult learners' experiential knowledge and established academic knowledge be viewed pedagogically? To what extent should students' prior experiential knowledge be drawn upon, or excluded, in the research-writing process?

Exploring the Relationship between Experience-Based and Academic Knowledge

Experiential learning theories place experience at the core of knowledge development, and have been central to adult education as a field of practice and research. Embedded in these theories is the assumption that the role of people's experience in learning and knowledge production should be celebrated and legitimated (Fenwick, 2001). As noted earlier, more radical approaches to RPL see experience-based knowledge as having the potential to enrich higher-education pedagogy and theory building.

Ironically, however, experiential learning theories do not provide the conceptual tools necessary for assessing the contribution of experiential learning to academic knowledge. By stressing the essential similarity and continuity of all forms of knowledge, they offer no conceptual language with which to talk about different kinds of knowledge or the relationships between them. If it is because of *its distinctiveness from* academic knowledge that experiential knowledge is seen as having pedagogic and epistemological value, then we need a conceptual language that allows us to describe different forms of knowledge as well as the nature of interaction between them. In addition, experiential learning theories tend to pay little attention to power relations, and are thus unable to account for why some forms of knowledge carry significantly more power in society than others (Fenwick, 2001). This social reality has significant implications for the conventions and genres of research writing that postgraduate students are expected to acquire.

Drawing attention to the power of formal, academic knowledge, writers such as Young (2008) and Muller (2000) have argued that the only way in which access to higher education can be widened to historically excluded constituencies is by giving them epistemological access to 'powerful knowledge'. This requires having a keen sense of the differentiated nature of knowledge (in particular, the distinction between scientific and everyday knowledge) and an understanding that everyday or experiential knowledge can never make the same kinds of truth claims as can formal, codified knowledge (Young, 2008: chap. 3). Muller warns that if this distinction is not made clearly visible to students, they might 'stub their toe[s] especially severely on the reefs of social hierarchy which are not displaced but merely removed from view' (Muller, 2000: 71). The implications of this position for postgraduate pedagogy are that students' experiential knowledge should, as far as possible, 'be kept out of' research writing, as it can potentially act as a barrier to their acquisition of academic discourse. Countering this view, it is arguable that the boundary between experience-based and 'schooled' knowledge *is always already breached*' (Walkerdine, 1988 cited in Michelson, 2004: 17, emphasis added). Furthermore, arguments in support of the differentiated nature of knowledge are often premised on a dualist view of 'everyday' and 'scientific' knowledge, which portrays formal academic knowledge as being relatively impermeable to knowledge developments outside of specialised sites of knowledge production. The problem is that such a view of knowledge making (like experiential learning theories) is unable to account for the outcome of the interaction between different forms of knowledge.

Claims that 'scientific knowledge' is – or should be – untainted by everyday experience have been critiqued by several critical feminist and post-modernist theorists. For example, Michelson (2004: 14) argues that the claims regarding the objectivity and universality of theory are part of 'Western, metropolitan and masculinist knowledge practices' that dominate conventional academic constructs of knowledge. Connell (2007) locates the origins of established social theory under colonialism, and argues that the social sciences have evolved historically via a one-way flow of information from the periphery to the metropole: while the periphery provided 'raw data', the metropole was where theory was built. Ideas and intellectuals from the periphery rarely shaped social theory, and forms of knowledge that did not 'fit' into established scientific genres were lost, erased and deleted. The consequence of this has been the exclusion of knowledge generated in the majority world at a serious cost to our collective knowledge archive. Connell (2007: 226) cites African philosopher, Hountinji, who argues that a sociology that is based solely on the experiences of the metropole results 'not in minor omissions but in major incompleteness'. Connell goes on to assert that knowledge contributions from the 'periphery' can add value to our understanding of human society because they 'multipl[y] the local sources of our thinking' (Connell, 2007: 207).

In the text that follows, I draw on these critiques of experiential learning theories and dualist views of knowledge in exploring the role of experiential, professional or work-based knowledge in adult learners' research writing. I position my argument within the traditions of post-Vygotskian and Activity Theory perspectives which, while maintaining the distinction between 'scientific' and 'everyday' knowledge, point to the centrality of each in the process of knowledge making. In other words, while scientific concepts gradually acquire meaning through being embedded in everyday referents, 'everyday thought is given structure and order in the context of systematic scientific thought' (Daniels, 2001: 53). This (more dialectical) view of knowledge making foregrounds not only the differences between forms of knowledge but also the relationships between them in the processes of research and knowledge making. The aim is not merely to find categories into which different kinds of knowledge may be 'slotted', but rather to explore their forms of engagement and patterns of interaction.[1] Such an approach values diverse ways of knowing and foregrounds the potential contribution that experiential knowledge from diverse sources can make to the knowledge archive of the academy. At the same time, it acknowledges the power of established conventions of research writing within the academy; as Blommaert (2005: 106) has noted, creative practice can only happen within certain contextual and structural constraints – within the 'borderline zone of existing hegemonies. It develops within hegemonies while it attempts to alter them'.

Methodology: From Pedagogy to Student Agency

In this section, I describe in some detail the methodological moves that I made in the process of my research for this chapter. I began with the assumption that the nature of the 'engagement and patterns of interaction' between experiential and academic knowledge are potentially shaped by three factors: (i) the nature of the knowledge/academic field; (ii) the pedagogic approach adopted by the supervisor; and (iii) students' own approaches and strategies. Initially, I was most interested in exploring the second factor – postgraduate pedagogy – and in particular, the ways in which supervisors advised their students on how to deal with their experiential knowledge in the research-writing process.

I selected three students with whom I had been involved, to varying degrees, in the supervision of their dissertations.[2] All three entered the university via RPL, and with considerable practitioner experience in adult education, and all had successfully completed their master's degrees. With the permission of the students and their supervisors, I embarked on a process of 'excavating' successive drafts of their theses. I focused initially on the supervisors' written feedback on sections of writing that drew extensively on the students' professional and life experiences, and attempted to identify the pedagogic strategies that the supervisors adopted. Did they value students' professional and life experience, and if so, in what way? What role did they see it playing in the making of new knowledge? What did they advise students 'to do' with their experiential knowledge in the research-writing process?

Working back through successive 'layers' of students' thesis writing, however, I found my attention increasingly drawn to the third of the factors above – namely, students' strategies involving their experiential knowledge. I was struck by the desire of students to give 'voice' to their experiential knowledge, and by the fact that their research writing – in its early stages at least – was motivated by the fact that they had something they wished to say rather than the desire to find answers to specific questions. I became aware of the considerable agency, expressed through the adoption of various strategies, which students employed to incorporate their experience into their research writing, and to create spaces (appropriately or inappropriately according to established research-writing conventions) to give voice to their experientially formed theories and explanations. What became apparent was that certain experiences were ultimately deleted from their theses, and I sought to find out why this was so. It is the set of moves that students made in their attempts to incorporate their experiential knowledge, and to negotiate the contours between their experiential knowledge and the codes and conventions of academic research writing, that form the focus of this chapter.

Drawing on drafts of students' theses, the critical feedback that they received from their supervisors and examiners, and on informal conversations with the students as well as one formal interview, I track the students' struggles to establish the status their experiential knowledge had, and the risks involved in deciding where 'to put it'. The experiences of two of the students illustrate how experiential knowledge has the potential to act as a barrier to the acquisition of academic research-writing conventions. I illustrate this, not just to argue for the exclusion of such knowledge, but to emphasise the point that drawing on such knowledge in the academic research-writing process is not uncomplicated; it involves risks for both the student and the supervisor. In the case of the third student, I make a systematic examination of successive drafts of his thesis to illustrate how it is possible to creatively negotiate the inclusion of experiential knowledge into academic writing. I probe the strategies that this student adopted to find expression for his experiential knowledge, the styles and genres of writing that facilitated its expression and the extent to which he was able to draw on this knowledge to develop a research-writing voice. I explore how the student negotiated the risks involved in drawing on his experience, and highlight those strategies that he adopted which were ultimately 'successful'. I then consider the insights that inclusion of experiential knowledge contributed to his research writing, and finally, evaluate what was 'lost' through processes of deletion and exclusion of this knowledge.

Is the Experiential Voice Too Strong?

In the two examples that follow, I show how students' prior work experience or professional knowledge may be a double-edged sword. For these two students, it served strongly to motivate and provide direction to their research, and facilitated deep insights and understandings; however, at times it also acted as a barrier – clouding their interpretations, clogging up their research writing, and presenting them with dilemmas about 'where to put' their experience.

Anna

Anna[3] had no prior degree, but had the British equivalent of a postgraduate diploma. Her work experience (mainly in the United Kingdom) had spanned a period of nearly 35 years, and included development work in the field of early childhood development. She had supervised and mentored senior local-government staff, and developed training programmes for women elected to local authorities. During her long career, she had completed numerous non-degree courses in community development, as well as psychology and counselling, and had gained extensive counselling experience, including counselling skills training. She had enrolled for a master's in management and organisational learning at a British university, but did not complete. During the seven years prior to starting her second master's course, Anna had been working with South African NGOs in the area of leadership development. She enrolled for her master's in adult education, keen to learn more about the South African context, but also motivated by a desire to have her experiential learning and attempts at theory-building recognised.

On completing her coursework, Anna embarked on an action-research project that involved the piloting of a community leadership-development course of an unusual kind; one which sought to embed the training within a psychodynamic framework. Anna sought, from the outset, to 'test' a theory of community leadership-building that she had developed through years of practitioner experience. To some extent then, she already had a good idea of what she wanted to say when she set out on the research. Having completed the empirical research, she submitted the first full draft of her thesis to her supervisors in October 2009.

What were some of the moves she made in this early draft to draw on her prior experience? Her first chapter reflects on her personal history, and this served to locate the origins of the research project; it also included lengthy sections in which she reflected on what she felt was her relative outsider status in South Africa, and her anxiety about her ability to make valid interpretations. The first two chapters clearly articulated her views on how psychodynamic factors might hinder or promote the development of leadership capacity in communities, and these views were further elaborated in the chapters dealing with her findings.

Feedback from her supervisors was that in various respects, her professional and life experience were frustrating her attempts to follow research-writing conventions. On the one hand, the lengthy sections dealing with her lack of familiarity with the South African context undermined her arguments as a researcher. On the other hand, and in apparent contradiction, her analysis of her findings strongly articulated her own 'philosophy of praxis', thus foregrounding her own voice when, in fact, the voices of her research participants needed to lead the analysis.

Anna spent months rewriting the thesis to address these problems. The final version of the thesis demonstrated that she had succeeded in 'mastering' the conventions of working with evidence in research writing. However, many of the original ideas that she brought to the research could not ultimately find expression as they lay beyond the scope of the evidence she was able to present. Furthermore, what emerged in written communication with her supervisor, more than six months after completion, was Anna's frustration with trying to reconcile her deeply held professional principles with the demands of academic writing:

> Interpretation in the world of psychoanalysis is not itself unusual, (the problem for me was) more the fixing of interpretation on paper, an ultimately non-dynamic process, lacking in ongoing and continuous relationship between me as practitioner and each and every community leader individually and collectively. (July 2011, email to supervisor)

Faeez

Faeez grew up in a working-class community on the Cape Flats and obtained undergraduate certificates and diplomas in adult education from two local universities and an institution in the United States. He describes himself as an organisational development and transformation consultant, and at the time that he was enrolled for his master's degree. He had been involved in training people in development organisations for 26 years, working across southern and East Africa.

At the point when the examiners' reports on his thesis came in, I met with Faeez and his supervisor to discuss the reports, and what follows represents a selective record of this informal conversation. Faeez revealed that his main motivation for choosing the focus of his thesis was tied up with his own political history and the questions that he had faced as a trainer of community leaders. He wanted to find out, 'Why [after the end of apartheid] did people leave this [NGO] sector and go "straight"?' In other words, why did they enter government or the corporate world, and seem to no longer share the values that inspired and motivated them during the struggle against apartheid?

Like Anna, Faeez began his research with a readymade thesis or hypothesis – in his case, a periodised explanation of changes in community leadership over time. In our conversation, he related how this conceptual framework 'evolved from my own experience – contact with leaders every day'. He was able to clearly articulate the conundrum that he had faced throughout the writing process: his explanations of how the nature of community leadership had changed over time predated his actual research, while research-writing conventions required that they emerge out of his research. As he put it: 'I [understood] knowledge-construction and everything but … I already kn[e]w [the answer]!' As he began to write, he realised that there was 'too much of "Faeez-the-activist" there'. As a consequence, at some point in the middle of his thesis writing, he took time off to publish a book on community leadership development; he described this as 'part of purging myself of what I already kn[e]w'. In retrospect, he felt that the publication of this book had subsequently helped him to make 'some amazing breakthroughs' in his thesis writing.

Despite recommending a good pass mark, the examiners' reports were critical of the final dissertation mainly on account of the student's own voice being 'too strong' and that the conclusions were not sufficiently justified by the evidence. One examiner wrote that 'The rationale for the study is somewhat peculiar since it justifies the study on the basis of its findings,' while the other argued as follows:

> the candidate makes claims about the macro context of NGOs which are not sustained by the limited data and methods of the study itself. These claims seem to come from the candidate's prior experience of the field and his insights as an activist. While they might well be accurate, the limited data in the study cannot carry certain generalisations asserted … In places, the candidate thus uses the study to 'confirm what he already knows'.

Thus, although Faeez recognised the problem, and his supervisor had pointed to the issue in earlier stages of the thesis writing, ultimately neither was able to find a fully satisfactory solution.

As noted earlier, both Anna and Faeez's cases illustrate that the drawing on experiential knowledge may present specific problems for postgraduate thesis writers. These problems are portrayed sharply by Morphet who – drawing on a Vygotskian perspective in a discussion of 'experience and adult learning' – argues that experiential knowledge can act in two ways. It may serve to illuminate understanding – 'make some kinds of learning easy, speedy and powerful and ... throw open the doors [to new learning]'; however it may 'also operate as a barrier, making other kinds of learning difficult and slow, keeping some doors closed'. The origin of the problem is not that we lack the information or skills to solve a particular problem, but rather that 'our own experiences get in the way. In confronting new learning situations, we inevitably bring our own "inner history" to bear on the matter and we try to make the problem fit into our [existing] framework' (Morphet, 1992: 94–95). The terrain that students need to navigate between their experiential knowledge and meeting the demands of academic research writing may be seen as a 'space of risk' that can potentially generate new insights and understandings, but can equally lead to the silencing or deletion of experiential knowledge.

How then, as postgraduate supervisors, do we ensure that adult students' prior experience helps to 'throw open doors' in the thesis writing process, rather than 'blocking access' to the forms of reasoning and writing that will ensure uptake and recognition in the context of postgraduate research writing? The cases of these two postgraduate students show how they struggled to find a legitimate way to locate their experiential knowledge within the accepted conventions for making arguments and valid knowledge claims when writing about their research.

The Strategic Use of Experiential Knowledge as 'Illumination'

My third example shows how a student managed, more successfully, to navigate the space of risk between drawing on his experiential knowledge to illuminate and enrich his research findings, and meeting the demands of academic writing.

Jerry

As Jerry's supervisor, I had fuller records of successive drafts of his thesis, and of my feedback on these. I delved into my computer to find (what I thought was) the earliest full draft of his thesis (from mid-2007). I then tracked forward through subsequent drafts of the thesis and noted that, until mid-2008, Jerry drew very minimally on his own life history, and his references to it were scattered across various chapters. Then, in the last three months of his thesis writing, following the suggestion of an advisor from the university's Writing Centre,[4] an account of his personal history, accompanied by a number of illustrative photographs, came to constitute a substantial portion of his first chapter.[5] Much of the account that follows of Jerry's life history is taken from the final version of the thesis.

Jerry was born into a poor, working-class family and grew up in Cape Town in the mid-1960s in the context of forced removals and an apartheid-divided city. His school days were 'filled with misery and mischief'; he started playing truant in Grade 4 and dropped out of school after he failed Grade 7. He saw himself as being 'prepared ... for a future of gangsterism and crime' and certainly never dreamed that he might study again. At the age of 14, he lied about his age and got his first job as a labourer in a factory. His memories of this period are of his 'hatred' towards the racism of his white overseers; however, he noticed that coloured workers were given the opportunity to develop skills in carpentry and furniture manufacturing.[6] 'I became inquisitive and curious to learn how to operate (the sanding) machines.' Jerry was promoted and became an apprentice 'hand sander', but this career was cut short when he lost his job and was 'drawn into various criminal activities under the guise of politics' (referring to some of the student protest of this time), and later into more serious 'gangsterism and crime'. In the late 1970s, however, Jerry converted to Christianity and decided to reform his lifestyle radically. In 1982, he managed to find a job as a labourer for the Cape Town municipality.

As a 'general worker' in the electricity department, Jerry found himself increasingly doing the work of a skilled electrician but derived no additional recognition or remuneration from this because he had 'no papers'. He returned to learning and completed his school-leaving certificate at a local government adult basic education and training (ABET) centre.[7] A fellow learner at the centre tried to dissuade him from studying, saying: 'This ABET story isn't for you. You are a practical person, a handyman, someone who fixes things with his hands ... this theory stuff isn't going to work for you.' Jerry writes that although 'my colleague's words haunted me', he came to see education and training as the key to workers gaining better job opportunities and better pay, as well as to 'gaining social and community status'.

In 1998, Jerry enrolled for a certificate course in adult education at a local university. He went on to complete a postgraduate diploma and an honours degree in this field, and finally enrolled for his master's in adult education in 2003. By then, he was employed as an ABET trainer at a local government training centre.

Jerry's master's research focused on trying to understand the factors that led municipal workers, who had previously been 'demotivated', to return to learning. From the outset, the personal, autobiographical origins of his question were obvious. From early on, Jerry seemed to adopt a strategic approach to his use of prior experience in his research writing. Drawing on extracts from the final written draft of his thesis, the following sections show how he deployed creative ways (agency) to make use of his experience in quite diverse but legitimate ways.

Jerry's personal history captures the complex and contradictory attitudes of workers to education and learning in the context of institutionalised racism, as well as the experience of working-class adult students who do not feel that they have the appropriate 'habitus' to study. Skilfully sketched as a particular example of 'the general', his personal history implicitly serves as a rationale for his study. As the following extracts show, he also draws on his experiences to provide a more explicit rationale for the focus of his study:

> This was during the apartheid era, when African and Coloured workers at most industrial, municipal and government sites of practice were discriminated against and their skills exploited. At the City of Cape Town,[8] I found that racial discrimination and all the other inequalities and injustices I had experienced at my former workplaces were even worse... My requests to study, for a study allowance and for time off to study fell on deaf ears as manager and supervisor alike ignored my interest in becoming an electrician. (p. 12)

> Most children who had some schooling, would be faced with making sacrificial decisions to end their own schooling careers in order to help their impoverished parents and siblings... this has helped to fuel and develop an ideology of negative attitudes towards any form of education or training which could perceivably benefit the employer. (p. 10)

While many black workers had negative attitudes towards education, it was also promoted as a means of 'liberation':

> I attended countless depot meetings organised by the unions. At most of these union meetings the issue of education and training would be discussed as a method of liberating disadvantaged workers from injustice, discrimination, and inequality, and as a vehicle to better job opportunities, job advancement, better pay, and to gain status in the community. (p. 13)

Jerry documents his memories of past traditions of communal knowledge making with painful emotion and nostalgia:

> Culturally, African and Coloured folks, especially before the advent of television in South Africa, would sit around with their families at night and discuss the day's proceedings... Folk tales told by our parents served as family entertainment while we all gathered around the old dining-room table or 'ghelly' (fire), and were at times filled with sadness, bitterness, fear and rebellion. It is these stories that allowed the youth to experience and understand the persecution, the practice of race discrimination and most of all, the dreadful living circumstances brought about by poverty. (p. 9)

He also draws on his experiential knowledge to justify some of his methodological choices in the third chapter, in particular, his choice of interviewees:

> The interviews were confined to eight coloured learners... The reason why I specifically chose these learners is that I was known to them and anticipated that they would give me their honest and full cooperation during the interviews. (p. 33)

Jerry then draws on this intimate relationship with fellow workers to strengthen his claims for the validity of his findings:

> During my research investigation, I tried to establish the validity of statements made by some of the respondents through my personal and intimate association with them... workers/learners were eager to share their personal and confidential information with me and mentioned names and job titles. They fearlessly exposed line-managers and supervisors who disregarded the rules applying to the implementation of [the City of Cape Town's] education and training policy by refusing workers time off to attend ABET classes. (p. 36)

While he draws on the use of self-narrative in Chapter 1, later in the thesis Jerry also deploys a narrative form to present his findings. He paints vivid, personalised portraits of each of his eight research subjects which might not have been possible had he not shared a personal history and intimate relationship with them. In the following extracts, italics are used to highlight how Jerry draws on his experience to interpret his findings:

> Victor has jokingly set a goal for himself, saying, 'I don't want to be an electrician, no, I want to become the city electrical engineer'. Maybe this

would have sounded ridiculous to his colleagues and family. Nevertheless, and bearing in mind that the slogan to the NQF's Outcomes Based Education (OBE) 'From a sweeper to an engineer' allows learners to envision their dreams therein. *It is this same slogan, which is dangled like a carrot in front of workers, by motivational speakers like others, and me in the quest for motives to encourage workers to enroll in training courses that would benefit them in achieving their future goals ...* (p. 53)

Nazley adopted an attitude renowned amongst many council employees and that is that she didn't need to know anything else and didn't think 'that anybody could teach her anything' about her present job. *As a labourer at the City of Cape Town, I have worked amongst and with many council employees and have at times identified this kind of attitude as being a shield which workers use to hide their anguish and fear of becoming a student/ learner in a classroom situation.* Some workers would say that they would rather be taught organisational knowledge at the workplace by observation where there is no need to read or write, than to risk sitting in a classroom and being found incompetent in dealing with theoretical tasks. (pp. 51–52)

Gregory Daniels's story is very much similar to my life story. Gregory's interest in education and training began when he moved from Vrygrond to move in with his in-laws in Mitchell's Plain. The fact that his brothers-in-law were all tradesmen, bricklayers and/or plasterers made him feel very uncomfortable because his brothers-in-laws were earning a lot of money compared to the money which Gregory receives from his low paid job at the CCT [City of Cape Town]. (p. 54)

Here, his 'prior experience' acted to afford insight, to enable him to contextualise his findings, and to make an interpretation that relied on his identification with the research subjects and on parallels within his own experience.

Finally, in his conclusion, Jerry presents a deeply personal ending to the thesis. Here, he gives full vent to the 'message' he wanted to give expression to right at the beginning – that to really understand workers' motivation to learn, or their refusal to engage in learning, one has to know them intimately. In contrast with Anna and Faeez, however, Jerry was more successful in making this voice heard in the academic research-writing context.

Municipal workers have a habit of sharing all the details of their activities with each other. When they sit down and have tea or lunch in their mess-room, they share stories, mutual needs and problems and create camaraderie. It is also during these discussions that workers listen to the different needs and shortcomings of their colleagues, and give advice or make decisions on how to approach the manager to discuss these needs and shortcomings. It is in this atmosphere that managers and those in supervisory positions should sit down, listen to and laugh with workers at their stories. It is during these discussions that line-managers and supervisors can become acquainted with workers needs and wants ... If line-managers are acquainted with workers' needs and problems, they will know how to rectify these either by motivating workers to enrol into education and training courses, or by advising workers to seek professional help if the problem is of such a serious nature.

I believe that education is power. As a former gangster and previously disadvantaged individual, I only got the respect of people because of my ruthlessness as a gangster. Today, having taken the initiative to educate myself, I enjoy the respect of people not because of their fear of me, but because of the status that education has afforded me. (p. 65)

Jerry draws on oral genres that are familiar to him to create a style of academic writing that facilitates not only the expression of his own experiential knowledge but also that of the collective, and in doing so, enables the development of an authentic writing voice. Throughout the chapter, the 'I' is prominent in Jerry's writing; this is not an individual voice but a 'community' voice acting as a ventriloquation of the collective.[9] This allows Jerry to identify with, and give voice, both directly and indirectly (through the stories of elders), to those who experienced racist and class oppression.

Jerry draws on speech genres and symbolic tools that are familiar to him, and commonly used in local working-class communities[10]: the construction of narratives (his own and that of his research subjects); the use of ventriloquation; his use of illustrative photographs (unusual in a thesis where they are not the object of analysis); and his mobilisation of emotional resources in his writing. His descriptions of past traditions of collective knowledge making and resistance, like his concluding comments, have an idealised ring to them, echoing the transformative orientation of the 'struggle' contexts that he participated in during his younger days. Portelli (1991: 2) reminds us that these idealised versions of the past (and of the future) allow us to 'recognise the interests of the tellers, and the dreams and desires beneath them', as well as to imagine alternatives. All of these writing devices serve to reaffirm and solidify Jerry's identification with black, working-class community and culture. In the context of South African higher education, in which the dominant genre of academic writing is modelled on the conventions of 'northern' or 'western' academia, the assertion of this identity must be seen as a move to challenge or at least disrupt the norm.

There may be a further function served by the deployment of these genres and tools. Wertsch (cited in Daniels, 2001: 81) has argued that 'utterances function to presuppose the context of speech in which they occur, on the one hand, or act in a "performative" capacity to create or entail the context, on the other'. It is possible to see Jerry's 'transcription' of elements of working-class oral genres in his academic writing as not only allowing the expression of his experiential knowledge and that of his community, but also as a move to reshape and claim greater ownership of the meaning-making function of academic thesis writing.

What Gets 'Lost'? Trails, Traces and Deletions

Despite Jerry's considerable achievements in terms of developing an authentic writing voice, and negotiating the contours of postgraduate writing conventions in a creative way, when I compared earlier drafts with later drafts of his thesis, it was clear that significant sections of his life and work experiences had been deleted over time. In particular, during the last weeks of thesis writing, very substantial sections of his personal narrative presented in the first chapter were pruned (mostly because of a rigidly enforced word limit imposed by the faculty), and some sections deleted. In an interview which I conducted with Jerry as part of the research for this chapter,[11] I asked him how he experienced having to progressively cut and trim sections of his life history; his responses demonstrate his frustration and sense of loss in being required to do so:

> I was so annoyed! I prepared that whole section where I had ... learners' photos and all that and I thought, yes Linda, you cut out all that ... I worked on this so long ... and I lost everything ... the gravy ... I trusted your judgement, I thought Linda says this, then it must be done, because you're my supervisor! But I felt deprived of what I wanted to say ... because of the limited words I had. But I [also] feel I have said enough ... That's enough – I brought most of my argument across.

At the time of this interview, I had gone a step further in attempting to retrieve the 'trails and traces' of experiential knowledge that entered Jerry's research writing at various stages. I had unexpectedly come across a copy of an even earlier full draft of Jerry's thesis dated more than a year earlier (January 2007) than the series of drafts that I originally analysed. In the earlier draft, I discovered that he presented an additional set of findings from his interviews with fellow workers, written up in the original Capetonian working-class dialect – a 'creole' version of Afrikaans – which is semantically rich and enormously expressive. An English translation of some extracts from these interviews is given below:

> No man, these fucking people always take other people for arses. I had to wait two fucking years before they decided to call me in for training. When I'm done studying here, then I will show those fucking bunch of bastards what an artisan looks like.

> Old J—, you know yourself how these bastard people thinks, now look at your situation, they didn't even want to pay your tuition fees. I came here for assessments in 2001 already, look at when the pigs decided to call me in ... after two fucking years ... look at all the time that has been fucking wasted.

> Look here my brother, there at our f—. Sorry brother, I almost swore in front of you, you're still converted aren't you? Now there at our depot are a lot of men who was assessed in 2001, they have all lost interest in this training shit ... I nearly never came to this training centre because the fucking larneys want to send you on the course which they prefer to send you onto and not the training which you've asked to be sent on.

These quotes with their exaggerations and strong emotions, raucousness and abusive language, bring to mind Bakhtin's notion of the carnivalesque – the potentially subversive discourse of the everyday (see Gardiner, 2000: 61–63). As noted, these quotes were completely deleted in subsequent drafts of the thesis. I wondered why Jerry had done this, while preferring to retain the more sanitised language of the vignettes sketched in subsequent drafts. When I pursued this question in my interview with him, he insisted that I had instructed him to remove these extracts from his interviews. I was horrified and claimed that I could not possibly have done so! But he held his ground. Whatever the case, it became evident that the deletion of this material represented a significant loss for him:

> I felt like we'd lost the value of the story – of that section – I sat there and I thought: everything is there; that's how we talk.

He argued that there are some things that you are only able to express 'in a mundane way', and when 'you are forced or compelled to say it in an academic way' it is not the same; 'it should be said in the way you can have expressed it'. He had this to say of academics:

> They want everything to be academic, not interested the mundane stuff. It's as if you're tainting the academic stuff with the mundane stuff, the experiential stuff. They've been working for years and years building their academic empire, and now you come with all your mundane stuff. 'No, what are you talking about? No, you must do it like this, speak like this. [It's] like going to Buckingham Palace: you must use your knife and fork, and must eat lovely and have table manners – you can't just come here and use your hands and that!'

Despite his intention (visible in this extract) to parody and subvert the power of academia, it seems that, in the process of his research writing, Jerry had understood that it would not be acceptable to the academic community were he to quote the bawdy and expressive language of some of his fellow workers.

The discovery of Jerry's deletion of this piece of his research material reminded me of Bowker's (2006) notion of knowledge as a 'dual archive'. According to Bowker, the formal (jussive) knowledge archive represents that which can be said, 'the story of how things should be'; it is bounded, linear and hierarchical; it represents that which is actually remembered but represents only a very small subset of the archive's potential memory. There is also always a 'trace archive' – that which cannot be told because it goes 'against the grain'; it is 'the place for transgression against laws and current official groupthink'. This latter body of knowledge always leaves traces of itself in the local environment and is 'recalled' through being performed as customs, habits, lived experience. Bowker (2006: 6–7) argues that each archive needs the other, that they are actually 'dual moments' of the same archive, and there is a complex interplay between the two: 'What we leave traces of is not the way we were, but a tacit negotiation between ourselves and our imagined auditors.'

What is lost in this process of negotiation 'between ourselves and our imagined auditors'? In Jerry's case, the deletion of the original quotes in later drafts of his thesis did not merely represent the loss of an empirical window on the kinds of barriers to learning that many workers face but it represented a loss to our formal knowledge archive of rich insights into the existential world of ordinary workers.

Looking Forward

In this chapter, I set out to explore 'what happens' to the experiential knowledge brought by adult learners who have entered postgraduate study via RPL, and to ascertain whether this knowledge contributes to or hinders the process of research writing and hence knowledge making. It is clear that adult learners' experiential or work-based knowledge has the potential to enrich our knowledge archive, but that drawing on experiential knowledge may also present specific challenges for the writing of research. Jerry's case demonstrates his considerable achievements in finding an authentic writing voice within the world of postgraduate writing. It illustrates the possibilities that exist when students grasp how to exercise their agency strategically; they may find ways not only to express their own experiential knowledge but also the knowledge of communities historically marginalised in the knowledge-making process, thus generating a productive interplay between the 'trace' and 'official' knowledge archives. There were clearly also losses sustained as he engaged in the process of negotiation between the experiential knowledge he wanted to express and his 'real or imagined auditors'.

Jerry ended our interview by expressing his view that we need a new form of academic writing:

> I do appreciate the fact that we can overshadow the whole thing by just talking about ourselves all the time ... I believe, yes, we can't just talk about ourselves, but there must be a section where you are able to say 'listen, this is my own experience'. So I've used my experience and I've gone back, and I've done some research around this and that, and I do agree with some theorists. I've looked back at my own life and this is my argument ...

My case study has echoes of Casanave's (2002: 149–176) case study of 'Virginia', who withdrew from her PhD a year after she had registered. One of the key factors leading to her withdrawal was that she felt that the requirements of strict adherence to 'scientific' language precluded her from communicating her studies to those around her that really mattered: 'they expect us to use that strict language – which isn't normal everyday language' (quoted in Casanave, 2002: 160). As a result, she felt 'she was aligning herself with scientists, not with the populations she wished to communicate with at home and in future work' (Casanave, 2002: 161).

Unlike Virginia who decided that 'the games of language, knowledge, and power that she encountered were not ones she wanted to participate in'

(Casanave, 2002: 149), Jerry found a way to complete his postgraduate degree and negotiated a space to express his experiential knowledge. In our final interview, he expressed the idea of publishing his thesis wherein he might experiment with a different kind of writing:

Jerry: Maybe in my book I will be able to (keep) all those little things that I couldn't use in the thesis!
Linda: If you'd had the freedom to write in the way that you wanted, how would it be different? How will you write that book?
Jerry: I will write it freehand. Not Afrikaans but with Afrikaans and other colloquialisms ... Maybe they should work out a strategy to try and maintain most of your experiential wording and so on and merge it with the academic thing and give it another name or something – but just to throw it out, it's our culture, man. It's not an American thesis that we're writing, or an English thesis that we're writing, it's a South African thesis that we're writing and it should be written in a South African way. Bring in our cultures, and we have diverse cultures, we should bring in our cultures.

Notes

(1) For this, I suggest that we need metaphors that are less static than 'knowledge boundaries' or 'structures' – concepts that suggest multiplicity and hybridity rather than dualism, and allude to movement, direction, conflict, uncertainty and emergence.
(2) I was sole supervisor of one of the students; secondary supervisor of another, and acted as an informal sounding board for the third student's primary supervisor.
(3) Pseudonyms are used for all three students.
(4) Email from Jerry, 21 July 2008.
(5) In the August 2008 draft, Jerry's life history occupies 13 of the first chapter's 16 pages, and in the final draft submitted a month later, it takes up 8 of 12 pages.
(6) Under apartheid, African workers were more strictly denied access to artisanal skills.
(7) ABET centres intended to offer an adult version of basic schooling and the equivalent qualifications.
(8) 'City of Cape Town' is the municipality's formal name.
(9) Bakhtin (1981, cited in Wertch, 1991) saw ventriloquation as the process whereby one voice speaks through another voice in a social language.
(10) See Cooper (2005: 127–128, 161).
(11) The interview took place in Maitland, Cape Town on 23 December 2010.

References

Blommaert, J. (2005) *Discourse*. Cambridge: Cambridge University Press.
Bowker, G. (2006) *Memory Practices in the Sciences*. Cambridge, MA: MIT Press.

Casanave, C.P. (2002) *Writing Games: Multicultural Case Studies of Academic Literacy Practices in Higher Education*. New Jersey: Lawrence Erlbaum Associates, Publishers.

Connell, R. (2007) *Southern Theory: The Global Dynamics of Knowledge in Social Science*. Malden, MA: Polity Press.

Cooper, L. (2005) Towards a theory of pedagogy, learning and knowledge in an 'everyday' context: A case study of a South African trade union. PhD thesis, University of Cape Town.

Daniels, H. (2001) *Vygotsky and Pedagogy*. London: Routledge Falmer.

Fenwick, T. (2001) *Experiential Learning: A Theoretical Critique from Five Perspectives*. ERIC Information Series No 385. Columbus, OH: ERIC Clearinghouse on Adult, Career and Vocational Education, Ohio State University. Online document: www.cete.org/acve/mp_fenwick_01.asp

Gardiner, M.E. (2000) *Critiques of Everyday Life*. London: Routledge.

Grossman, J. (1999) Workers and knowledge. Paper presented at the conference on Researching Work and Learning, Leeds, September.

Michelson, E. (1998) Re-membering: The return of the body to experiential learning. *Studies in Continuing Education* 20 (2), 217–233.

Michelson, E. (2004) On trust, desire, and the sacred: A response to Johann Muller's *Reclaiming Knowledge*. *Journal of Education* 32, 7–30.

Morphet, A. (1992) Introduction to the problems in adult learning. In B. Hutton (ed.) *Adult Basic Education in South Africa*. Cape Town: Oxford University Press.

Muller, J. (2000) *Reclaiming Knowledge: Social Theory, Curriculum and Education Policy*. London: Routledge Falmer.

Portelli, A. (1991) *The Death of Luigi Trastulli and Other Stories: Form and Meaning in Oral History*. New York: SUNY Press.

Ralphs, A. (2009) Specialised pedagogy: A comparative study of RPL practices within the changing landscape of the NQF in South Africa. A research proposal submitted to the South African Qualifications Authority: February.

Wertch, J.V. (1991) *Voices of the Mind: A Sociocultural Approach to Mediated Action*. Cambridge, MA: Harvard University Press.

Young, M. (2008) *Bringing Knowledge Back in: From Social Constructivism to Social Realism in the Sociology of Education*. London: Routledge.

2 A Lovely Imposition: The Complexity of Writing a Thesis in isiXhosa

Somikazi Deyi

This chapter documents my experiences as a postgraduate student writing a master's thesis in isiXhosa, my mother tongue. South Africa's Language Policy for Higher Education (Ministry of Education, 2002) provides students, particularly second-language speakers of English, with the option of writing in their mother tongue. Section 6 of the policy reads as follows: 'The challenge facing higher education is to ensure the simultaneous development of a multilingual environment in which all our languages are developed as academic/scientific languages, while at the same time ensuring that the existing languages of instruction do not serve as a barrier to access and success.' It was hoped that the policy would help to enhance overall academic performance and improve outputs at postgraduate level.

While the policy may work reasonably well for students studying African languages or African literature, for those like me, who attempt to write in the mother tongue in other disciplines, it can be a struggle. There is the risk that while policy might appear to be implemented, at the same time there are inadequate student support systems in place.

My master's thesis examined the teaching and learning of mathematics using isiXhosa to formulate equivalents of concepts that seemed to create difficulties for learners. Writing my thesis in isiXhosa presented several challenges: (1) the supervisory pool was inadequate to provide the necessary supervision of my thesis; (2) the written vocabulary is still being standardised and terminology is still being developed; and (3) the issue of external examination had not been thought through and this delayed my graduation. Although I succeeded in writing a thesis in isiXhosa, and graduated in 2007, facing these challenges meant that I had to compromise some of my initial hopes and dreams about how I wanted to write. In other words, meeting the demands of academic writing and 'scientific' discourse jeopardised (and ultimately silenced?) the rich modes of expression I desired to achieve in my home language.

In planning this chapter, I first wrote an account of my experience and then engaged in face-to-face conversations with the volume editors – both former lecturers of mine. Additional dimensions of meaning associated with my experiences emerged during our conversations. Thus, drawing on the notion of a 'dual archive' (Bowker, 2006), the volume editors argued that my spoken account could act as a 'trace archive' – a reservoir of experiential knowledge that could complement my written account, and serve to better illustrate what happened, and why I was unable to write the thesis in the way I had initially hoped. This chapter is, therefore, a combination of two accounts: an edited version of my original account of the experience, interwoven with thoughts that surfaced in conversation with one of the book editors, who helped me to reflect further on aspects of my written account.

African Languages and Academic Writing

The intellectualisation of African languages has been an issue of debate for some time. Many scholars claim that African languages do not have adequate terminology to function as languages of academic proficiency but little has been done to assess this empirically. Scholars such as Vygotsky (1962) and Alexander (1989) have contended that learning in one's mother tongue during the first six years of schooling forms a strong foundation for conceptual development and that, once learners are able to conceptualise and think critically in their mother tongue, they are in a position to perform better in an additional language. Writing in the popular media, Emeritus Professor of African Languages at the University of Cape Town, Sandile Gxilishe (2002) argues that learning in one's mother tongue has cognitive advantages, and adds depth, meaning and value to education. Thus for me, deciding to write my thesis in an African language was partly an attempt to contribute to the debate as to whether African languages can be used as languages of academic writing.

Context and Motivation for Writing a Thesis in My Mother Tongue

I have long had an interest in working with languages, not just as tools of enquiry but also as tools for change. I grew up writing, and have always seen writing as one of the gifts that I was born with. I also loved reading and was attracted to literature at a very young age. I would see a tree and I would write about it. I would compose a poem and a short story on each subject of interest. If I had had the opportunity, I would probably have published about 10 books by the time I reached Grade 5 at school as I was writing constantly. I loved writing to the extent that I felt language was part of my breathing. Writing comes from within, and I had that fire within me all the time. I created topics to write about, putting stories together about anything that touched me.

After I completed my first degree, I worked for the National Language Project (NLP) for a period of six years. NLP was an NGO that existed in South Africa's Western Cape province from the late 1980s to the mid-1990s. It was set up to promote African languages, and particularly isiXhosa, which was marginalised in the Western Cape at the time. The organisation's aim was to lobby for isiXhosa to attain equal status with English and Afrikaans in educational, political and commercial contexts. My work convinced me that one's mother tongue is capable of mediating any kind of concept. When I started working at NLP, there was no language policy that encouraged the use of African languages in teaching and learning, particularly in higher education. The argument was that the terminology and vocabulary in African languages were inadequate to qualify them as academic languages. Some of the leading sceptics were themselves mother-tongue speakers of isiXhosa, who had high regard for research in African languages, yet they dismissed the effectiveness of writing in their mother tongue. They saw attempts to prove otherwise as impractical and ideological, and saw African languages as having no significance in terms of contributing to scholarship. The more this notion gained popularity, the more I desired to prove it wrong. I wanted to prove that it was possible to produce a scholarly contribution in an African language, and this aim developed into a personal agenda.

Although I had a desire to showcase the potential of African languages to be exploited as languages of scientific engagement, there was initially no opportunity for me to do this. However, after I completed the coursework for my master's degree, and began to work towards my thesis, my supervisor (an educationalist whose mother tongue is English) asked me to consider writing my thesis in isiXhosa, my mother tongue. He had various reasons. To begin with, he was concerned about my ability to write in English in an acceptably academic manner, and said he thought I might not succeed in obtaining my master's if I submitted it in English. Initially, this made me angry because, as a supervisor, he had offered me no assistance with my writing. He seemed to simply assume that students who reached the master's level would know how to write a thesis. However, instead of feeling unworthy, I saw this as the opportunity I had been waiting for – to explore using my mother tongue to write about the use of isiXhosa in teaching and learning mathematics. In other words, his suggestion promised to provide a platform for what I had always wanted to do, and so I readily agreed to it.

My supervisor's second motive was that he, too, wanted to prove that African languages have the potential to be used for academic purposes. He wanted to show that, although he does not speak an African language, he was right about the capacity of African languages, and that someone was willing to write in isiXhosa in a scientific field. Although his understanding was that I was going to write in isiXhosa because he found my written English problematic, we also planned to use the data collected to write a paper for a language conference showing how, for isiXhosa speakers, learning mathematics concepts in isiXhosa improves their understanding. Indeed, the process led to conference papers, and eventually a book on understanding mathematics and science concepts in isiXhosa.[1] Being a co-author on these papers and publications helped me discard all the negativity accompanying the initial suggestions.

Two Supervisors: A Complex Space in Which to Manoeuvre

It was agreed that I would write my thesis in isiXhosa on condition that I had two supervisors: the primary supervisor (an English speaker and educationalist), would act as the research overseer (content supervisor) of the study, and a secondary supervisor (an isiXhosa speaker and African languages specialist), would advise on, and make judgements about the language used. The plan was that each chapter would be written in isiXhosa and then summarised in English. The task appeared laborious but I wanted to do it.

The process never seemed to work as planned, however. Much of the supervision, including of the content, was left to the secondary supervisor, as it was virtually impossible to discuss language devoid of content. As an African-language expert working with the thesis, he needed to understand the depth of the content. This meant that I generally received two sets of feedback. This became a bit much, and I had to carve out a space in which I could work independently. I would think hard about both sets of feedback and decide whether I should use all the feedback given or accept certain aspects and discard others. This was especially the case when the two supervisors addressed the same issues very differently. Instead of being frustrated, I found that receiving two sets of feedback actually gave me some latitude to make my own decisions. My primary supervisor could not check the isiXhosa version to see whether I had followed through on his recommendations, and realising that opportunities for surveillance were diminished in this case, I was able to achieve a degree of agency that I might not have enjoyed otherwise.

Scientific Writing, Language Standardisation and Silencing the Breath and Movement of a Language

I wanted my thesis to conform to the criteria set for scientific studies because I wanted to show that African languages can be useful in any scientific field. My secondary supervisor (the language expert) was also keen to prove that isiXhosa could be used for scientific discourse, but he did not always approve of the manner in which I wrote. His words were: 'I don't want this to be a fashionable thing, I want it to be something you can feel good about and be proud of once it is done. At the end you should be proud of yourself especially when the next person reading it is able to see the scientific engagement.' These words were encouraging. It occurred to me that since mine was the first such study of mathematics to be written in isiXhosa, the secondary supervisor wanted to ensure that the norms of western scientific writing were maintained for the sake of his reputation (as both a proud isiXhosa speaker and as an academic supervisor). I assume he did not want my qualification to be viewed as having been 'given away' simply because it was written in isiXhosa.

I pleaded with him not to cut out certain issues, but he explained that the study was intended for teachers of mathematics and that we should focus on their requirements. The study was not about my feelings and we were definitely not trying to create anything other than a scientific study in isiXhosa. It soon became evident that the thesis was not about what I liked but about the requirements of academic writing. Therefore, I had to adhere to that.

The difficulties were made even more complex by the fact that isiXhosa language scholars appeared not to agree on certain terms and concepts. While I was writing the thesis, several language bodies and groups of scholars[2] were busy debating and developing technical terminology in African languages, and also debating the appropriateness of the existing terms across various learning areas in an attempt to standardise the written forms of South Africa's nine official African languages. In this context, it was important for me to tread carefully around use of terms, concepts and the language itself. Each term used in the thesis had to undergo intense scrutiny related to its etymology, and the contexts within which it was used, before my supervisor and I could agree on whether it was appropriate or not to use in teaching.

If I had had my way, I would have brought in many more proverbs and idioms. In isiXhosa, one never makes a point very precisely in the first instance. Instead, many examples are presented, using different forms of the language, and many synonyms are used to explain the issue at hand. The use of idioms and synonyms in African languages is generally known to give spoken or written isiXhosa a 'rich effect'. Even if one is writing something scientific, there is a tendency, when elaborating on an issue, to borrow from poetic styles of expression to put across an idea. For me, writing in an African language has rhythm, almost like a voice, a sound. It has breath, and one can feel the breath of the language moving from deep within. This movement of the language seems important to me, and made it very difficult for me to cut the text.

The academy does not easily allow this particular way of doing things, however. Drawing on predominant isiXhosa culture and genres through, for example, the use of synonyms for emphasis, tends to be judged as repetitious when seen through the lens of western scientific modes of writing. In English, an idea tends to be conveyed once, and repetition is 'not allowed'. The tensions involved in moving from a poetic to a more rhetorical genre required many drafts by me before it was deemed to have reached a form that was satisfactory for an academic thesis.

My secondary supervisor constantly reminded me that we were using the language as a vehicle and not as an end in itself. He reiterated that I needed to forget about the lovely language patterns that are characteristic of isiXhosa, and rather maintain a scholarly, academic style of writing. The thesis had to be flawless and squeaky clean, and contain nothing that might make it unfit for academic purposes. Although he shared my burning desire to showcase an African language functioning as an academic language, he argued that there were norms and standards that had to be maintained if I was to attain academic success. Maintaining these standards seemed to be his way of minimising the risk of failure, and hence I had to adhere to the advice he offered. Often, I tried to leave in some of the writing he suggested I should remove, but he had a very fine eye and was thorough with every chapter. I was caught out several times. I would simply say, 'I thought you wouldn't notice that,' and then do as I was told.

The process made me aware that a postgraduate thesis does not belong to the student at all, but is determined by the audience it is intended for (the external examiner and other possible readers). The supervisors made me aware that the people out there should see no fault with my study, my use of language or my style of writing. I finally understood that I had to cut all evidence of my emotions out of the study. This was a struggle, but apparently it had to be done for the benefit of the audience – in other words for the sake of the supervisors' reputations, those of the examiners and of the academy itself. I wanted to push the boundaries, but found that this could not be done. To keep things simple one had to comply with the supervisors although I was tempted to write the thesis in the way that felt significant to me. Initially, I thought I could challenge the process because there seemed to be little point in using isiXhosa if it was going to be denied its naturalness. However, it became clear that the supervisor was bound by standard academic writing norms, so I had to refrain and do as advised.

However, removing the characteristics of the language meant that there were times when it did not feel as if I was actually writing in isiXhosa. Removing my feelings for the language meant that all intimacy was lost. In fact, the process defeated what I imagined could be achieved by writing in my mother tongue. I wanted to write in a way that included all the ingredients that make isiXhosa the beautifully rich and creamy language that it is, to exploit its full potential. Unfortunately, scientific discourse had to be observed and this left little space for what I wished to do. I must say that I still see this as a loss.

Administrative Bungles

Despite the difficulties, writing a thesis in isiXhosa proved doable until it became clear that there were administrative issues that the institution had not thought through or communicated clearly to my supervisor or the administrative staff of the department. First, if a student plans to write a thesis in a language other than English, the department in which the thesis originates has to notify the faculty. In my case, this did not happen until I was ready to submit my thesis. I then had to withdraw my work until these issues were sorted out. Second, it seems that few examiners are qualified to evaluate work in the field of language as it is used across a school curriculum. Most of the available examiners were isiXhosa language specialists, but none were expert in the issues related to teaching mathematics through isiXhosa. Identifying a suitable external examiner took a long time. Eventually, I even asked if I could submit the thesis in English because of the cost I was incurring by having to continually reregister as a student. Luckily, this was not necessary in the end, but it took me a few years to pay off the fees incurred. Clearly, institutions should explore *all* the necessary requirements before encouraging students to write in languages other than those that are mainstream within the organisation.

A Case for Retaining the Rich and Creamy Nature of Language in Scientific Texts

I conclude this chapter by reflecting on lessons for supervisors and postgraduate pedagogy. There is a need to encourage scholars to explore the possibility of using the beautifully rich and creamy nature of their languages. In relation to isiXhosa, this richness tends to be displayed best when one is writing without boundaries. It is crucial to point out that this does not mean removing or ignoring scientific norms and standards. But when writing is confined to western scientific ways of using a language, much is lost. The 'being of the language' can be jeopardised in order for a writer to meet the standards of academic writing. It felt to me like taking a part of myself right away.

This raises the question of whether there has ever been a thorough discussion among higher-education authorities about accepted thesis formats. This question should have been proactively explored before the implementation of the language policy in education (Ministry of Education, 2002). It is extremely difficult to write in an African language and, at the same time, use methods of argumentation that are foreign to that language. Confining the thesis to scientific writing standards created a cold distance between me and my own words; I had to totally remove myself from the study. This was a challenge because African languages are essentially intimate, emotional and absolutely spiritual. As noted earlier, expanding on a point by using excessive emphasis, bringing in idioms or recalling what a great speaker once said on the topic is normal in isiXhosa, although this is considered repetitious in western scientific discourse.

The issue of postgraduate writing needs further discussion. The dilemma for me is that it is supposed to be the student's work but, at the same time, the process of thesis writing does not appear to be intended for the benefit of the student but for someone else. If the writing was the student's, it would pose the student's questions, answer those questions, and the findings would convey the student's particular message or argument. What is clear to me is that, as a student, one can claim only limited ownership of one's own study. I can, however, claim that I achieved some of my aims in writing the thesis in isiXhosa. As a result of the study, I have been involved in programmes that seek to promote the use of African languages in learning and teaching, and particularly in teaching concepts that English second language students tend to grapple with. I have also co-authored a book on the teaching of mathematics using isiXhosa, thus sharing knowledge and enhancing broader understanding.

Notes

(1) *Understanding Concepts in Maths and Science: A Learner's and Teacher's Resource Book*, which I co-authored, was published by Maskew Miller Longman, Cape Town, in 2005.
(2) These organisations included the South African government's Department of Arts and Culture, the Pan South African Language Board, and the Project for the Study of Alternative Education in South Africa, to name just a few.

References

Alexander, N. (1989) *Language Policy and National Unity in South Africa/Azania*. Cape Town: Buchu Books.
Bowker, G. (2006) *Memory Practices in the Sciences*. Cambridge, MA: MIT Press.
Gxilishe, S. (2002) Language the determinant of a child's success in education. *Cape Argus*, 19 June, p. 14.
Ministry of Education (South Africa) (2002) Language policy for higher education, accessed 18 November 2010. www.dhet.gov.za.
Vygotsky, L. (1962) *Thought and Language*. Cambridge, MA: MIT Press.

Part 2

Strategies for Hybridity: Writing Together

3 Negotiating Alternative Discourses in Academic Writing and Publishing: Risks with Hybridity

Suresh Canagarajah and Ena Lee

> *Autoethnography, transculturation, critique, collaboration, bilingualism, mediation, parody, denunciation, imaginary dialogue, vernacular expression – these are some of the literate arts of the contact zone. Miscomprehension, incomprehension, dead letters, unread masterpieces, absolute heterogeneity of meaning – these are some of the perils of writing in the contact zone*
>
> Pratt, 1991: 37

There is a new openness to alternative discourses in the academy. Perhaps, the backlash against modernist orientations to knowledge construction has cleared the way for a search for other modes of inquiry and writing. To some extent, the mythical data-fronted, detached introduction–methods–results–discussion (IMRD) structure (see Swales, 1990) of the research-article genre received its justification from the positivistic research tradition of modernity. The realisation that knowledge is frankly value laden, if not personal and ideological, has created a readiness to search for alternative ways of representing research knowledge. In recent years, we have found research articles adopting more narrative, personal, self-reflexive, and dialogical structures (see Canagarajah, 1996a). There is more scope for voice for authors in the research-article genre, especially from those who have traditionally been excluded from mainstream publishing forums – such as, women, minority, and multilingual scholars. However, it is not easy to adopt alternative genres in refereed journal publications. This forum is strictly guarded by many of the major journal editors and publishers (known as gatekeepers). To a considerable extent, articles published in academic journals still adopt structures approximating the IMRD genre. Hence, although some movement has been made towards greater openness to alternative discourses, research articles – and academic writing in general – remain resistant to change. In this context, there are still many dilemmas and much uncertainty.

The notion of hybridity, however, provides a way out for writing scholars/teachers. Hybridity is a pragmatic response, which seems to accommodate both the voices of the authors and established discourses of the field. In this sense, it eschews the extremes and stakes out a middle path between tradition and change. Hybridity has also been made fashionable by contemporary theories in cultural studies and philosophy. Postmodernity critiques all forms of essentialisation, and the mixed and mediated nature of identities and texts has emerged as common sense. The contact between cultures and languages, even in power-ridden contexts such as under colonisation, has been theorised as engendering new genres of communication and culture (as the above quote from Pratt indicates). Reversing the modernist valorisation of pure and discrete constructs in communication and social life, hybridity now helps define texts and identities as open to negotiation.

These developments have emboldened writing scholars to promote hybridity as the answer to the writing challenges facing multilingual scholars and students. Zamel's (1997) article on the implications of hybridity for multilingual writers is illustrative. She argues that it would be a mistake to view genres of writing as preconstructed and rigid in conventions. Referring to Pratt's (1991) concept of 'transculturation' to challenge these essentialised and reductive conceptualisations, Zamel says, 'Transculturation assumes and celebrates the selective, generative, and inventive nature of linguistic and cultural adaptation and thus reflects precisely how languages and cultures develop and change – infused, invigorated, and challenged by variation and innovation' (Zamel, 1997: 350). If languages and cultures always change and proliferate, why should anyone fear genre conventions? Similarly, she criticises attempts to fix the writing of multilingual students or to limit their discursive possibilities to 'legitimate [linguistic] moves': 'There is evidence all around that individuals have access to a range of complex linguistic moves that are not taken into account in the tendency to delineate, objectify, and rationalize' (Zamel, 1997: 344).

At this point, hybridity and transculturation might seem a bit too triumphalistic as they seem to defy all norms, rules, regulations and conventions in writing. It might appear as if we are taking the resistant and empowering potential of hybridity too far. Although anything is possible in communication, there are still strong notions about what genres are permitted in certain domains of communication, and, as noted, the boundaries of these domains are zealously guarded. Similarly, although anything is possible for writers/students, social and historical contexts have created preferences for certain writing styles and resistance to alternative languages and genres. These constraints create tensions that can sometimes be difficult to negotiate.

There are other limitations to treating hybridity as an answer to all writing problems. As Williams (2003: 600) has observed, 'The idea of a hybrid re-inscription of the symbols of authority ... or the idea of a "third space" has been employed to describe a benign and ultimately progressive and positivist multicultural synthesis that creates a new culture of pluralistic tolerance'. In other words, the pragmatic middle path provided by hybridity can lead to conservative and compromising outcomes: in having to merge one's preferred discourses with the established ones, the critical edge in alternative genres might be lost. Thus, it is possible for hybridity to serve as a vehicle for containing and managing difference, limiting its potential to initiate meaningful change.

Despite these possible limitations, the case for hybridity had been made so forcefully in academia that when Suresh took over the editorship of *TESOL Quarterly (TQ)*, he treated this as a useful construct in his effort to internationalise the journal and diversify its knowledge representation practices. This is how he announced his mission when he became the editor:

> I intend to help *TQ* keep up with changes in scholarly research practices. In many disciplines, research has become more participatory, reflexive, critical, and local. The research approaches in TESOL [the teaching of English for speakers of other languages] still largely follow the controlled, impersonal, and positivistic mode of traditional modernist inquiry. *TQ* has to present a wider range of research approaches.
>
> I intend to help the journal negotiate more boldly the diverse modes of representing research findings. In many journals, introspective or narrative writing sits side by side with the more impersonal articles reflecting the traditional introduction, methodology, results, discussion (IMRD) structure. I would like *TQ* to be more open to atypical forms of scholarly rhetoric.
>
> I also want to facilitate a more inclusive international conversation on mutual disciplinary interests. Linguists and teachers in places such as India, Singapore, South Africa, and the Middle East are developing interesting new orientations that fall outside the current paradigms in the profession. Their work gets published locally, if it gets published at all.

I intend to be more proactive in accommodating the work of nontraditional researchers. I want to explore ways to mentor new authors, encourage referees to provide more constructive commentary to help these authors in the revision process, and increase *TQ*'s readership outside elite research and academic institutions.[1]

Suresh mentions that in order to help non-traditional authors (i.e. those from multilingual and international contexts) succeed in having their work published he would like to introduce a system of mentoring. Although it would take two years to formally establish a mentoring system, whereby rejected authors with promising work would be invited to correspond with selected members of the editorial board to revise their work before a fresh review, he immediately started offering additional help to authors and inviting reviewers to offer constructive suggestions. Ena was one of the first authors to receive this extended help because her article reached Suresh as he was settling into his editorial position. Her narrative and self-exploratory approach to her professional status in the field was the type of alternative genre Suresh had envisioned would broaden the discourses in the journal. However, in this case, the mentoring and negotiation unexpectedly resulted in a failed publishing outcome.

We recount the negotiation process here to consider the challenges and possibilities involved in publishing alternative genres by novice authors. Rather than brushing aside the failed encounter, we prefer to open it up for analysis so that both authors and gatekeepers can explore the conditions for the negotiation of voice in academic writing, particularly in relation to novice scholars. Both parties have to develop a critical understanding of their mutual roles and responsibilities. The narrative that follows demonstrates that writing is always risky – a condition that cannot be avoided – and is negotiated by all parties in publishing for voice. As Arnoldi (2009: 1) rightly argues, 'we constantly accept and/or take risks because accomplishing anything necessarily entails risks of all sorts'. And for novice scholars the risks are even bigger. Our narrative illustrates that hybridity is not a solution to the challenges of alternative genres but is itself the issue that needs negotiation. For while hybridity opens the doors to alternative discourses, it can simultaneously be a means through which the risks entailed in the publishing of these discourses are both mitigated and regulated in order to maintain the hegemonic norms of writing and knowledge within a particular field. Ang (2001: 197) argues, 'What we need to question ... is not so much hybridity ... but the depoliticization involved in the reduction of hybridity to happy fusion and synthesis'. Note that in the epigraph, Pratt (1991) calls attention to the 'perils' in hybrid literacies even as she articulates their creativity. Hybridity in the context of academic writing and publication thus poses the following important question: to what extent must novice/multilingual authors accommodate established discourses in order to ensure voice?

Background to this Study

It was in a face-to-face meeting at a late stage of the publishing negotiations that both of us realised that the mentoring process had not gone the way we thought it had. The epiphany motivated us to revisit the experience for an understanding of what had gone wrong. We analysed all our correspondences. We came up with prompts to elicit and reconstruct our attitudes and responses at every stage of the review process. After we journaled our experiences and recollections individually, we had an opportunity to reflect on them further when we put our narratives together for a presentation in a panel during the 2006 TESOL convention (Wei et al., 2006). Hearing each other's perspective, together with the questions raised by panel members and the audience, helped us to analyse our experiences further before we wrote this chapter together. In combination with the different artefacts relating to the review – that is, multiple versions of Ena's article, reviewer comments, editorial decision letters and other correspondence – we reconstructed the negotiation process with sufficient descriptive thickness (Geertz, 1973). In constructing our narrative jointly in this chapter, we attempted to arrive at some common findings without suppressing the tensions and differences; concerns regarding story ownership and representational power, however, must thus be approached differently and critically in this kind of method (De Fina & Georgakopoulou, 2012: 153).

Specifically, it became clear to us as we drafted this chapter that we had differing (and sometimes divisive) interpretations of events as they happened. Thus, arriving at 'common findings' would be a problematic process, illuminating the challenges of narrative meaning-making when both authors (simultaneously researchers and under research) are equally 'present' in events, but not equally situated within them (i.e. one is very well established and the other is a novice researcher at the start of her career). Disjunctures in understanding of and reporting on the events would inherently impact any analysis of the narrative; thus, the process of reconstruction and storytelling, itself, needed to be a negotiated process. Ironically, the difficult mentor/mentee lessons we both learned from the events recounted in this chapter assisted us to negotiate the writing of this piece with greater wisdom. The lessons learned have enabled us to both acknowledge and attend to notions of power and positionality in the construction of a joint narrative and in the collaborative analysis that follows. The result – the current chapter – aims to highlight rather than suppress the tensions and differences of our shared experience. An appreciation of the risk involved in writing an *equal co-authored* chapter was thus not lost on either of us.

We are of the opinion that our approach provides an insider perspective on the dilemmas and tensions that characterise the apprenticeship experience. A limitation in some of the previous studies on mentoring is the lack of a sufficiently emic perspective on the interaction. In studies such as Belcher (2007) and Flowerdew (1999, 2000), researchers approach the publishing experience objectively. Although some attempts are made to solicit their views, authors are not drawn directly into a collaborative research relationship or invited for a member check on the researcher's reading of the outcome. This study adopts autoethnography as its method. Like ethnography, this method focuses on developing a thick description from a holistic and emic perspective. However, it features the researcher as a full member of the community or experience being studied (see Anderson, 2006; Chang, 2008); the ethnographer is fully visible. Indeed, in this study, the subject/researcher roles are fused. The ethnographic method also focuses on evoking the experience with emotional richness, in most cases as a narrative, before facilitating an analysis. The narrative is seen as the basis, method, and the eventual result of ethnographic research and is privileged over more general theorisation.

Within autoethnography, many types of interviews can be conducted to generate narrative and reflection (see Ellis, 2004). We opted for interactive interviews, in which, typically, two or more people who share similar experiences act as both participants and researchers. Ellis describes this type of interview as a 'more self-conscious, collaborative process' and states that 'interactive interviews try to access a deeper level of information – the emotional, intimate realm' (Ellis, 2004: 64, 65). These interviews led to a co-constructed narrative; thus, the narrative that follows develops from questions we posed to each other as we acted as both participant and researcher to dig into this particular publishing and mentoring experience.

In this chapter, we first quote directly from our own journals (where we recorded our answers to the questions we posed to one another) to present our experiences in our own voices. Our journals have been lightly edited for coherence. At times, we use italics to evoke our stream of consciousness. In quoting also from multiple texts (i.e. versions of the draft, reviewer commentary, decision letters, and formal and informal correspondence), we give multiple perspectives on the experience to complement our voices. What emerges from the narrative is something akin to a textual history study (see Lillis & Curry, 2010). A close analysis of the evolution of a single article is developed, revealing the ways in which it was shaped by the different investments, motivations, and objectives of different parties in the publishing and writing process. Through this process, we demonstrate the challenges and risks inherent in attempting to publish an alternative discourse or genre in a mainstream academic journal.

Our story also goes beyond some of the more usual differences that occur in such disciplinary or publishing engagements. While the best that multilingual authors can usually hope for are friendly and understanding native-speaker editors, the editor in this case was himself a multilingual (and non-native) speaker of English, a fact that one might expect would make the negotiation process easier and smoother for multilingual writers. The author, although of Chinese descent, was born and raised in Canada and English is her dominant language. While her linguistic identity considerably reduces the alienness that other multilingual authors may face, she experienced other forms of disempowerment. As a female graduate student adopting a theoretical framework (critical race theory) that was underrepresented in the fields of applied linguistics and TESOL at the time she wrote the article, she faced considerable rhetorical challenges. The objective of her article was to convey the struggle for voice by a TESOL professional who queries the place of 'race', and offers a critical understanding of the native/non-native dichotomy through an analysis of her own experiences as a 'native-speaker' from a visible minority. Her article was a narrative, an alternative genre of writing that the editor and the journal were somewhat ready for. Although the terms of this publishing engagement do not display the more stereotypical and extreme differences between an unsympathetic native English editor and an under-resourced author of limited proficiency from a remote third-world country, the experience is uniquely revealing. It illustrates some of the more nuanced yet equally intractable features of academic socialisation, rhetorical expectations and publishing conventions that can be challenging for any author, mentor or editor to negotiate. The discourses dominant in each discipline, and in the publishing world, shape our interactions and negotiations despite good intentions on all sides relating to the publishing of alternative genres.

The Narrative

ENA: My interest in writing the article I submitted to *TQ* derives from my racialised identity within the TESOL field. For many years, I had been struggling with issues that would arise in classrooms and staff lounges regarding my 'race' – seeing that I was Chinese, most students and colleagues would assume that I was an English second-language (ESL) student, rather than a teacher. When recounting these experiences to family, friends and colleagues, oftentimes I was made to feel that this situation was of my own doing: *I didn't dress appropriately; I didn't do my hair and wear makeup; it was an isolated incident; it wasn't about race, but because of other situational or personal factors instead.* Reading Bourdieu (1977) and learning about his construct of legitimacy during my doctoral studies helped me theorise my identity within the TESOL field for the first time. As a Chinese subject, perceived as non-native, I lacked the legitimacy to become an insider and to succeed in my profession. In thinking later of writing about my identity, I figured that Bourdieu's work might offer a good theoretical framework because I was aware that an explicit theoretical component was needed in order to strengthen my arguments in the eyes of other TESOL scholars.

An opportunity presented itself in the colloquium on 'Theorizing race in TESOL' at the 2003 TESOL convention, where I presented my paper, 'Reflections on illegitimacy in teaching ESL' (Lee, 2003). I had specifically written the piece as a conference presentation for the colloquium without fathoming that anything would come of it later. I framed it as a journal entry, with a strong narrative voice. I adopted a tone of simply recounting my story to my friends and colleagues – as I had in fact done on many occasions before the colloquium – struggling to understand my place in the discipline. I wanted to use my own voice and my own experiences to query the need for change in the field, and using personal narrative to do so was a deliberate decision as it allowed me to illustrate how seemingly innocuous everyday experiences can reveal how discourses of racism connect with the native/non-native construct.

However, on my return from the convention, my supervisor encouraged me to submit the article to *TQ* because she thought it was a piece that the journal might find interesting. She felt that its ideas had not been addressed in the field before. Although I agreed with her, I followed up with some reluctance due to the personal nature of the piece – exposing my private concerns in my field's most influential journal wasn't very appealing to me. Besides, I was concerned about changing the voice and genre of the personal writing to suit the usual requirements of publication in a research journal. So when I revised the conference presentation for submission, I decided that I wouldn't radically change the structure, style or tone, because I felt that doing so would be insincere. *This is my story, this is exactly how it went, this is exactly how I felt; and to describe it otherwise would be to invalidate my own experiences and feelings.* I also decided to request that it be treated as a 'think piece' for the Forum section of the journal.² I didn't want it to be in the main section where full-length research articles are featured. I figured that in the Forum section, even if I was asked for revisions, I'd still be able to maintain the narrative tone that I thought was crucial to my piece. I didn't want reviewers to tell me that it wasn't empirical enough or make me 'scientify' or theorise my life story so that it would qualify as a full-length article. I figured that as a 'think piece' it wouldn't have to replicate the rigid structures and requirements of a research article.

I wrote a covering letter thinking that, as an amateur, I didn't have much chance of getting it published. *Who will value the story of an insignificant graduate student, let alone a story that may be viewed as just a 'poor me' piece? And will it be seen as 'academic' enough for a highly selective academic journal?* Matters became complicated when I sent my manuscript to my supervisor before sending it to *TQ*. She was disappointed with me for my decision to submit it as a Forum piece and felt that it should be sent as a full-length article. Although I didn't agree, we came to a compromise: I would (very reluctantly) write in my covering letter that I didn't know whether my article should be a Forum piece or full-length article, and that I (in fact, my supervisor) felt that 'it would be at home in either venue'. *How could it ever be accepted as a full-length article? As a Forum piece, I may have a better chance of getting it published.*

SURESH: When Ena's submission reached me in February 2004, I was surprised to see how close I was to realising some of my publishing dreams so early in my editorial tenure. I had always wanted to publish more diverse genres and research approaches. I was impressed by the timeliness of the subject matter and the audacity of the tone. I initially wanted to hurry the refereeing process as I had the dream of publishing Ena's article as the lead piece in my first issue. (The manuscripts for the March 2005 issue had to be sent for production around December 2004.) By publishing Ena's article, I would be able to make a statement on my readiness to publish non-conventional research and writing. Such a gesture would announce to multilingual and novice authors that *TQ* was open to new voices.

There are ways to nudge submissions in positive directions even though refereed publishing may seem impersonal and mechanical, leaving little room for editorial intervention. One way to do this is through the strategic choice of referees. I chose to send Ena's submission first to two scholars who had previously published non-traditional writing in *TQ*, and represented unconventional professional identities in TESOL.³ I assumed that they would be supportive of the genre of writing Ena was engaging in. They were both women (although I didn't think gender was foregrounded in Ena's argument or discourse). They also happened to be 'native speakers' of English. I assumed that Ena had to convince the TESOL field's membership and the journal's dominant audience as to the worth of her article. Therefore, although I chose a somewhat supportive set of referees, I still wanted Ena to receive rigorous and constructive criticism.

On reading the article more closely, however, I realised that more work would be required before Ena's article would reach publishable standard. Let me share my initial impressions. Ena's article began thus:

On race and illegitimacy in teaching ESL

> Whiteness and the native speaker construct are in a complicit relation, forcing nonnative English teachers of color to face challenges White colleagues do not usually experience. (Kubota, 2002a: 87)

The above quotation from one of Ryuko Kubota's most recent papers highlights the relationship between current *constructions* of *whiteness* and the 'nonnative' speaker. She asserts that nonnative English teachers of color often struggle with particular issues of *legitimacy* in the English as a second language (ESL) classroom that white teacher do not; however, I would argue that Kubota's use of the word 'nonnative' is actually superfluous as her observation reflects a reality experienced not only by nonnative English teachers of color, but by all English teachers of color. I frame this observation in my own experiences, conflicts, and intersections of being a Canadian, an ESL teacher of color, and a native speaker of English. I also draw on Pierre Bourdieu's (1977, 1982/1991) notion of *'legitimacy'* in order to explore these challenges and the implications they have on the field of ESL. (first draft: 1, emphasis added)

Ena jumps straight into her topic, introduces the argument, and locates the discussion in her personal experience. She frames the argument well by invoking Kubota's arguments published in this very journal on non-native identity and race (indeed, at the time, the work referenced was one of Kubota's most recent papers). But she also critiques Kubota slightly to argue that the very concept of nativeness is at issue as all teachers of colour face marginalisation, irrespective of native-speaker status. Thus, she identifies the niche she wishes to occupy with this article.

However, inadequate attention is given to *TQ*'s audience. It appears as if Ena assumes that the journal's readership is familiar with the discourses of poststructuralism, critical race theory and postcolonialism. Even if the audience was familiar with those discourses, it is advisable for authors to be sparing with jargon, yet in her opening paragraph, Ena uses the term *legitimacy* before introducing it in relation to Bourdieu's work. Other seemingly innocuous terms, such as *race, whiteness* and *construction,* also come with theoretical baggage. More controversially, Ena uses these terms in the title and the epigraph, failing to realise that they could be question-begging and provocative for some readers, especially when she has not yet made her case in the article. The rapidity and casualness with which she uses these terms and theories assumes a sympathetic audience who shares her radical perspectives. However, for *TQ*'s readership, which includes teachers who are not conversant with contemporary theories and/or researchers who are largely positivistic in disposition, the tone and style are inappropriate.

Then follows Ena's richly personal narrative. In a dramatic switch of discourses, Ena adopts the strategy of foregrounding the narrative and sending citations to endnotes. For example, she recounts situations where she experienced racism in her school, but attaches endnotes in appropriate places that lead to scholarly references:

> I vividly remember, however, retorting to him, 'I'm Canadian, stupid,' as if he were too dumb to recognize the difference.[1] (p. 5)

> This was, ironically, in direct contrast to reasons why I had started to develop more of a Chinese identity to begin with – namely, because I felt that both in school and out, I was seen and treated as a Canadian 'outsider'.[2] (p. 5)

The related endnotes read as follows:

> 1. Like Bannerji (2000), Fleming (2003) and Ng (1993), I see a clear relationship between being a Canadian and being white. I will discuss the connections between race and 'national identities' in the following sections.
> 2. See Li (1999) for similar observations on being 'on the periphery of both worlds' (p. 43) and being positioned as an outsider in one's own communities.

This approach of foregrounding the narrative and backgrounding the citations has been used by many established scholars, most eminently by Heath (1983) in her ethnography, *Ways with Words*. However, even a narrative can be problematic in a journal that mainly publishes quantitative and controlled studies. In 2004, this strategy was somewhat unconventional for the

TESOL community. *TQ* readers would probably want to see more analysis of the narrative and direct interpretation of the implications for her argument. They would expect an amplification of works cited in the body of the text. The narrative might be perceived as too impressionistic and personal, and written in too relaxed a tone. In my view, the stories thus could have been introduced and framed better in relation to the overriding argument. Ena's topic sentences reveal that her stories lack good framing:

> The first episode that confirmed for me the relationship between race and legitimacy... (p. 9)
>
> In another instance... (p. 11)
>
> A more thought-provoking incident occurred when... (p. 12)

The development of her argument had a loose episodic structure and the stories could be more tightly integrated into it. When she reached the section on pedagogical concerns, Ena did not have good stories. Her narratives were mostly experiences with her peers (when she was a student) and with colleagues in the staff room. It seemed as if, since she did not have any classroom stories of her own, she had latched her argument onto other people's stories:

> As with the teachers of color in Amin's (1997, 2000, 2001) study, *I too, have always felt* the need to work particularly hard in establishing my legitimacy in the classroom. The initial looks of doubt that I receive each semester from students is a more than obvious hint that I will, indeed, have to 'prove myself' as an authentic teacher, native speaker, and Canadian. In some cases, this exercise may take a few days, and for other students, a few minutes; however, one semester, intervention from administrators and fellow instructors resulted when one student's challenges to my legitimacy severely affected the classroom atmosphere and dynamics. *Like Thomas (1999), I was disappointed...* (p. 14; emphasis added).

Ena began her argument by attaching her stories to Amin's quote but then merely stated that she shared similar experiences, rather than explaining the details of the stories that would assist readers in better understanding the 'similarities' of which she spoke. In addition, the stories that Ena recounted in the earlier sections of her piece were based on her experiences as a student rather than on experiences more closely related to TESOL pedagogy (the focus of this particular section of her article).

Ena concluded her article with the implications of her narrative. The concluding section had the following subtitles: 'Issues of Identity,' 'Issues of Legitimacy' and 'Issues of Race.' Although these points are relevant and in keeping with *TQ*'s requirement that all studies offer pedagogical implications (*TQ* is a practitioner-based research journal), the presentation was a bit diffuse. The sections overlapped in some ways and some aspects were redundant – for example, 'issues of race' are already part of 'issues of identity'. Furthermore, these sections could also have been better integrated into the overarching argument, rather than being framed separately and worded vaguely as 'issues'. The problem was that Ena's stories of personal discrimination covered different contexts (viz insults experienced as a student from fellow students, as a teacher from fellow teachers, and both inside and outside the classroom). I felt that if she focused her stories on those she experienced as a teacher, she could offer better lessons to other TESOL professionals – *TQ*'s readers are teachers, not students. Besides, Ena's stories showed her as a victim of racism, but not how she negotiated each event. Such information would have provided some pointers for other visible-minority teachers on ways of dealing with bias, both in the classroom and within their institutions more broadly.

After waiting for some time and failing to receive the second referee's comments, I sent Ena an update on her article. I indicated to her that the first referee (who had already sent her comments) felt that the article needed more work and another round of revision. In a lengthy letter, where I shared the reading articulated above, I decided to give her some points to consider and concluded with the following recommendation:

> This paper might work better as a multivocal essay. That is, you must try to merge the narration and analysis. In some of the early pages you relegate comments relating to other scholars and studies to footnotes (see p. 3, 4, 6, 7). If you can use the scholarship more actively to interpret and analyze your narrative, you might convince our readers of the research-worthiness and scholarly stature of this article. See if you can switch between narrative and analysis more fluidly. (Editor's decision letter #1, 10 May 2004)

What motivated my decision was my orientation to publishing as a conversation. To bring in a new contribution, the author has to enter into the ongoing conversation in a relevant way. Therefore, I expected Ena to engage more closely with the current discourses and conventions of the journal. It appeared to me that Ena was not framing the article relevantly. I also realised that although I valued hybridity, there are different levels and extents of discoursal merger; Ena's approach kept dissimilar discourses too far apart rather than merging them seamlessly.

> **ENA:** I was surprised to receive a lengthy and affable letter from the editor of *TQ*. I was shocked, exhilarated, and then daunted (all in that order) by the editor's response. Shocked because the editor (not just a reviewer) would do such a careful reading of my submission, and then go on to provide two full pages of suggestions to assist in getting it published. Excited that he even suggested that it might be a full-length article. Daunted about what that now meant: it might actually see the light of publishing day (and in *TQ*, no less), and I now had an obligation (as the new editor was obviously sticking his neck out for me!) to do a good job with the revision. He had written: 'I'd like to see one more round of revision to see if we can feature this as a full-length article ... Feel free to call me or email me for further advice or clarifications' (Editor's decision letter #1, 10 May 2004). *Call him or email him? Personally? As if Suresh Canagarajah really has time to help an unknown grad student with their research, on top of the one million other things on his 'to do' list each day.*

Excited that I was so close to getting published at such an early stage in my academic career, I calmed myself, and started slowly on the revisions. I figured that I needn't rush as I was still waiting for the referees' comments.

> **SURESH:** When the second review reached me a month later, I was impressed by the remarkable unanimity between the three of us. This realisation gave me confidence in the refereeing system. Our assessment of the article didn't seem too subjective or idiosyncratic. The first referee had written a shorter response as she felt that the article was more appropriate for the Forum section. Her note read:
>
> Recommendation: Revise
>
> This manuscript deals with an issue that deserves more attention in the *TESOL Quarterly*; it's well written and will appeal to a wide audience... However, the article is not as focused as it could be and I would recommend that the author shorten the article and that the editor publish it in the Forum section of the journal ... The most important contribution the article makes is its focus on the teacher. The author could shorten the manuscript by eliminating the sections on students, which, at any rate, are speculative. (Referee comment 1.1, 7 June 2004)

The second referee encouraged the author to develop the piece as a full-length article. She wrote:

> Recommendation: Accept with revision...
>
> I think the paper in its current state reads more like a (successful) conference talk or an expository essay than a featured article for the pre-eminent research journal *TQ*. In terms of publishing it within *TQ* I see two alternatives. One would be to shorten the paper considerably so that it would fit within the forum section of the journal... My suggestions below, however, concern how to revise the paper to make it more suitable as a featured article by, in short, engaging the key issues in ways that are more depthful, critical and detailed.

In terms of reworking it as a featured article, I would pose three sets of questions for the author's (and editor's) consideration. The first concerns the research approach:

> 1. How might you characterise, and justify, the research approach/design/methodology that you are using? What literature, from ELT or from education research more broadly, might be of use in this endeavour? (As a starting point, see Canagarajah's 1996 paper in *TQ* 30 (2))[4]
> 2. How can you sharpen the focus of the paper and strengthen its argument? In the main the paper reads smoothly and clearly, which is good, but ironically, perhaps slightly too seamlessly – given the fraught subject matter and the critique of simplistic notions of identity. How can you add specificity, theoretical complexity, texture, dynamism? Are there any messy aspects that have been left out or simplified?

By the final section I would like to have a sharper sense of the new ideas that your paper is contributing to existing literature... What was 'known' before versus what is now 'known' as a result of your analysis – this may be some interesting questions or paradoxes that you are formulating.

> 3. Are you using the concept of race but at the same time querying it? If the aim is to produce a featured article, might it be useful to more explicitly foreground this tension? (Referee comment 2.1, 1 May 2004)

It is clear from the comments of the second reviewer that she expected Ena to be a bit more analytical. She wanted Ena to merge her narrative more closely with her argument, be a lot more rigorous and balanced in her analysis of her examples, and to provide a justification for her unconventional research approach. In all this, she seemed to share my assumption that publishing is a conversation, where the new entrant speaks relevantly to the ongoing discourse. In her conclusion, she made her assumptions very explicit:

> I do not think it will be too onerous to make a case for the self-reflexive approach (a narrative approach? – you will need to choose a term that suits) that you are taking here, but I do think that a case will need to be made (because a case always needs to be made for one's research approach, not because this one requires particular justification). In my view, if you do not make such a case then you run the risk of readers dismissing your experiences as anecdotal evidence, and only one person's at that. You also run the risk of presuming that the reasons for valuing one teacher's experiences are self-evident – which is not necessarily the case in a research journal, but certainly not in a journal such as *TQ* that encompasses a variety of qualitative/quantitative approaches. (Referee comment 2.1, 1 May 2004)

When I sent my official decision letter, I had to take into account the different impressions of the referees. However, I had some reservations about publishing the article in the Forum section. I was mindful that the Forum might become a way of sidelining nontraditional genres. While we do give such articles space in the journal, we don't treat them as fully-fledged research articles. Forum articles don't get institutional credit, and nor are they treated as enjoying equal stature with full-length articles. I wanted to explore whether we could publish the article in the main section as it would help introduce alternative genres and oppositional knowledge to challenge dominant tradition. Therefore, I sent a decision of 'revise and resubmit':

> I like to see one more round of revision to see if we can feature this as a full-length article. Perhaps you can send me a revision before the end of summer. If the referees are still dissatisfied, then we can move on to consider other options, including a Forum article. (Editor's decision letter #2, 10 June 2004)

ENA: About a month later, I received the reviews from the editor via email, apparently to speed up the revision process, before the official letter reached me by regular mail. I was happy to hear that both referees at least told me to revise and didn't 'reject' the submission outright.

However, I was confused by the two reviewers because their comments seemed to contradict one another. Moreover, the first referee (hereafter Ref#1) barely wrote half of a page, while the second referee (Ref#2) wrote a whopping four pages. I didn't know which to prefer! Although the detailed review provided useful information for a good revision, the vague review seemed to leave the revision process more 'open' for me to pursue changes as I saw fit.[5]

Ref#1 liked the article as a Forum piece – which was what I wanted anyway. However, her comments were much too general for them to be helpful to a 'newbie' in publishing. General questions were posed, with no specific highlighting of particular passages or ideas in my article. Ref#2 was more detailed, and I was surprised that she thought that it might actually be acceptable as a full-length article. I was shocked by the amount of detail in her review. The referee had gone through my paper page by page and carefully documented her comments.

Ref#2 seemed to have understood the context of the article quite well. But I was taken aback by some of the terms and phrases in the review such as, 'research questions', 'data' and 'contributing to existing literature'. The use of these terms in relation to my submission confirmed why I wanted my article to be a Forum piece. I felt that trying to qualify my experiences or legitimise them through objective research or 'empirical' studies would devalue my story and my point that stories such as mine are often silenced due to 'lack of proof'. *It's tiring, the whole 'burden of proof' thing – where minorities always have the burden of proving that they are discriminated against.* As I proceeded through the review, I felt more and more discouraged. I contemplated not resubmitting because I was resistant about doing the requested revisions. I was afraid that the change in tone and approach would take away the voice I wanted to use in the paper.

Five months passed and I felt bad for not communicating with the editor and letting him know what was going on. So I wrote and apologised for the delay in my response and tried to frame the reason for delay in a way that wouldn't let on that the revision was delayed because I actually felt paralysed about the direction I should take with this article. The editor's response to my email scared me. He observed: 'I was in fact thinking that you were mulling over the direction your revision should take! ... We have had some scholars resubmitting their articles after a year or more of interval!' (email: 28 October 2004). I responded in (pseudo) jest: 'Many thanks for understanding, Suresh. As always, much appreciated. Let's just hope it doesn't take me "a year or more", however!' (email: 30 October 2004). *Would I be able to find a voice and develop it through negotiation with the referees? After all, isn't revision always supposed to be a good thing? Doesn't it make the article even better in quality and effectiveness? These senior scholars are the very people who will decide whether I 'belong' in the profession and whether I might be worth publishing. So I have to engage with them in some way, and I really don't have much choice about this. If I want my story to find an audience, I have to make the changes that the gatekeepers in publishing expect.*

When I finally got around to doing the revisions, I approached them methodically because, for the most part, I didn't feel I had any option but to revise as requested. I compiled the three reviews into one document, merged any similar thoughts and comments, and then arranged them in point-form. I then initialled each comment with 'Ref#1', 'Ref#2' or 'E' (for Editor) to see which concerns were shared by all of them. The common points were the ones that I figured were non-negotiable. I had to address them as I figured that the similarities indicated the main weaknesses of my paper. Then I worked backwards from there, moving to the comments made by two out of the three. However, I always weighted the editor's views as the most important as I felt that, of the three, he seemed to best understand the perspective I was taking and the reason I was writing this piece. *Where there are comments that I don't agree with? I'll just pretend that I didn't read those ... or that they don't exist.*

SURESH: By the time Ena sent her apologetic email, the material for my signature issue had already been sent for production. My hopes of carrying Ena's article in that issue had been dashed. *You certainly can't make the horse drink the water! Too bad, it's against publishing protocol to compel authors to resubmit their articles.* Ena's revised version arrived two months later. What was initially surprising was that she offered no explanation of the revisions done or response to the suggestions of the referees. *TQ* instructs authors to include this explanation in their revised resubmissions, so this omission made Ena seem to be a real novice. But a closer look at the manuscript revealed that, in her second draft, Ena had responded carefully to the suggestions; she had simply not explained her decisions in her covering letter.

Once again, I contemplated how I could use my editorial power strategically to shepherd Ena's article into print. Since Ref#1 had made up her mind that this was a Forum piece, I thought of soliciting a new referee who might read the article from the perspective of a full-length article. The scholar I chose was another female, 'native' speaker, who is open to new modes of writing. I retained Ref#2 who had commented extensively on developing the piece into a full-length article.

While the second draft of the article was being read by the referees, I reviewed Ena's changes to consider the prospects for publication. In general, I was impressed with the changes. The title was more focused and accessible to readers who were not theoretically informed – she had changed the title from 'On race and illegitimacy in teaching ESL' to 'Race: A third voice in the native/nonnative speaker debate.' The abstract had also been rewritten with polemical rigor, analytical clarity and thematic focus. The differences were striking: The first abstract was written as follows:

> This paper represents a unique point of view on the contentious issue of the 'native/non-native' English-speaking teacher as it presents an analysis of my own conflicting identities as a teacher and researcher of color in the field of ESL. Specifically, I address the intersections of race and the native/non-native dichotomy; however, I do so from the perspective of a 'native' English speaker of color – a voice thus far unrepresented and untheorized in ESL literature. I frame my arguments through the lenses of anti-racist as well as sociocultural theories and attempt to bridge these theories with ESL praxis. Further, I address the implications of this research on classroom relations and ESL pedagogy and I conclude my research by proposing suggestions for engaged and transformative paradigms and practices to address social and structural inequities in English language education.

The revised abstract read:

> Literature regarding the 'native/non-native' English-speaking teacher (NEST/NNEST) construct in TESOL has primarily focused on language and notions of linguistic ability. In this paper, I add a third voice to the debate that could serve to recomplicate our understandings of what it means to be a NEST/NNEST and its implications on issues of equity in the field of TESOL. Specifically, I discuss the salience of race in the continued production and reproduction of this dichotomy, and I frame this discussion in the experiences of a 'native' English speaker of color – a voice thus far unrepresented and untheorized in NEST/NNEST literature. Through a recounting and analysis of my own experiences, conflicts, and intersections of being a NEST and a visible minority, I argue that the dichotomy is maintained not merely to delineate and discriminate based on one's language, but more controversially, I attempt to argue here that the dichotomy is more so to delineate and discriminate based on one's race. I highlight how minority teachers can negotiate their identities with their students and fellow teachers and

propose that this reinvestigation of the NEST/NNEST construction can serve as an entrance-point into wider discussions of issues of race and racism in TESOL.

The second abstract contains less jargon from critical race theory or post-structuralist discourses. There is no impression of theoretical posturing. The revision also focuses more on teacher development, whereas the earlier version attempted to make applications to students, teachers and scholars from a limited narrative. The revision uses a more analytical language. Where the earlier version dealt with 'representing' and 'addressing', the revision promised to 'complicate', 'frame' and 'argue'. Furthermore, the revision was more qualified and humble. It did not promise a 'unique point of view', but 'adding a third voice', 'attempt(ing) to argue' and 'highlighting'. Finally, the sustained focus on the theme of 'third voice' created an effective niche for Ena's paper in the scholarly literature and provided an integrated perspective for her various experiences.

The changes in her draft showed me that Ena was focusing well on the views of the referees. For example, Ref#2 had wanted 'a clearer sense of what the discussion [of] your experiences have [sic] added to existing literature?' Ena was already addressing this concern in the abstract. She develops it further in the body of the article. It is also noteworthy that while the research literature had been relegated to endnotes in the previous version, it was now actively employed in the body of the article to make a space for the author's experience and argument – as we see in her introductory paragraph:

> In this article, I present an additional perspective on the NEST/NNEST debate. I argue that the NEST/NNEST dichotomy is maintained not merely to delineate and discriminate based on one's language, but more controversially, I attempt to argue here that the dichotomy is more so to delineate and discriminate based on one's race.
>
> There is a need to reconceptualize the notion of native/nonnative within the framework of race and racism as these discourses have been glaringly absent from the large majority of work on the native/nonnative construct. Except for some recent exceptions, such as Amin (1997, 1999, 2000, 2001), Brutt-Griffler and Samimy (1999, 2001, 2003), Kubota (2001, 2002a, 2002b, 2004), Liu (1999) and Thomas (1999), the concept of race has not been addressed in native/nonnative speaker debates. (p. 5)

Our concerns about methodology were also addressed well in the new draft. Ena states: 'I frame the discussion in my own experiences, conflicts, and intersections of being a "native" speaker of English and an ESL teacher of color. Through a recounting and analysis of my own narrative, I theorize the intersections of identity, legitimacy, and race in TESOL' (p. 6). These changes help her to move towards a hybrid text that provides an argumentative framing for her personal narratives. They prepare the reader well for a genre of writing that is unusual for this journal. In answer to the questions raised by Ref#2, Ena goes on to provide a rationale for the genre she uses, showing how it was motivated by her atypical methodology. She explains:

> In grounding this article on race and identity within my own narratives, I am cognizant of the possible critique that those reading my stories may relegate my experiences as anecdotal, 'isolated, random, individual happenings' (Lin et al., 2004: 494); however, I argue that attempting to write this article using the academic genre representing past scientific-empirical research traditions continues to reinforce the mythical notion of the objective researcher who is both disconnected and disaffected by her/his research (Canagarajah, 1996). If we claim to have a more progressive understanding of research and if we claim to be aware of our own biases and their possible influences on our research, this progression in research ideology needs to be represented not only in our methods, but in our reporting. Thus, Canagarajah advocates 'energetic experimentation with alternate forms of research reporting that would better reflect our emerging realizations on the nature of research and knowledge production'. (Canagarajah, 1996: 7, 321)

This paragraph reveals how the revision process had generated an increased reflexivity on Ena's part. She is more aware of her writing strategy and context. Ena is also more cognisant of some of the tensions and ironies in her frames of analysis. In fact, Ref#2 had pointed out 'a central tension' inherent in 'using the concept of race but at the same time querying it'. Ena addresses this dilemma in a footnote linked to her first use of the term 'native speaker':

> I recognize that it seems paradoxical to want to apply the concept of race to the native/nonnative debate while, at the same time, want to question, and even reject, the very conceptualization of it. I turn to Ang (2001), however, for a retheorization of race and the ambiguities of racial identity as she recognizes 'the inescapable impurity of all cultures and the porousness of all cultural boundaries in an irrevocably globalized, interconnected and interdependent world' (p. 194). Thus,

by characterizing racial identity as 'together-in-difference', where one's identity can be 'embedded ... yet always partially disengaged; ... disembedded ... yet somehow enduringly attached' (Ibid.), she reconceptualizes a notion of race which allows for the sorts of complexities and variances that I illustrate as operating in my own stories and narratives. (p. 6)

Ena thus builds on this tension to develop a nuanced perspective on race and identity.

She also provides other qualifications to guard against essentialising her identity, in deference to Ref#2's suggestion that her claims sound too pat, she argues:

Before I begin framing the complicated entanglement of my identity in relation to the NEST/NNEST dichotomy specifically and issues of race and racism broadly, I feel it is important to provide readers with insights into my experiences both in and out of the ESL classroom. While doing so, however, I recognize that there is no one Chinese-Canadian experience and point out that this ambiguity is exhibited in my own continual process of reinvention and renegotiation of identity throughout the years (cf. Norton, 2000a, 2001; Ang, 2001). (p. 8)

Her approach to voice has also changed. Whereas she had earlier foregrounded the theoreticians, and latched on her narrative to amplify their points, now she had reversed the order. The new strategy conveys more authority for her claims and more confidence in her voice. It also helps her to weave together her experiences and other scholarship more effectively to form a hybrid text. In response to a racial insult from a boy at school, she says:

I vividly remember, however, retorting to him, 'I'm Canadian, stupid,' as if he were too dumb to recognize the difference. This connection between race and national identity that I had unconsciously assimilated as a child has been hypothesized by Bannerji (2000), Fleming (2003), and Ng (1993), who all see a clear relationship between being a Canadian and being white. Little did I know, however, that I would be forced to revisit this connection on a more conscious level in my identity as a TESOL professional. (p. 9)

The narrative is also better organised, further integrating the chronological and theme-specific considerations. The headings and subheadings of her final implications section reveal the way her ideas are structured according to their relationship and importance:

> Race and (il)legitimacy ...
>
> ... In the Classroom
>
> ... In the Staffroom
>
> ... In the Industry

Ena goes on to address well my request for ways of negotiating her conflicts, in an effort to provide some constructive pedagogical suggestions for non-native teachers and students. She narrates some modes of negotiation in the final part of her paper, after analysing her conflicts:

> My positioning as a teacher of color at this ESL program provided me with a unique opportunity to use my hybrid identity as an interesting source of conversation and an important catalyst for critical analysis in the classroom; however, while many students attempted to now reconceptualize their understandings of the native/nonnative construct, simultaneously, in many other instances, my hybridity became a point of contention and contestation for those students unable to see beyond the powerful discourses of race. (p. 13)

However, the narrative here still lacks detail and sounds vague. Similarly, I felt that the positives Ena developed at the end of the article were not concrete enough. Ena was resorting to clichés from other researchers, rather than providing constructive strategies for negotiating these tensions in her own voice. She concludes thus:

> Lin *et al.* (2004) believe that 'under the communicative ethic of risk, no one is exempt from the obligation to dialogue with others to discover and transcend the blind spots inherent in their respective subject positions' (p. 499). Indeed, it is through the initiation of these critical dialogues that the road towards change begins. For this reason, it is my hope that this article will help to bring to the forefront the salience of race and racism in the NEST/NNEST debate. (p. 24)

I planned to push Ena further on these points and ask her to develop her pedagogical implications and recommendations after I heard from the referees.

ENA: I didn't talk with anyone other than my supervisor during the revision process as no one in my department was doing race-related research, and I was very aware of the controversial nature of the topic. Additionally, since this article features my personal story and I feared that its status as scholarship might be questionable, I felt uncomfortable consulting anyone who might not understand my voice and objectives.

When I initially showed my supervisor the three reviews, she was really happy. She thought the comments were positive and boded well for the publication of the article. She wanted me to get on with the revisions right away. When I shared with her my reluctance to resubmit, she convinced me that the paper was worth publishing and asked me to figure out a way that I could still have my voice present even with more theory and objective analysis. My supervisor helped me to understand the reviewer comments in a more balanced way, but I was worried when she told me that I had to address *all* of the points brought up by *all* of the reviewers.

When I was done with my revisions, I showed my supervisor my final product. She didn't comment much on the need for substantial additional changes. She pointed out a few things here and there. But her biggest concern was the title. She didn't find it focused and catchy enough. She talked to me about how important a title is, and how she felt people didn't put enough thought into titles, not realising how significant they actually are. I told her that I liked my title (On Race and Illegitimacy in Teaching ESL) because I was trying to make my article narrative and indirect. The title was inspired by Ang's (2001) book *On Not Speaking Chinese: Living between Asia and the West* – a book that Ryuko had introduced to me after hearing my paper at TESOL 2003. My supervisor persisted, however, and after reading the paper and picking out the key ideas, she suggested, 'Race: A Third Voice in the Native/Nonnative Speaker Debate.' Initially, I thought the new title was too much of a change to my desired tone. Eventually, I realised that it was a stronger title and that it really did encapsulate the article better. I am thankful to my supervisor for pushing me to think about the title in a more focused way and for convincing me that it was worth revising the article for publication.

I was happy with the piece after the revisions, and I was particularly thankful to Ref#2 and to the editor for their insightful comments and detailed suggestions. The paper would never have reached the next level without them as I essentially followed all their suggestions and tried my best to answer their queries as thoroughly as possible. I figured that this course of action would give me a much better chance of getting accepted. However, I still wanted the article to be a Forum piece. I knew I still had to go through at least one more round of review, and I didn't want to have to sacrifice more of my voice in the piece. Although I had read articles on how one's voice is always mediated and negotiated, I wasn't comfortable with the thought of further losing a sense of voice in this particular piece.

In the covering letter that I sent with the revision, I wrote that I didn't think my article was a 'research piece' and it was, therefore, not really suitable as a full-length article. I said that I would, however, leave it to the editor and reviewers' discretion. *I was really hoping that they would get my hint that I wanted it to be a Forum piece. Needless to say, I didn't show my advisor the covering letter for this revised resubmission because I didn't want her to be upset when she saw that paragraph.*

SURESH: Ref#2 (retained from the first round) was mostly happy with the way Ena had made concessions to the dominant genres in the discipline, developing a more hybrid text. She recommended acceptance 'with minor edits'. She observed: 'It was with immense pleasure that I read the revision of this manuscript. The revision is substantially improved, with more sophisticated (and more solidly referenced) theorisation, and a tighter integration of theory with lived experience... I think the paper makes some excellent points and does so persuasively, with an appealing combination of accessibility (using clear examples to illustrate the points to readers who will find them new and novel) and scholarly referencing (drawing on a wealth of studies from within and beyond the field)'. (Referee comment 2.2, 22 March 2005)

However, the new referee (whom I will call Ref#3) saw some problems in presentation. She wrote:

Recommendation: Revise.

The issue of race in TESOL is an important topic and the author's personal narrative is compelling. I would very much like to see this article accepted for publication. I've asked the editor to allow me to comment on the m.s. by using the 'tracking changes' function since I'm suggesting relatively minor changes that involve organization, avoiding repetition, and providing supporting evidence.

The following is an example of the types of changes she made in Ena's text (note the 'track changes' convention, underlined statements for additions and strikethrough for deletions):

<u>Discrimination against non-white ESL teachers gets played out in classroom practices in different ways. For example,</u> ~~It is unfortunate~~

~~that s~~Some students believe 'only a White accent qualifies one to be a native speaker' (Amin, 1999: 97) without necessarily understanding on a conscious level what these sorts of discourses imply. <u>Such is the case when students (and colleagues, for that matter) compliment me on the fact that they 'can't hear my accent.'</u> ~~In this case, t~~ The underlying discourse ~~that cannot be denied~~ is that a 'white accent' has more to do with facial features than with linguistic features. ~~Such is the case when students (and colleagues, for that matter) compliment me on the fact that they 'can't hear my accent.'~~ (Referee comments 3.1, 15 April 2005)

The third referee's preference is clear. In general, she more explicitly subsumes narrative to argumentation. As in the example shown, she sees the need for better topic sentences for the paragraphs, thus foregrounding the main points from Ena's examples. Similarly, she lets the moral of the examples conclude the paragraph ('The underlying discourse is that ...'), reminding readers of the point behind her story.

In the light of the minor changes in paragraph development and rephrasing requested, I felt confident in giving a decision of 'accept pending changes' to Ena. My decision letter stated:

Thank you for your patience during the review process of your manuscript. I am pleased to inform you that your paper has been accepted for publication in *TESOL Quarterly*, pending your response to the points raised by the reviewers.

Before submitting the final version of the paper, consider the reviewers' comments, make any additional changes that you feel would improve the paper, and explain decisions not to respond to suggestions on a separate page. In addition to addressing the concerns of the reviewers, note also that you have to flesh out your pedagogical application. Your anecdote about a case of classroom interventions in page 20 lacks development. Give more context and develop the case more fully. (Editor's decision letter #3: 18 April 2005)

I sat back, proud of the investment of time on this manuscript. *It is gratifying when an editor's assessment of an article's potential is validated by the referees. How satisfying when the author and mentors are able to agree on the final shape of the manuscript and shepherd it into publication. It is even more satisfying when the article in question involves alternative discourses. Mentoring seems to have worked. All that remains is to receive the final version and copyedit it for publication.*

ENA: Four months after sending my second version, I got an email from the *TQ* editorial assistant, rushing me a decision letter that was to reach me later by regular mail. The words that stood out were 'pending' and 'satisfactory response to the points raised by the reviewers'.

Ref#2 had written another two and a half pages of comments on editing matters. (I knew it was the same reviewer as the text was formatted in the same way as the first round of revisions with the same sort of commenting style). But, then, there was another set of comments done using (MS-Word) 'track changes'. *This is weird as it is obviously not the same person as before (who had written a vague short paragraph). I wonder what happened to the other reviewer?* Putting the reviewer comments and the editor's letter together was even more confusing than the first time around. Moreover, although the editor and reviewers may have thought of the changes as inconsequential (as suggested by Ref#3's mention of 'relatively minor changes'), they were not so for me. Out of 24 pages of my text (not including the references), Ref#3 wanted me to change almost eight pages (cumulatively). *I've always appreciated the track changes function in MS-Word when I do my own copyediting because of the way it clearly highlights changes made. But I didn't realise how incredibly jarring it could feel when in abundance. There were strikethroughs covering entire paragraphs, and on some pages, more than 70% of the words were crossed out or underlined.*

In the very brief, six-sentence long comment that Ref#3 made before doing the track changes, she simply said: 'I'm suggesting relatively minor changes that involve organization, avoiding repetition, and providing supporting evidence.' *I've just been asked to revise one third of my paper. These are 'minor' changes? And since when is a perceived lack of supporting evidence a 'minor' issue?* As I looked through the changes, I felt that the suggested revisions were watering down my arguments. For example, in my introduction, I was trying to distinguish myself from other writers who have theorised the NEST/NNEST debate. By comparing how 'different' I was, but at the same time how similar our racialisations were, I thought I had made my argument more compelling. This section had actually been added in response to comments made by Ref#2 in the previous round. But Ref#3 struck out that entire section of my paper. Furthermore, the conclusion, in which I tried to re-emphasise my most significant points, was deemed redundant and completely eliminated. I felt that a lot that the reviewer edited into/out of the paper for reasons of 'organisation' and 'avoiding repetition' thus took me further away from my intended narrative and tone.

The editor's decision letter only compounded the problem. His letter said: 'I am pleased to inform you that your paper has been accepted for publication in *TESOL Quarterly*, pending your response to the points raised by the reviewers.' The letter went on to say: 'Before submitting the final version of the paper, consider reviewers' comments, make any additional changes that you feel would improve the paper, and explain decisions not to respond to suggestions on a separate page. *All I see is 'consider reviewers' comments', 'make any additional changes' and 'explain decisions not to respond to suggestions'.* I figured that like the first time around I was expected to follow what the reviewers wanted, and make these changes. If I were gutsy enough, or had higher academic credentials, I could try to explain to the reviewers why I didn't agree with them. But, as a graduate student and novice author, I didn't feel I had room to negotiate the process. Instead, I faced two options, neither of which was favorable: either make the changes requested or not make the changes and sacrifice the publishing opportunity.

I took stock of the situation: Ref#2 liked the revision; Ref#3's tracked changes seemed to indicate that there were major issues; and the editor thought the article still needed work. I didn't want to resubmit. I didn't want to change my argument and voice any further. Although I knew it could be a much stronger paper in *TQ's* sense, making further changes would take the submission in a direction that was contrary to why I had chosen to write it in the first place. Therefore, although I had felt a renewed enthusiasm for the article after the first round of revisions (resulting in changes to the article that I felt had indeed brought it forward), I was now dejected to find that I was expected to make even more alterations – revisions that I felt were now moving the piece backwards.

I remained paralysed by the revision process and couldn't bring myself to do the changes. So when the editor wrote to me about my final revised version, I kept giving him excuses. I just couldn't tell him that I was, once again, feeling paralysed about the revisions. As we continued to correspond about a TESOL paper we planned to present together, I was very careful not to mention the resubmission. Four more months passed (it was now seven months since I had received the second set of reviews), and I received another prod to complete my manuscript. I hedged my reply with a humorous response, throwing in the 'grad school deadlines are getting in the way' thing. Even now, years after the experience, I find myself almost back at the paralysis stage. It is hard to forget the final reviews, which still echo inside my head as do the images of all the tracked changes. If those responses even remotely reflect the feedback that I might receive once the paper is actually published, I want to address those issues now; but then, the changes might take me away from my desired voice. And so the circle continues...

Discussion

In this section, we reflect together on the lessons learnt from this experience for negotiating alternative discourses in academic publishing. We benefitted from trying to look at the experience through each other's eyes, and accept that there might, at times, be irreconcilable differences in the perspectives and practices of the different parties in a mentoring process. However, if we are able to develop some level of consensus on what went wrong and how to proceed from here, there may be more hope for mentoring and for developing alternative discourses in academic publishing.

So, how do we explain this failed publishing experience? Although there are many issues at play, we want to focus here on how the mentoring process, correspondence and other texts – such as the reviewer feedback and decision letters, which Canagarajah (1996b) labels para-research article texts – had implications for the final product and its publishing prospects in the process of negotiating hybridity.

We must first note that the much-touted hybridity cannot be treated as a monolithic product. As Shohat (1992: 110) reminds us:

> As a descriptive catch-all term, 'hybridity' per se fails to discriminate between the diverse modalities of hybridity, for example, forced assimilation, internalized self-rejection, political cooptation, social conformism, cultural mimicry, and creative transcendence. The reversal of biologically and religiously racist tropes – the hybrid, the syncretic – on the one hand, and the reversal of anticolonialist purist notions of identity, on the other, should not obscure the problematic agency of 'post-colonial hybridity'.
> (Shohat, 1992: 110)

Just as hybridity is constructed differently and assumes different significance in various historical and social contexts, it takes different forms in publishing. It can be realised differently by different authors for different contexts and different audiences. In the episode narrated above, the author and the gatekeepers make different assumptions about the levels of hybridity that are acceptable for the context. Although Suresh and the reviewers are open to alternative forms of writing, they assume that authors should engage closely with the current discourses of the journal. Their sense of an acceptable level of hybridity operates within a narrow range of divergence from the journal's established discourses. Ena's aim, however, is to deviate more widely from the established discourses. Although she is interested in merging personal, narrative and academic discourses – and, in fact, does a good job of bringing alternative discourses much closer to the established publishing discourses – her effort doesn't come close enough to the expectations of the gatekeepers. In this sense, what both parties mean by hybridity is not the same.

Behind the shapes of the desired final product are varying assumptions about the publishing process and its conventions. Suresh and the reviewers are motivated by the well-known metaphor that publishing is about joining a conversation. From their perspective, for Ena to enter relevantly into the ongoing conversations in a specific journal, she has to engage more closely with the established and dominant discourses. As Tardy and Matsuda (2009: 45) have noted, 'although readers [that is, academic journal manuscript reviewers] may find certain breaks from convention to be refreshing and thus rhetorically effective, those ruptures generally still have to occur within particular parameters'. As gatekeepers, the editor and the reviewers are still concerned about the expectations of the profession. Violating the dominant discourses of a particular journal too radically (particularly one which is seen as being pre-eminent within a profession) may create a lot of controversy and complaints from readers about falling standards. Therefore, their expectations tend to be relatively conservative. Ena, however, wants to disturb the conversation. Although she understands that the text and voice are always mediated by the discoursal and the social, she expects that her objectives in this article are better served by resisting the dominant discourses. There is a performative dimension to her writing strategy as well. It is precisely by deviating starkly from the dominant discourses, that she can dramatise her differences, articulate her critique and reclaim her voice. The expectations of the two parties appear to be at cross-purposes – that is, while one party focuses on their concern about sustaining tradition, the other focuses on resisting that tradition.

They also have diverging expectations about the publishing outcomes. Ena expects and would prefer to see the article as a Forum piece, while Suresh and the reviewers feel that it would work better as a full-length article, assuming that a Forum piece would perhaps marginalise its status as a research piece. Featuring Ena's work as a full-length article in the main section would introduce the possibility of narrative research. Here, Suresh and the reviewers have more radical expectations for the article than Ena. Her expectations are more humble. She assumes that sidestepping the dominant conventions of a full-length article and speaking through the space for reflection and opinion in the Forum section provides a better outlet for her views. However, Suresh and the reviewers see an opportunity to expand the genres accepted as full-length articles in the journal by publishing Ena's piece in the more important section. In aiming high, they also raise the stakes for the article. If published as a full-length article, it would have major significance for the mission of the journal and for the profession as a whole. However, such high expectations also increase the risk of not getting published. Should the gatekeepers have opted for a more limited and safer option?

The attempts at a negotiated shaping of the text make us realise that hybridity can involve a loss of voice. Although we often focus on the positive experience of new genres and styles entering the discourse through a case of successful negotiation, we have to also consider what is lost in the process. Although Ena was sufficiently aware of poststructuralist discourses to understand that there is no pure or unmediated identity, could she have negotiated a voice that would have been acceptable to everyone concerned, given the fact that the negotiation process was an unequal one? It is clear that Ena's readiness to engage in the review process was often affected by her awareness of the power of the editor and the referees. Her frequent perception of imposition has to be taken seriously. For example, the reviewers' asking for more proof for her claims, even though she had referenced similar narratives by more established researchers such as Nuzhat Amin and Ryuko Kubota, among others, is interpreted by Ena as insulting, and as if an argument based on her own life is not seen as sufficiently convincing by the referees. Furthermore, when Suresh and the referees consider edits and paragraph restructuring as 'minor changes', Ena sees these as laden with ideological values that have serious implications for her voice and her writing objectives; the changes are not minor for her.

In publishing, there seems to be an expectation that it is the author's responsibility to make a new genre acceptable. The onus is on the author to make a successful case for the shifts in discourse (as is made explicit by Ref#2 in her review, point 2.1). The professional community may not bend to accommodate any and every rendition of the established genres. Obviously, this puts authors on the defensive. Needless to say, it is the less powerful in the negotiation process (i.e. novice authors, multilingual scholars) who are expected to make more sacrifices such as limiting the critical edge of their intentions, arguments and voice. Rather than considering those who are not willing to make compromises as 'uninformed about the way writing works', we have to ask how we can expand the possibilities available for everyone to represent their voices. We have to consider the extent to which we can adopt more flexible norms and mutual negotiation in the publishing process.

Similar to power, there are other historical factors that shape publishing negotiations. From this perspective, good intentions on both sides are not enough. There are somewhat impersonal constraints on the extent to which discourses and publishing conventions can be expanded. To begin with, we have to be mindful of the history of the journal and the discipline. John Swales (1988), analysing a 20-year corpus of articles in *TQ*, sees a tendency in both the TESOL field and in *TQ* to build their scientific credentials. As a young field, with a professional organisation that started only in 1966, there is a need for TESOL to establish itself according to the dominant knowledge-making practices in the academy. Swales' study reveals that the field is professionalising itself according to the tenets of modernity and empirical science. Therefore, quantitative studies and data-driven articles have constituted the dominant discourses of the journal. Although there are signs of deviation from such discourses after Swales' study, especially since the 1990 s, critical discourses have not eclipsed modernist approaches completely. Specifically in relation to Ena's research topic, *TQ*'s special issue on 'Race and TESOL' was not published until 2006, while an issue on 'Narrative research in TESOL' was published as recently as 2011. In that issue the editor (Gary Barkhuizen), 'invites readers, particularly novice narrative researchers, to explore their epistemological and methodological selves [as] ... the field is wide open, especially in the diverse world of TESOL'. After this initial invitation, he notes, however, that 'narrative research has only fairly recently begun to gain traction in TESOL' (Barkhuizen, 2011: 410).

Bell (2011: 582–583) further brings to light how the stories presented through narrative inquiry may initially 'baffle' readers; but she makes the case that 'the very bafflement serves to alert us to important differences in basic assumptions that might otherwise have gone undiscovered'. Thus, while Ena attempts to use her stories to query 'commonsense' understandings of the native/non-native dichotomy, Suresh and the reviewers clearly had the history of *TQ* in mind as they negotiated the extent to which they could allow Ena to deviate from the established discourses and conventions. They encouraged Ena to engage more closely with the modernist discourses, as evident in their requests that she provide more evidence, justify her methodology and adopt a more objective tone. They are wary that the readers of the journal might consider Ena's article an abrupt and unceremonious violation of the established conventions of the discipline.

The authors do need to be mindful of a journal's dominant discourses and audience when they situate their articles in the historical flow of discourses. They have to calibrate the extent to which they can adopt alternative styles in relation to the different historical trajectories of both the journals and their disciplines. In the field of language teaching, there are other disciplinary communities and journals that accommodate a greater degree of personal voice and narrative. For example, the community of compositionists are more critical in orientation, and moved away from the positivistic tradition of inquiry much earlier. Other scholars have studied the differences between first- and second-language writing/teaching to bring out the cultural and ideological differences between these communities (Atkinson & Ramanathan, 1995). Thus, in journals with more pronounced traditions of mixed-genre writing (such as *College, Composition & Communication*), Ena's options would have been different. Referees of such journals might have said that Ena's article was not narrative enough, and asked for more creative and bold rhetorical moves. There would have been less of a need to foreground her argument. Even non-prestige dialects (such as, African-American vernacular English or Spanglish) have been used in some such journals (see Smitherman, 1999, for an example of an article that uses African-American vernacular English in *College, Composition & Communication*). Thus, within the same profession, new forms of expression are accommodated differently, depending on the history of the discipline and the journal. It would have helped if Ena and the gatekeepers of *TQ* had been more conscious of the considerable ways in which their negotiation was being shaped by history.

We must note that the extent to which compromise is acceptable in hybridity is unclear. To what extent should one sacrifice one's voice in the name of revisions? Different authors have varying levels of tolerance for compromise, balance and merger. Although Ena knows that research articles are co-constructed, negotiated and shaped products (Swales, 1990), and that the personal is mediated by the social, her tolerance level for compromise (like that of her gatekeepers) has limits. After a point, she experienced the merging of discourses asked of her as a loss of voice. What one person may perceive to be a hybrid genre may thus be too compromising for another. Too often we focus on issues of mediation and the co-construction of written products without problematising the level of compromise expected from different parties in the publishing process. Closer analysis of the discursive constructions of 'risk' as they relate to the publishability of Ena's article warrant particular attention. As Arnoldi (2009: 182, cited in Wilkinson, 2010) warns us:

> risk is literally a powerful concept. It renders areas of society governable ... It is used to create common fears and enemies, to mobilize people, but it is also used for conducting conduct – for governing free subjects at a distance.

Reviewers' perceptions of the risks involved in the publication of Ena's article may have influenced their conceptualisation of what they would deem 'acceptable levels' of textual hybridity for their field.

The phrase 'run the risk', for example, occurs twice within a short span in Referee comment 2.1 (1 May 2004; excerpted in the initial narrative). Both sentences in which the phrase occurs refer to how Ena's submission may be rejected by those in the wider field, due to unmet expectations regarding how the research is reported (leading to its devaluation and interpretation as merely 'anecdotal'). Phrases such as 'run the risk' represent 'risk-talk' – language that communicates as well as constitutes and controls risk. Risk-talk enables us to deal with risk by the labelling of something *as* risk and thereby producing parameters for manageable interaction. As such, negotiations between novice authors and gatekeepers (while in the process of publishing para-research article texts for example) may serve to 'manage' risks posed by the introduction of alternative discourses to a field of inquiry not fully open to this progress. Important to note, however, is that the referee whose comments included aspects of risk-talk was clear in her supportive intentions. Detailed suggestions were explained in depth to assist Ena with her revisions in concrete ways. Concomitantly, however, each subsequent reviewer report further assimilated Ena's discursive difference to the norms and standards of publication as conceptualised within the TESOL field. Thus we see how, as Lupton (1999: 122) argues, 'risk discourses operate as strategies of normalization, of exclusion and inclusion ... Notions of Otherness remain central to ways of thinking and acting about risk'. Consideration of sociological theories of risk may have assisted the parties in this negotiation towards a more complex understanding of how hybridity as a counter-discursive response to risk may have been both strategic and, at the same time, problematic.

It is also interesting to note that while Ena's perceptions of risk in her research were situated within her own constructions of her racialised and gendered identities – theorised by Lyng (2008: 113) and Wilkinson (2010: 72) – within TESOL, these perceptions were further constructed (and acted on) via internalisations of academic writing and publishing and of what constituted writing and knowledge within her field. For example, her strong preference for her paper to appear as a Forum piece rather than as a full-length article was a deliberate strategy to mitigate the possible risk of receiving harsh critique or feedback from the *TQ* readership. Ena had read 'Response to author' critiques of articles addressing similarly controversial topics by researchers of high stature in the field, and these heightened her sense of the risks entailed in the publication of her piece as a 'more legitimate' (read: held to a higher standard) full-length article, especially given her status as a novice scholar. Additional strategies used by Ena in addressing risk are similarly informative.

In making her revisions, Ena adopts a number of strategies to sidestep the expectations of the referees. She avoids explaining her refusal to take on board some of their suggestions by pretending they 'didn't exist'. Although she includes a covering letter with her revision resubmission, she fails to justify the changes she did make. Such non-participation strategies can sometimes constitute constructive resistance to community expectations; however, certain forms of non-participation can be ineffective. Ena may have benefitted from being more upfront about her resistance and reservations. She could have expressed herself more confidently because the gatekeepers had expressed sympathy for novice/multilingual authors and consciously adopted a mentoring relationship. Ena could have taken up the editor on his professed openness to new genres of writing and research approaches and perhaps explored how much further she could go in constructing an article with alternative discourse that would also preserve her interests and her voice. It is possible that had she made a strong case for adopting her style, she could have persuaded the gatekeepers to concede as has been done before (see e.g. Bhatia 2001).

Ena's perceptions of her article as risky (as it clearly subverted expected writing norms and involved highly charged content), and her fears of appearing too demanding and entitled as a novice scholar, however, prevented her from confidently asserting herself to the gatekeepers. Hence her inability to query reviewer comments, and make her own desires for the piece clearer. When considering notions of risk and risk-taking in contexts of unequal power relations, we must consider whether a novice scholar presenting alternative discourses is able to take risks. Similarly, this explains why, although Ena wrote to the editor to clarify some of the publishing conventions (such as the deadline for resubmission), she did not discuss questions about the product at the same time. She could have clarified the meaning and import of the final decision letter (i.e. whether the article had been accepted or not), played up the differences among the referees in her favour, or argued that she is more comfortable revising the article along the lines of a particular referee or the editor. However, engaging in discussions of 'less risky' administrative items (such as due dates) surrounding the publication of one's article are much easier dialogues to engage in with the editor of a prestigious journal.

In this vein, Ena's perception of risk led her to isolate herself during the writing process. But not seeking help from those around her (such as her supervisor or other potential mentors) is arguably not an ideal strategy for a novice. More senior scholars could have voiced the concerns of the diverse readers in the field, and helped Ena consider other perspectives for her revision. They could have suggested options for revision, as well as ways of understanding the conventions of the publishing process and negotiating with the gatekeepers. Such mentors may even have made Ena more comfortable about accommodating the expectations of the readers and gatekeepers, and thus able to adopt a more mediated voice in her article. Conversely, however, they could have assimilated Ena's article even further towards 'safer' discursive practices, and moved it further away from her desired voice as they were similarly situated in the authoritative discourses of the discipline (which Ena was attempting to subvert). Thus, 'supportive' responses from colleagues, peers or faculty may have further heightened Ena's perception of the possible risks involved in publishing this controversial piece, and may have also adversely affected, rather than improved, the publication process.

It is useful (for both gatekeepers and authors) to remember that hybridity is itself a strategy. It is not an identity (as Ena seems to assume) nor is it a type of text (as Suresh and the reviewers assume). As Bhabha (1999: 39) reminds us: 'Hybridization is a discursive, enunciatory, cultural, subjective process having to do with the struggle around authority, authorization, deauthorization, and the revision of authority. It's a social process. It's not about persons of diverse cultural tastes and fashions.' From this perspective, Ena and the gatekeepers should have negotiated different positions surrounding the text to discover spaces that are available for change. Since the gatekeepers themselves are committed to alternative discourses and knowledge, they can engage with authors to consider ways of finding a critical edge in the dominant discourses. Similarly, authors should consider the best way to represent their voice and interests, and abandon notions of a preconstructed voice or knowledge that must gain representation at any cost. The challenge for both parties is one of positionality, not a construct (either a type of product or voice). Bhabha goes on to say:

> Hybridization is really about how you negotiate between texts or cultures or practices in a situation of power imbalances in order to be able to see the way in which strategies of appropriation, revision, and iteration can produce possibilities for those who are less advantaged to be able to grasp in a moment of emergency, in the very process of the exchange or the negotiation, the advantage. (Bhabha, 1999: 39)

One way to go forward with the publishing of alternative discourses is to focus more on negotiation strategies than on the publishable product. While much has been done to describe research-article genres and to train novice authors on composing strategies, little has been done in terms of exploring effective negotiation strategies. We have to train novice scholars to negotiate with the multiple parties and texts involved in the publishing process so as to make space for alternative voices and genres. Scholars of the processes of socialisation into academic discourses have also found that negotiation strategies would help students in their academic career (see Duff, 2007; Lillis & Scott, 2007). But we wonder if mentorship and socialisation into discourses of academic publication are necessarily the answers to the challenges facing novice authors. Casanave (2010), considering the reluctance and wavering of graduate students on adopting alternative genres, argues that mentors and advisors can do much to minimise the risks and encourage students to confidently adopt creative strategies. Similarly, in the publishing context, Belcher (2007) recommends that constructive and patient commentary by referees and editors can serve a mentoring function and provide more successful outcomes for novice authors. However, the experiences recounted here show that mentors are not free of ideological influences, vested interests or rhetorical biases of their own, nor is anyone exempt from the misunderstandings that derive from different expectations and objectives. Tardy and Matsuda (2009: 46) thus recognise the need for explicit discussion, between all involved in publication processes, of the 'socio-political dynamics of scholarly publication' embedded in the negotiation of the context-specific complexities that can compound the challenges involved in publishing atypical subject positions and agendas (see also Aitchison *et al.*, 2010; Mullen, 2003). Risks cannot be minimised or avoided. They have to be taken by the horns.

Further, in comparing Casanave and Belcher's studies, we must recognise how risk for novice scholars is situated differently within the microcosm of graduate writing versus the macrocosm of scholarly publishing. As Casanave (2010: 13) observes, 'the bottom line for every dissertation writer is acceptance or rejection by one small group of dissertation evaluators. Strong support from advisors is therefore crucial'. Alternative discourses may, therefore, be easier to negotiate within the relatively insular context of dissertation writing than in the broader context of scholarly publishing for one's entire field. In our narrative, we see that although an editor or (multiple) reviewers may be supportive of alternative research and writing such as Ena's, accountability to the peer-review process and its responsibility to uphold the 'rigour' and 'standards' of an entire field of inquiry (influenced, in part, by the field's social and historical trajectory, as discussed earlier) presents additional pressures and paradoxes for gatekeepers even if they wish to see systemic change within a field. Therefore, we mustn't consider the negotiation of academic writing (whether in graduate work or in scholarly publication) as immune from the hermeneutical and ideological challenges inherent in the publishable product. Our experience suggests that both parties (i.e. mentors and mentees; authors and gatekeepers) have to consider how much they can revise their assumptions to accommodate alternative discourses. This negotiation cannot be one-sided. Both parties have to consider how they can be self-critical while acknowledging the limitations of dominant genres as well as the extent to which they can push the established discourses to accommodate alternative genres.

Hybridity, as a strategy of compromise, does not favour extreme forms of resistance. For this reason, it is in some ways a 'safer' and, hence, more useful strategy for negotiating the risks of voice and individuality in academic writing and publishing. However, despite the adoption of a complex and dynamic negotiation strategy where all parties attempt to engage fairly, critically, and flexibly, success is not guaranteed. New forms of writing and knowledge are risky, and as Lupton (1999: 132) elucidates, 'hybridity is always risky... because of its unbounded nature, its defiance of taken-for-granted categories'. Thus, while Pratt (1991) reminds us that engagement in the academic contact zones can bring forth novel genres, it may also be misunderstood and underappreciated. While creative new hybrid products can arise in academic context zones, she warns that, 'Miscomprehension, incomprehension, dead letters, unread masterpieces, absolute heterogeneity of meaning – these are some of the perils of writing in the contact zone' (Pratt, 1991: 37). Risk is not something that can be managed or side stepped. It is present in any rhetorical endeavor. Attempting to write and publish alternative discourses is always risky. However, risk allows for discourses to be expanded and new knowledge to be created. As such, Casanave's (2010: 12) reminder that 'dissertation writers who work under a cloud of fear and intimidation are more likely to give up before they finish, or to find the processes of research and writing so distasteful that they do not pursue their projects post-dissertation' is crucial when considering Ena's experience, and those of other novice researchers. In the final analysis, we have to prepare students and novice authors to face risk – even the risk of losing a publishing opportunity in a leading journal, as in this case.

Epilogue

Ena's article has still not been published. But through the writing of this chapter and the opportunity to gain further clarity and critical understandings of why the publication process may have failed, she now feels more able to revisit the challenges associated with her first ever peer-reviewed academic publishing experience. And while the fate of her original article is still unresolved, there may be a silver lining somewhere: it has engendered the current chapter using a still more atypical genre and shares lessons for more complex consideration of notions of risk for all involved in academic publishing.

Notes

(1) See www.tesol.org/s_tesol/sec_document.asp?CID=209&DID=3150 (accessed 7 November 2011).
(2) In *TQ*, the main section of the journal is devoted to data-driven articles (called full-length articles). Reflections and think pieces appear in the Forum section. While full-length articles are usually about 8500 words, Forum pieces are about 3400 words.
(3) Permission was obtained from the three referees who read Ena's manuscripts to quote from their comments. They remain anonymous, however, including to Ena.
(4) Suresh had made a case for alternate genres of research reporting in *TQ* years earlier – see Canagarajah (1996a).
(5) We have to conduct more research on the kinds of referee comments that are helpful to writers. Tone (evaluative or process oriented), length (long or short) and content (focusing on argument or editing matters) seemed to make a difference to Ena's reception of their comments. For a related inquiry, see Belcher (2007). See also Flowerdew and Dudley-Evans's (2002) study of editors' decision letters.

References

Aitchison, C., Kamler, B. and Lee, A. (2010) Introduction: Why publishing pedagogies? In C. Aitchison, B. Kamler and A. Lee (eds) *Publishing Pedagogies for the Doctorate and Beyond*. New York: Routledge.
Anderson, L. (2006) Analytic autoethnography. *Journal of Contemporary Ethnography* 35 (4), 373–395.
Ang, I. (2001) *On Not Speaking Chinese: Living Between Asia and the West*. New York: Routledge.
Arnoldi, J. (2009) *Risk*. Cambridge, UK: Polity.
Atkinson, D. and Ramanathan, V. (1995) Cultures of writing: An ethnographic comparison of L1 and L2 university writing/language programs. *TESOL Quarterly* 29 (3), 539–568.
Barkhuizen, G. (2011) Narrative knowledging in TESOL. *TESOL Quarterly* 45 (3), 391–414.
Belcher, D. (2007) Seeking acceptance in an English-only research world. *Journal of Second Language Writing* 16 (1), 1–22.
Bell, J.S. (2011) Reporting and publishing narrative inquiry in TESOL: Challenges and rewards. *TESOL Quarterly* 45 (3), 575–584.
Bhabha, H. (1999) Interview. Staging the politics of difference: Homi Bhabha's critical literacy. In G.A. Olson and L. Worsham (eds) *Race, Rhetoric, and the Postcolonial*. Albany, NY: SUNY Press.
Bhatia, V.K. (2001) Initiating into academic community: Some autobiographical reflections. In D. Belcher and U. Connor (eds) *Reflections on Multiliterate Lives*. Clevedon: Multilingual Matters.
Bourdieu, P. (1977) The economics of linguistic exchanges. *Social Science Information* 16 (6), 645–668.
Canagarajah, A.S. (1996a) From critical research practice to critical research reporting. *TESOL Quarterly* 29 (2), 320–330.

Canagarajah, A.S. (1996b) Non-discursive requirements in academic publishing, material resources of periphery scholars, and the politics of knowledge production. *Written Communication* 13 (4), 435–472.

Casanave, C.P. (2010) Taking risks? A case study of three doctoral students writing qualitative dissertations at an American university in Japan. *Journal of Second Language Writing* 19 (1), 1–16.

Chang, H. (2008) *Autoethnography as Method*. Walnut Creek: Left Coast Press.

De Fina, A. and Georgakopoulou, A. (2012) *Analyzing Narrative: Discourse and Sociolinguistic Perspectives*. New York: Routledge.

Duff, P. (2007) Problematizing academic discourse socialization. In H. Marriott, T. Moore and R. Spence-Brown (eds) *Learning Discourses and the Discourses of Learning*. Melbourne: Monash University Press.

Ellis, C. (2004) *The Ethnographic I: A Methodological Novel About Autoethnography*. Walnut Creek, CA: Altamira Press.

Flowerdew, J. (1999) Writing for scholarly publication in English: The case of Hong Kong. *Journal of Second Language Writing* 8 (2), 123–145.

Flowerdew, J. (2000) Discourse community, legitimate peripheral participation, and the nonnative-English-speaking scholars. *TESOL Quarterly* 34 (1), 127–150.

Flowerdew, J. and Dudley-Evans, T. (2002) Genre analysis of editorial letters to international journal contributors. *Applied Linguistics* 23 (4), 463–489.

Geertz, C. (1973) Thick description: Toward an interpretive theory of culture. In C. Geertz (ed.) *The Interpretation of Cultures: Selected Essays by Clifford Geertz*. New York: Basic Books.

Heath, S.B. (1983) *Ways with Words: Life and Work in Communities and Classrooms*. London: Cambridge University Press.

Kubota, R. (2001) Discursive construction of the images of U.S. classrooms. *TESOL Quarterly* 35 (1), 9–38.

Lee, E. (2003) Reflections on illegitimacy in teaching ESL. Paper presented at the colloquium, 'Theorizing race in TESOL: Exploring critical practice', Convention of the Teachers of English to Speakers of Other Languages, Baltimore, Maryland.

Lillis, T. and Curry, M.J. (2010) *Academic Writing in a Global Context: The Politics and Practices of Publishing in English*. London: Routledge.

Lillis, T. and Scott, M. (2007) Defining academic literacies research: Epistemology, ideology and strategy. *Journal of Applied Linguistics* 4 (1), 5–32.

Lupton, D. (1999) *Risk*. New York: Routledge.

Lyng, S. (2008) Edgework, risk, and uncertainty. In J.O. Zinn (ed.) *Social Theories of Risk and Uncertainty: An Introduction*. Oxford: Blackwell Publishing.

Mullen, C.A. (2003) Shifting the odds in the casino of academic publishing through mentorship. In F.K. Kochan and J.T. Pascarelli (eds) *Global Perspectives on Mentoring: Transforming Contexts, Communities, and Cultures*. Greenwich, CT: Information Age.

Pratt, M.L. (1991) Arts of the contact zone. *Profession* 91, 33–40.

Shohat, E. (1992) Notes on the 'Post-Colonial.' *Social Text* 31/32, 99–113.

Smitherman, G. (1999) CCCC's role in the struggle for language rights. *College Composition and Communication* 50 (3), 349–376.

Swales, J. (1988) Twenty years of *TESOL Quarterly*. *TESOL Quarterly* 22 (1), 151–163.

Swales, J. (1990) *Genre Analysis*. Ann Arbor, MI: University of Michigan Press.

Tardy, C.M. and Matsuda, P.K. (2009) The construction of author voice by editorial board members. *Written Communication* 26 (1), 32–52.

Wei, Z., Xiaoming, L., Canagarajah, A.S., Lee, E. and Leung, C. (2006) Periphery scholars publishing in professional journals. Paper presented at the TESOL Convention, Tampa, Florida.

Wilkinson, I. (2010) *Risk, Vulnerability and Everyday Life*. New York: Routledge.

Williams, B.T. (2003) Speak for yourself? Power and hybridity in the cross-cultural classroom. *College Composition and Communication* 54 (4), 586–609.

Zamel, V. (1997) Toward a model of transculturation. *TESOL Quarterly* 31 (2), 341–352.

4 Academic Writing and Research at an Afropolitan University: An International Student Perspective

Aditi Hunma and Emmanuel Sibomana

We are PhD students from two francophone African countries, Mauritius and Rwanda. While writing this chapter, we were studying at two different South African English-medium universities. We met via one of the editors of this book, a lecturer at the University of Cape Town (UCT), who happened to be Aditi's supervisor for her master's and PhD and Emmanuel's external examiner for his master's. She noticed that both our research projects examined the challenges faced by students from francophone backgrounds studying at South African universities, and focused particularly on the issue of academic literacy. We both found the topic of academic literacy interesting because of the high value attached to writing at universities, and because of the challenges we ourselves had to face in this, especially as we transitioned into two relatively elite South African universities. In this chapter, we share our stories, our challenges, our motivations and shifting understandings of postgraduateness in the volatile and risky landscape occupied by international students and novice researchers – an area we have decided to name 'the contact zone', a term derived from Pratt (1991).

We have not known each other for long. We met face to face only once in Cape Town in August 2011 to brainstorm ideas for this chapter. Since then, we collaborated online, and our relationship was enhanced by openness, flexibility and frankness in offering and receiving constructive criticism. Co-authoring a chapter involves not only sharing a thinking space with another but, in the process, allows one to refine, enrich and articulate one's perspective in a more audible or resonant way. Owing to this, our working/authoring relationship has been exciting, inspiring and productive.

The writing process itself was well structured. We first agreed on the story we would tell, then we decided on the headings, and allocated tasks and deadlines for each section. Each of us contributed equally to the chapter, kept our promises and met all the commitments and deadlines for the different activities. We wrote our own stories separately and worked on other parts together, editing each other's work in a critical and constructive manner. Communicating about what we had written became as important as the writing process itself. Given that we met only once, and wrote separately for much of the time – in different South African cities and at times from Rwanda and Mauritius – the use of email, online chats and telephone conversations proved crucial to reach a consensus. Our narrative is thus interspersed with excerpts from some of the online conversations we had while writing the chapter.

These conversations revealed a number of similarities and differences in our early academic experiences, and particularly in connection with our experiences of academic literacy. The similarities relate to the fact that in our early years at school, little emphasis was placed on reading, and there was less exposure to English texts. This would have put us in a vulnerable position when we came to South Africa had we not both made use of out-of-school opportunities to develop our reading, writing and critical-thinking skills. Regarding the differences, Aditi had had more access to English texts at school and at home than Emmanuel. It follows, then, that Aditi may have been better prepared for the challenges of study at an English-medium university, and that Emmanuel may have faced more difficulties. However, while Aditi arrived in South Africa as an undergraduate, Emmanuel had already obtained an honours degree in Rwanda and so may have been better prepared for the demands of tertiary studies. Certainly, we arrived with different expectations of ourselves in our new environments and of the ways in which our universities might accommodate us.

This chapter takes as its starting point the narratives of our journeys from two 'third-world' francophone countries to South Africa. We share our experiences at our respective universities and those of fellow francophone students who later became participants in our research. We then discuss the relevance of our experiences to broader themes, such as Afropolitanism, existing knowledge in new settings, critical thinking at the centre and on the periphery, and coping strategies used by international students through what we have termed *'nou base'* and 'proxy persons'. We then revisit these coping strategies in relation to ourselves and others, and reflect on notions of risk as experienced by international students. In our conclusion, we pose questions about the opportunities and challenges that lie ahead, and consider how international students can participate in the dialogue surrounding this issue.

From Francophone Contexts to English Afropolitan Universities

Aditi

Born and brought up in Mauritius, I was always eager to explore and encounter the vibrancy, the explosion of cultures and knowledges in the world out there. Mauritius brings together a mosaic of people from different parts of Africa, Asia and Europe, and I am a product of its rich post-colonial reality. I speak four languages, Hindi, French, Mauritian Creole and English. I agree with linguists that knowledge of different languages gives one access to a range of world views. Growing up in an environment in which life was constantly celebrated, I looked forward to travelling and learning about new ways of being, languages and cultures.

While applying to UCT, I became interested in the country's history. I imagined Cape Town as one of the most diverse cosmopolitan hub on the African continent. It seemed starkly different from the war and famine-struck parts of northern and western Africa. I was aware, however, that free movement across South Africa's inner and outer boundaries had not always been a given. Reading Nadine Gordimer's *July's People*, I sensed a degree of social and political malaise across the nation's racial boundaries. Yet, despite its wounded apartheid past, I imagined the country would be quite similar to Mauritius in its cultural diversity. As well-known religious leader Desmond Tutu often stated, post-apartheid South Africa could be a country of hope and rich potential. When the plane landed in Cape Town, I looked forward to an experience of a lifetime.

As we drove from the airport to the university, we could see a neat but dismaying agglomeration of shacks made from corrugated iron sheets and blue plastic on either side of the road, just before we drove past an area of gated suburban houses. The social disparities became blatant. The driver dryly pointed out that the slums sheltered approximately 1 million people. The figure still rings in my head; it would have almost absorbed the entire Mauritian population. Nine years later, my eyes still scan those shacks. Poverty bursts at the seams crying malpractice and corruption. Few people have been rehoused, and the grass has simply grown taller in front of the shacks.

UCT intrigued me, being in some ways a miniature world that reflected South Africa's cultural diversity. I was sure that many of the kids from the shacks never made it to university even though UCT offered student loans and other incentives, such as extended degree programmes to improve access for South African students from underprivileged socio-academic backgrounds.

Starting out as an undergraduate, I chose English, linguistics and philosophy as my three majors because of my natural inclination towards languages and arts. The courses and modules reflected the nation's identity and ethos. For example, while studying South African literature, we immersed ourselves in unsettling novels such as Zakes Mda's *Ways of Dying* and Sello Duiker's *Thirteen Cents*. In linguistics, we learnt about the lost language of the Khoi San. It was alarming to think that a language could die when its last speakers ceased to speak it, especially considering how English presently takes precedence over other local languages. South African students may have related to such topics easily, while I had to read around the broader history first. This meant that I took longer to write the essays. Still, because I approached them from a fresh gaze, the topics became more interesting for me.

In terms of academic writing, I coped quite well. I studied French and English literature for Cambridge A-Levels. My literature studies gave me some skills for a fairly perceptive, critical and nuanced appreciation of texts, as well as thorough writing practice. My father who had been a creative English teacher in his early career always encouraged me to question commonplace assumptions about particular topics, to read widely and write carefully with the reader in mind. Reading and writing became quite a creative and liberating activity in high school.

Still, during my first year of university, my marks fluctuated in some courses. This was less due to content and more because I was not aware of UCT's writing conventions or the scope of critical thinking required in academic essays. How critical were we allowed to be? What made the critical enterprise successful? It took me a while to find answers to these questions.

Moreover, the answers differed across departments. While searching for answers, I am now aware that I took the fewest possible risks in venturing outside what I perceived to be the lecturers' or tutors' expectations. I knew, however, that those expectations were blind spots that I needed to resolve, and I met with my lecturers and tutors to ask them how much I could explore without digressing from their expectations.

Throughout my undergraduate years, I observed how other Mauritian students coped with the new academic environment. I was surprised to see that despite obtaining good A-Level results, many struggled with academic writing, even in generic writing courses designed to help science and engineering students to think critically or to develop 'people skills'. Unfortunately, many scored in the borderline 50s. Some even failed modules where essay writing was a requirement, and had to repeat them, twice in some cases. Many of these students had not studied literature at high school, and had never expected academic writing to take on such significance in order to obtain their science or engineering degrees.

By the time I embarked on my master's in applied language and literacy, I had become increasingly intrigued by Mauritian students' writing experiences at UCT, and decided to make this my research topic. Using ethnographic approaches, I explored their writing difficulties and their coping strategies. The findings revealed that, instead of consulting with lecturers and tutors, many chose to rely on their senior peers, to whom they could speak Mauritian Creole and more easily express their concerns. Although some of these senior students had done well, many had just scraped through. In general, the seniors were ill-equipped to satisfy the academic needs of first-year students, and the advice they were able to offer seemed inadequate.

The presence of subcultures[1] and subculture practices at an internationalising university is alarming, especially in view of the time, energy and funding that the university has invested in developing an internationalisation policy, promoting aims such as 'Equity and Institutional Culture' (UCT, 2012). These mushrooming subcultures run counter to the university's efforts (or at least its intention) to integrate students from different backgrounds into the university.

My master's research led me to explore new spaces and methods related to teaching academic writing to international students, and this then developed into the topic of my PhD. I decided to set up a series of writing workshops for first-year international students from various parts of the southern African region. The workshops were designed to create semi-formal yet democratic spaces for students, leveraging on the appeal of subcultures. The pedagogies used were designed to be innovative and well suited to the needs of this diverse cohort, making use of their 'brought-along' knowledges as a starting point. On the whole, five sets of workshops were conducted, impacting on about 60 students. The workshops catered specifically to students who had studied for and written the Cambridge A-Level or International Baccalaureate exams.

Through these workshops, I realised that the stories told by international students were similar to my own first-year experiences, not only in relation to our prior socio-academic experiences but also in our desire to make a difference, and to make our families back home proud. The students' brought-along stories and aspirations became a propelling force for our workshops. Although the workshops provided safe spaces for students to share a range of issues, the topic of conversation rarely strayed from the expectations of the university's academic departments. In fact, during the sessions, students were offered tools to better negotiate their identities at UCT, to hone their critical-thinking skills, and to express these in their writing. The issue of identity is discussed in greater detail later in the chapter.

The workshops initiated a larger conversation about students' academic and cultural experiences at UCT, and led participants to exchange texts, even after the workshops ended. At times I, or other participants, became a port of call for ongoing discussion and queries. These contacts seemed to reassure students that they were not alone on their academic journeys.

Thinking back on my own journey as an international student, I wonder how international students at other South African universities experience the complexities of sociocultural and academic access. It cannot be denied that universities worldwide are broadening access to tertiary education across regional borders. Yet, to what extent are they widening access within their institutions through offering learning support or internationalising their curricula? For instance, while international students are immersed in the knowledges of their adopted land, often without any much-needed mediation, to what extent are the students' existing knowledges acknowledged?

Emmanuel

Born in a remote rural area in Rwanda, I began primary school at the age of six. In my early years at school, I believed that teachers were special people who knew everything and were right in whatever they said. When I started high school, my concept of teachers did not change. I was encouraged to depend on what teachers said, usually without question. I recall once being punished for pointing out a mistake in what a teacher had written on the blackboard – he seemed to think I wanted to undermine his knowledge and/or portray myself as more intelligent than him. At the time, his reaction convinced me that teachers always have the final word, irrespective of whether they are right or wrong.

I grew up in a linguistically and culturally homogeneous community. Although Rwanda had two official languages at the time (Kinyarwanda and French), Kinyarwanda was the only language of everyday communication in the area where I lived. Kinyarwanda is thus my first language (or mother tongue). I studied French as a school subject from my fourth year of primary school and English from my second year of high school. Kinyarwanda was the medium of instruction in my primary education, French was used when I reached high school and a combination of French and English was used at the Rwandan university I attended. It should be noted that in Rwanda, I encountered English and French almost exclusively in classroom settings – outside the classroom all interactions were in Kinyarwanda, while inside the classrooms code switching and the mixing of French and English with Kinyarwanda was routine. As is the case for many educated Rwandans, this prevented me from achieving real fluency in either French or English, but having chosen languages as my major subjects, I looked for opportunities to speak and write in English; generally these were quite limited.

At high school and at university, it was clear that examiners expected us to simply reproduce their notes. In studying towards my Bachelor of Arts degree, lecturers' handouts were almost the only reference required for passing exams; input from us and critical thinking were hardly required. I had the same experience during two trimesters that I spent studying towards a master's in education via a Ugandan university. At these levels, I successfully fulfilled the requirements without difficulty and was among the top students.

During my undergraduate years, I was never initiated into academic literacy in any specific or systematic way. Nevertheless, in my final year I was expected to do research and to write a research report. This was the first time I had been expected to deliver an assignment using 'academic writing'. I relied on what my predecessors had done: most of my peers had written in descriptive way, and I too took this route. For me, knowing a concept or a theory meant being able to summarise, explain and/or reproduce it, usually without analysing or expressing my own opinion about it. I was not familiar with approaching issues from different and sometimes conflicting perspectives, creating a debate or constructing an argument using other people's ideas. In short, I was educated using the 'banking approach' described by Freire (1968).

After receiving my BA degree in 2007, I obtained some work translating documents (including different types of reports) from and into Kinyarwanda, French or English for various organisations and individuals. In addition, I worked as a tutor at an institution of higher learning in Rwanda, and had to read several books and scholarly articles to prepare handouts for students. This time, I was not reading for exams but for understanding. This was when I first got a glimpse of the art of critical thinking, and of addressing issues from different perspectives. Had it not been for my involvement in these activities, I suspect that I would have struggled more than I actually did while studying towards my master's and doctoral degrees at the University of the Witwatersrand (Wits) with regard to learning the skills of academic writing and critical thinking.

I had long aspired to postgraduate study outside Rwanda, but for years I did not have the financial means to do so. Fortunately, as a result of a government policy aimed at revitalising the Rwandan education sector, I was sent to do a master's in applied English at Wits. My studies here marked a turning point in my approach to academic writing, but my adaptation to the university's academic writing discourses was not achieved without challenges. From being a top student and a university tutor with some additional work experience as a translator, I became a struggling student, faced with four main challenges: writing economically, synthesising other writers' ideas, developing an argument while making my own voice heard and ensuring that my style did not sound odd.

Writing economically was a challenge because up to this point in my academic career I had been rewarded for writing as much as I could. I recall one of my lecturers stating that 'the bigger the piece of writing is, the more ideas it contains', and the phrase 'in not *less than* __ words' was common in essay questions. I, therefore, cultivated a habit of striving to write extensively and exhaustively.

Related to this challenge was the difficulty of synthesising the ideas of other scholars. Instead of producing a concise summary of ideas, I would want to provide their extended expositions. At first, I failed to fit my written assignments and research work into the lengths required by my supervisors at Wits. Cutting the work down was a challenge because I thought deleting some of the important ideas would compromise the quality of my work. Fortunately, my supervisor and I established a relationship in which we were able to negotiate what to delete and what to retain. Thus, I would sometimes retain some of the things that my supervisor wanted deleted, and reduce my anxiety about losing any of my precious ideas. Conversely, I sometimes reluctantly let go of chunks of my texts, and was left feeling that something important had been lost. Most of the time, my supervisor would allow me the final choice.

One of the most important things that I learnt in this process was to always ask myself what claim I want to make before I start to write. I also learnt that I should continue with this process at every level of writing: headings, subheadings, paragraphs, and so on. This is something I did not know before. I would just have a claim for the essay, but not for paragraphs – these would flow spontaneously. This was one of the reasons why I found it difficult to develop an argument. When I started to apply this 'rule', I found the process of writing easier than I knew it to be.

As for the problem of making my voice heard, I came to realise that the challenge was not so much about putting my voice into what I wrote. Instead, it was to know how and where to put it, to identify it in my writing and know whether I had put it in or not. While I always worried about voice, I received no feedback from my lecturers that my voice was absent. When I eventually raised this with my supervisor, she told me that my voice was evident in what I had written. However, I am still unable to adequately explain how this is achieved. I expected some explicit guidance with regard to putting voice in one's writing, but this is not something I have ever received.

Since English is my second additional language, I was particularly unconfident about writing in English. Thus, while working towards my master's, I revised and proofread my work several times before submitting it but still felt anxiety about my style. The successful completion of the research part of my master's engineered a degree of self-confidence in me, and now that I am doing my PhD, I am less worried about the four challenges outlined earlier. I feel that I can read any book with a critical mind, take a position on it and defend that position, irrespective of whether it agrees or disagrees with what other people have to say.

The challenges I faced during my master's studies prompted me to think about how my compatriots were coping at Wits. I assumed that, for them, writing was even more challenging and risky given that I, as a student who had majored in languages, was finding it difficult. After talking to some of my peers, I discovered that many Rwandan students who registered at the university's School of Education in 2009 had hoped that they would first have some initial training in using English for academic purposes, as was the case for their colleagues at the university's law school. They assumed that the university knew that English had been neither their first (nor first-additional) language, and that it may not have been a language in which they had ever received instruction. They assumed that they would be treated accordingly but this was not the case. Instead, they were immediately integrated into honours, master's and doctoral programmes, and the education faculty assumed that, as university graduates and professionals in different educational institutions in Rwanda, these students had no need for such a course. This mismatch of assumptions was worrying many of the students I met and some were considering returning to Rwanda rather than facing failure. This aroused my interest in researching the challenges that these students were facing in their studies generally, and in their writing, in particular.

Our Shared Experiences

Clearly, there are common themes in our personal narratives and in the studies we conducted as novice researchers. We now delve a bit deeper into some of these themes with regard to the experiences of the international students who participated in our research,[2] and in relation to academic writing, research practices and challenges.

Risk manifests itself in various ways. In this chapter, risk is analysed with regard to three scenarios: researching and writing at an Afropolitan university, writing and critical thinking and strategies to cope with writing challenges in postgraduate studies. In these scenarios, risk becomes visible in students' fear of stepping into the contact zone, the erasure of several ideas, and conformity to the university's academic standards, usually without questioning them. The experience of international students at Afropolitan universities can be characterised as risky in some aspects. We suggest that 'Afropolitanism' may remain a myth for now and that the university structures and norms of correctness are still defined by Western standards, hence in part limiting the freedom of international students from parts of Africa and Asia to innovate or draw on their brought along knowledges. Within the universities, the admission policies and practices also heighten experiences of risk, being based on general assumptions and expectations of international students' academic performance. The risk can be overt when students are required to pass entrance tests to be admitted and covert when it is assumed that they are proficient and they now have to deliver without the additional support some may require. In such cases, the risk and pressure to conform lead to the reproduction of expected forms of knowledge. In academic writing, risk may be experienced when students are required to critically analyse texts and take a position on a particular subject matter. How much critical thinking is permissible? What if I digress? These are some of the questions that sometimes remain unanswered. To allay their fears, some international students seek the assistance of senior students. We share the students' coping strategies and discuss how unsuccessful they are in reducing the risks involved in the contact zone. This is the case when they simply shelter students and mimic the mainstream structures, providing no definitive solutions to their problems. Consequently, some were labelled as at-risk students and seen as potential threats to the universities' reputation; others were denied access by the universities' border guards.

Perspectives on Afropolitanism

Since our two South African universities define themselves as Afropolitan, it seems appropriate to begin by exploring what the term Afropolitan might mean. In the view of Max Price (UCT's vice-chancellor at the time we were writing this chapter), 'Afro connotes an open, assertive engagement with the world from the standpoint of Africa... Politan signals cosmopolitan, and signals a sophisticated and future-oriented approach to understanding Africa.'[3] Furthermore, according to the institution's mission statement, as an Afropolitan university, UCT aims to 'expand [its] expertise on Africa and offer it to the world, extend [its] networks on the continent... engage critically with Africa's intellectuals and world views in teaching... contribute to strengthening higher education on our continent' among other things.[4] In fact, for Price, 'UCT needs to be an African university in order to be a global university.'[5]

Furthermore, several South African universities make provision at policy level to meet the diverse needs of international students and to ensure that they succeed. UCT, for instance, has a policy which stipulates that 'internationalisation should contribute to an institutional culture which values diversity. Every effort must be made to integrate international staff and students fully into the life of UCT' (UCT, 2012). In our own cases, however, and those of all the international students we interviewed, the universities' internationalisation ideals do not seem to have been put into practice and very few practical measures have been taken to respond to the need for integration.

We tried to define the concept for ourselves, as shown in the following extracts from our online chats:

Aditi: In many ways, I think that UCT is an Afropolitan university.
Emmanuel: What do you mean by that?
Aditi: To me, the word Afropolitan brings to mind 'diverse', 'cosmopolitan' and yet 'African' in its roots and principles. And u?
Emmanuel: For me it is a hybrid institution that some practices from the centre have permeated while it still clings to its African roots. But do we have African roots in these universities? In effect, the university culture is not African! For example, what African roots can we find at UCT or at Wits? Black people? African languages?
Aditi: Yes, to respond to your first comment – 'hybrid' would mean not just the one or the other. The word does spark discussion. If we say that the institution is hybrid, is it just a happy blend of African and western? Or is it something new, something richer than the sum of both? In terms of roots, one does begin to ponder too. If Black people and African languages form the roots of an institution, then surely African indigenous knowledges would need to be

Emmanuel: promoted too. Is that just an elusive promise? Or are the knowledges really present at our institutions?

Emmanuel: I do not think it to be a sum of both. These universities' programmes and working systems are almost totally western! That is what I am questioning here. Or is it the fact that these universities are on African soil that makes them Afropolitan?

Aditi: I guess you are right here. Location cannot be the only criterion for calling an institution Afropolitan. It has to differ. Yet the western gaze is hard to avoid, when it is the sole measure by which our local texts and their thinkers are validated.

Emmanuel: True. But I also think that the location makes it difficult for these universities to escape their 'Africanness'. I agree with you; we cannot avoid western influence as we want to be part of the world academic and research community.

Aditi: I agree with you that 'Afropolitanism' may well begin as a geographically situated idea, but it needs to move beyond this, to inform practices at other sites of knowledge production.

Emmanuel: You are right but our universities are judged on the basis of how much they conform to the centre. So they are left with no other choice!

Mthembu (2004) presents an African perspective on 'internationalisation' and focuses on how African universities appropriate the discourses of internationalisation. He argues that African universities can participate in internationalisation in three ways: by the 'embedding of an external space into an internal space', by the 'embedding of an internal space into an external space' or by an 'isomorphism of the two spaces' (Mthembu, 2004: 81). The first form occurs when more influential, often western institutions impose their norms or knowledge on African universities. The second form occurs when African universities decide on and stipulate acceptable forms of knowledge for foreign universities – this is less common as African universities may perhaps have more authority on the historical, cultural and linguistic facts specific to their local geographies, but little beyond that narrow purview.

Mthembu's suggestion that there is a third type of internationalisation which occurs when both African and international universities share equivalent – not necessarily similar – values, and can mesh together to generate world knowledge, foresees a partnership that is yet to happen in the case of African universities (see also Kraak, 2004; McLellan, 2008; Rouhani, 2007).

Mthembu's interpretation of internationalisation on the African continent is pertinent since Wits and UCT, as Afropolitan universities, demand their own recontextualised definitions of the 'internationalisation' concept. One can imagine an Afropolitan university that would be cosmopolitan in its interactions with foreign institutions and African in its key principles and practices.

As noted by Todd (1997), many international students bring with them distinctive learning traditions with regard to expectations and academic requirements, and the effects of mobility are borne by international students long after their arrival in new institutional spaces. Although they are perceived (and like to see themselves) as providing a neutral space for exchanges between diverse national groupings, universities impose their own rules for the negotiation of power and selfhood. The institutional space can breed angst, fear and defiance when familiar signs of acceptance and success learned in one country's education system are nullified and shattered in another.

Of course, interactions in an institutional site can be hazardous to both insiders and newcomers if neither group is in a position to impose rules. In most cases, the insiders impose the rules – on the two campuses we have experience of, local students tend to do this by enacting what count as the norms of social interaction, while lecturers specify academic norms and standards. Outsiders, in these instances, may not feel empowered to initiate conversations or share their ways of seeing, possibly because of the perceived inferiority or irrelevance of the different cultural resources they bring.

In our view, an Afropolitan university cannot begin to respond adequately to its diverse international student body until it has explored those students' prior socio-cultural, political and academic contexts, and taken into consideration the knowledge and educational practices that they bring with them. Until then, the production of knowledge especially among postgraduate students may remain a risky venture.

Existing Knowledge in a New Setting

Arguably, the successful transfer of previously acquired discourses depends on the assumptions and expectations of key players in tertiary institutions. It is worth noting that some faculties (and some students) assume that their (Mauritian) Cambridge A-Levels, plus the additional year of schooling involved, gives those who have obtained these qualifications an advantage over South African students. However, because the quality of their schooling tends to rely too much on a banking model

(Freire, 1968), students with these backgrounds are often dependent on being 'spoon fed' when it comes to learning and assessment, and tend to battle just as much as South African students do. Unfamiliarity with English as a medium of instruction is another huge disadvantage for many international students.

In contrast to students who think they may be bringing some learning advantages with them, those who have academic backgrounds in languages other than English often expect to be 'apprenticed' into the use of the English academic-writing practices prevailing at the university before they are expected to undertake degree courses and research. Their assumption is that the university knows their backgrounds and will therefore provide training both in English and in academic writing. University lecturers, however, tend to assume that, as many of these students have undergraduate degrees (at least), and have done research before, they are academically literate. As discussed later in this chapter, the mismatch that surfaces exposes students, lecturers and the broader institution to a variety of risks, and a range of risk-management strategies have developed in response. For example, in trying to manage the risk for the university, some departments test new students' writing and other abilities. The following extract gives some insight into our experiences of this.

Emmanuel: On my arrival at Wits my writing abilities were tested in a way. I was given a writing task, so that my lecturers could see what my level was. This gave the impression that they were doubtful about my ability for postgraduate studies. Was it because I was from a more 'peripheral' university? Don't know.

Aditi: Do you think so? At undergrad level, we also all had to do an entrance test called a PTEEP [Placement Test in English for Educational Purposes].

Emmanuel: I did my best to save my face and I gave the lecturers a good impression.

Aditi: I'm sure. You must have been a bit stressed too.

Emmanuel: This was not an entrance test. It was a kind of informal task. I came three weeks after the beginning of the 2009 academic year and I was the only student who arrived in the department then. Whether the same test had been given to other students before I came I do not know.

Aditi: Perhaps that's the case here too. But mostly for postgrad students who enter in the 'non-traditional' way.

Emmanuel: I guess I would have been frustrated if I had failed the test. But my success with it increased my self-confidence.

In discussing this issue further, it became clear that we both felt that our new contexts were initially very demanding, given the academic writing skills we had brought with us. Our francophone backgrounds influenced our style of writing and argumentation in particular ways. French tends to use extended turns of phrase and allows for the construction of exploratory syllogisms and the derivation of a claim at the end of a discussion. This gives (especially beginner) writers the impression that they have to write as extensively as they can about a topic in order to put their points across, and helps to explain why Emmanuel initially exceeded the word limits set for his essays; he was accustomed to providing a wide context for any points he wanted to make. In the English-speaking academic world, however, we had to move from Montaigne's (1923) definition of an essay as an *'essai'*, a trial or a testing of ideas, to one that involves stating a thesis upfront and proceeding to prove or disprove it.

Universities, on the contrary, seem to assume that academic literacy can be reduced to a pack of skills that can work equally successfully across all cultural or academic contexts. In fact, what counts as academic writing is relative, and each university seems to consider their version of academic writing as 'the actual version', the 'divine discourse' (Cadman, 2005). On this basis, each university ends up making students who join it from other contexts believe and internalise a construct of that university's practices as though it were the only 'correct' approach to academic writing. For example, one of the Wits students interviewed noted:

> When I consider what is required in this university in terms of writing, I cannot say that we had any academic writing skills before coming to Wits.

Since this student had been a university lecturer back in Rwanda, where he had conducted his own research and supervised undergraduate students, one may wonder how this can be the case. What may be true is that academic writing at Wits is different from what he (and his colleagues) had known academic writing and research skills to be at other institutions.

In this way, students who are considered competent academic writers in one context may be seen as incompetent in another. Here, the issue of 'whose language' is both controversial and debatable since each discourse community has its own literacy practices (Gee, 1996). For instance, Bartholomae cited in Zamel (1993: 1) challenges students, stating that 'they must learn to speak our language', while Rose (1985: 134) argues that 'they have to speak as we do, to try [the] peculiar ways of knowing, selecting, evaluating, reporting, concluding and arguing that define the discourse of our community'.

Critical Thinking: The Centre versus the Periphery

Perhaps, the most challenging aspect of academic writing for the international students we interviewed was their inability or rather their reticence to display critical thinking. In fact, the question of critical thinking seems to be so strongly emphasised at some South African higher education institutions – heavily influenced as they are by academic practices in the United Kingdom and the United States – that this might be considered a factor in creating and/or furthering the distinctions between the centre and the peripheries of scholarship. In relation to this, some lecturers tend to label international students in somewhat fixed ways and then treat them accordingly. For instance, after realising that some of the Rwandan students were struggling with developing an argument, one lecturer remarked that these students were 'not able to think critically' and that 'deep down some students should not even be acceptable at master's level'.

'Not being critical' appears to be another way of constructing the 'other'. Certainly, some of the undergraduate and postgraduate students' writings studied did show very little evidence of critical thought. The students were used to summarising and reproducing what they had been taught without critically analysing it, and were repeating this practice in their new contexts. Yet, it is likely that each time one normalises the lack of criticality in international students' writings, one perpetuates its occurrence. Prejudgment partly conditions one's interactions with the 'others' and the subsequent responses from them: first, one begins to accept this 'lack' more easily, then one labels those students so as to better remedy the deficit or to expect less of them. Since the students themselves cannot deny the 'lack', they, in turn, begin to expect less of themselves. A vicious cycle of self-fulfilling prophecies is set in motion on both sides. At the core of the matter though, it needs to be acknowledged that the cause of any 'lack' may rely on a range of external factors, and should not be hastily attributed to a student's inherent aptitude or intelligence.

With regard to criticality, the main question asked by international students seems to be, 'how much is permissible?' While Aditi approached her tutors to enquire about these conventions, Emmanuel had to second-guess them from his lecturers' and supervisor's comments on his work. In a desire to play safe, the international students surveyed tended to refrain from taking a stance or taking ownership of their ideas. In some cases, this resulted in them being 'seen as not having any ideas, and as being incapable of doing academic work' (Kutz et al., 1993: 78). Such beliefs are detrimental to a student's expression of ideas in writing; they make students feel incapable of putting any ideas across and prevent them from seeing 'writing as a place to have a position to argue or an experience or an idea worth communicating to others' (Sheridan *et al.*, 2000: 152). Many of these students felt they occupied an inferior position in the academic world and thus restrained their voices when writing. This may also explain why some students interviewed had been accused of plagiarism – feeling that their own arguments were inadequate when placed alongside those of renowned scholars, they may have opted to simply reproduce the latter. As Sheridan *et al.* (2000: 152) note, 'viewing oneself as an "author" – feeling authoritative and feeling the right to exert a presence in the text – is often related to the sense of power and status writers bring with them from their life history'.

It has been shown that what this group of international students brought with them in terms of literacy was not valued, and this is likely to have disempowered them. In addition, since literacy practices are constitutive of identity and personhood (Pahl & Rowsell, 2005), rejecting these students' past literacy experiences constituted a rejection of their identities, and made them feel unfit for their new institutions. As Jones *et al.* (1999: 14) put it, 'when students have their experience and their questions not taken up, when institutional knowledge is being privileged over students' knowledge, students may have a sense of being deprofessionalised'. This seems to have been one of the reasons that international students we interviewed began to internalise the label of incapacity, and this ultimately affected the ways in which they coped with risk.

This rejection might be the result of a university considering some categories of students (mostly international) as 'other', and marginalising them or seeing them as problematic (Haugh, 2008). But then again, students placed on the margins by one university may be treated differently by another, which raises questions of who and what constitutes the centre or the periphery. For instance, after completing a language-training course and obtaining a certificate from one university's language school, a student was refused registration for a master's programme by another department on the same campus, on the grounds that his performance in the English course was poor. Interestingly, the same mark got him accepted by another South African university, which admitted him on the basis that his certificate proved his capabilities in English. The fact that two universities in the same country made two different decisions on the same case, challenges the binary divide between universities in the centre and those on periphery. It raises questions of whether some universities are more peripheral and/or more central than others. Similarly, due to their apparent 'incompetence' in academic discourse and research skills, several graduates of peripheral universities in other African countries have been unable to pursue their studies at peripheral universities in South Africa (such as Wits and UCT). Yet, all these universities see themselves as using western styles of education and championing writing conventions from the centre, regardless of whether these be French or English. With regard to academic writing, universities seem to hold diverse views as to what really constitute the traditions of the centre.

We chatted about this issue online too:

Emmanuel: So, do you think we're studying at the centre or on the periphery?

Aditi: As Afropolitan universities, UCT and Wits aspire to being on a par with makers of global knowledge. They ought not to merely emulate other institutions but to share their uniqueness with them. Your question about the centre and periphery is an intriguing one ... It feels as though we study at the centre of the peripheries, but at the periphery of the centre.

Emmanuel: I agree with you. But I think we are more central than peripheral. I think your description fits us.

Aditi: Which could also be a good thing?

Emmanuel: As long as we do not compromise our uniqueness. By conforming blindly.

Aditi: Yes. Such a hard balance to strike. We need to move with the world, can't be left behind, yet stick to our traditions, principles.

Emmanuel: True. We do not live in isolation. With globalisation, we also need to be part of the bigger academic world.

Aditi: And in the end, who judges us? Can we be in equal partnership with other global players?

Emmanuel: I don't think so. Our history is likely to put us in an inferior position compared to the west. Conformity seems inevitable.

Aditi: If the judging happens on both sides, like in a partnership, it would be ideal. If we could have our African representatives on board in the making and appraising of world knowledge ...

Emmanuel: Because of power relations and related factors, this partnership is hard to achieve.

The 'Nou Base' and the 'Proxy Person'

For the students who participated in our research, the failure of their existing knowledges and writing skills to transfer into their new contexts, affected not only their academic writing, their alignment to ideas and the projection of their voices, but also, in some senses, their academic identities. How could they share critical views in this new setting without an awareness of the acceptable conventional ways of doing so, and in writing? In response, both Mauritian and Rwandan students developed their own coping strategies.

Typically, students withdrew into subcultures and developed a fear of the contact zone. That is, both Mauritian and Rwandan students who participated in our study tended to seek advice and support from senior colleagues in their respective subcultures. The students seemed to avoid the broader student community mainly because they wanted to save face; they feared that if their weaknesses become obvious to others, they would be ridiculed and excluded. They felt more comfortable in their subcultures than they did in the broader campus community, but the support and advice available to them within these groups tended to be ineffective, particularly when it came to the writing difficulties they faced.

Initially, the Mauritian participants were confident that they could write well, but gradually became disillusioned by the low grades they received in assignments. Having tasted failure or near failure, most of the students felt too intimidated to venture outside their own group. Thus, instead of seeking advice from their faculties to help them manage the risk of further disillusionment, they turned to senior Mauritian peers, referred to as *nou base* – a Mauritian Creole phrase meaning 'our nook'. While postgraduate students from Rwanda articulated their need for particular ESL interventions, first-year Mauritian students, perhaps primed for subculture practices in some way, preferred to resort to *nou base*, with its informal, fluid democratic structure, hoping to avoid being labelled as 'at-risk' students. For many, it was a question of pride: they were reluctant to admit that they were struggling in any way. *Nou base* allowed them to nurture a sense of (false) confidence both within and beyond the group, by letting them believe that their seniors would help them to resolve all their socio-academic challenges.

Nou base's appeal was also hinged on the fact that it allowed members to communicate in their mother tongue, Creole. But the role of Creole among Mauritian students goes beyond communicative purposes. As Bourdieu (1991: 18) suggests, one needs to acknowledge that different linguistic utterances are not produced in a vacuum but within different 'markets'. If speakers enter the market with sufficient 'linguistic capital', they can enjoy the 'value' that the market places on the utterances. From observations and interviews, it was evident that, when using Creole, the students possessed more 'linguistic capital' than they had when conversing with faculty members or fellow students in English. In addition, with respect to academic work, participants could express their difficulties and anxieties far better in Creole than in English, which had thus far been the province of dispassionate writing only, and had never been used to convey their feelings.

These benefits were juxtaposed with their perceptions of the rigidity and judgmental nature of the university's institutional structures. These were some of their comments:

Aryan: With peers, you can understand easily. You can ask them more questions.
Rohit: You can swear at them if they don't ...
Rohit: And also the way peers and lecturers think is differently [sic]. You can easily connect with peers just like you would when you work in a team.
Aryan: The lecturer may ask you something that you don't know. He may say, 'You didn't read this about demand and supply?' Normally with peers, you don't face that problem.

This intimate site, where outside risks and perceptual barriers were continually reinforced, is what Canagarajah (2004: 121) refers to as a 'safe house', that is: 'A site that [is] relatively free from surveillance, especially by authority figures, perhaps because these are considered unofficial, off-task or extrapedagogical.'

Reflecting on the purpose of 'safe houses', Canagarajah notes,

> minority communities have always collaboratively constructed sites of community underlife wherein they can celebrate suppressed identities and go further to develop subversive discourses that inspire resistance against their domination. (Canagarajah, 2004: 121)

Nou base provided a safe house where a minority could assert its voice and marginal identity, swear and be subversive, as opposed to the mainstream institution where they were forced to conform or reproduce conventions. At the same time, *nou base* attempted to fulfil a pedagogical role by dispensing advice and notes to its new members. In that sense, it attempted to mimic the institution's academic practices.

Thus (unlike Canagarajah's 'safe house', where individuals oppose the yoke of a superior, if not oppressive, social dispensation), in this case, senior students used the space to mirror the norms and practices of the institutional space. If there is any form of resistance in this, it is in the fact that the imitation was a poor one. In Hegelian terms, *nou base* was a space where the students flouted authority through imitation, that is, by sustaining a 'mushfake' (Gee, 1996) version of the institution and finding their own role models within it. The seniors, hardened 'bondsmen' if you like, offered their services without proper training or guidelines themselves. As one student commented, 'Nina [another more senior student] just explained the format and where I could get the facts. I didn't think referencing was so important.'

Moreover, their support created a cycle of dependency which indirectly ensured that members remained staunchly tied to the group. The students seemed to expect that *nou base* would allow them to 'rehearse' their minority voices before they stepped back into the mainstream spaces, hence offering them a productive opportunity to learn the ropes of academic life. However, what it actually did was to short-circuit the 'mainstream' and keep students in the 'safe space' for as long as possible.

Researcher: But will you consult with the faculty in future?
Aryan: No ... Normally ... they won't get time [to see us] ... with all the people who go for consultations ... There are too many other students [who need help].

Aryan's excuse shows the reluctance felt by many members to step out of *nou base* where they derive comfort from intimate, one-on-one informal dialogues with someone they consider to be an informed peer. Students' poor performance in writing further increases the risk, fear or sense of intimidation with respect to the faculty and strengthens the push towards *nou base*. At postgraduate level, the push or pull towards *nou base* seems less strong. This is probably because there are fewer postgraduate Mauritian students to sustain the sense of community; the disparities between their disciplines increases, and those who pursue advanced studies may gradually realise the myopic purview of such subcultures.

In the case of the Rwandan students, risk was internalised too, and this greatly influenced the strategies that these students adopted in striving to cope productively. Like the Mauritians, their most prominent strategy was to retreat into subcultural groups, within which they discussed their writing tasks, and where they always had recourse to a more knowledgeable person in the circle. This person became a kind of proxy, and the authority and trust invested in them was so strong that it could make a significant difference to students' academic work. In one instance, a student nearly dropped out of his study programme altogether when his 'proxies' were unavailable to help him with a text.

Despite the existence of free academic-writing assistance offered to students by the university's Writing Centre, Rwandan students did not make use of this, even though they badly needed help. They seemed to fear exposing their weaknesses as regards writing in English, and were anxious to avoid any embarrassment that might result. Indeed, they reported feeling ashamed of being master's or PhD students, and researching in a language that they did not understand or speak well.

In addition, some of these students may have experienced difficulties related to switching between identities. They had several of these – being struggling postgraduate students on the one hand, while on the other hand, also being qualified university lecturers and research supervisors or respected ministry or district officials; being uncertain of their academic English but fluent in the discourses of language and learning in French.

This conflict was evident when some students withdrew from a training course on academic writing that had been organised by the university: one of the students commented that 'those who taught us considered us as children who are learning to speak a language'. The statement indicates that these students wanted to preserve their dignity and identity as respected postgraduate students. Unfortunately, while they wanted to address risk productively, by acquiring or adjusting to their university's academic discourse, they could hardly achieve this without venturing into the contact zone mentioned earlier. In fact, as Gee (2001) argues, one acquires a discourse by acculturation (apprenticeship) into social practices through supported interaction with people who have already mastered the discourse.

Revisiting Coping Strategies

Proxies and their relations to self and other

Confining themselves to subcultural groups prevented some Rwandan students from blossoming and affected the ways in which they coped with risk, because this strategy did not allow their horizons to expand. Similarly, while *nou base* seemed to mitigate risk by providing a safe space for Mauritian students, the increased confidence that the strategy seemed to promise did not actually transfer into mainstream institutional sites. In neither case did subcultures facilitate knowledge production (which would require the reappropriation of relevant old and new academic discourses) or even knowledge reproduction since its senior members were not fully equipped to translate the institution's known academic conventions for the newcomers. If anything, *nou base* reproduced the values of the subculture, whereby risk was perpetuated, or became productive of itself. In Hegelian terms, *nou base* created a strong sense of selfhood in juxtaposition to 'others', and allowed its members, in the true spirit of a subculture, to assert a semblance of independence which inadvertently also inhibited their growth alongside the 'other'.

The lecturers' behaviour also affected the ways in which students managed risk. Certain lecturers functioned as gatekeepers, assigning students to somewhat fixed categories and treating them accordingly. Assuming that the students had educational deficits of one kind or another, these lecturers considered them a potential threat to the university – some even publicly expressed their regret that the students had been admitted to the university. One student pointed out that some lecturers' comments were shocking and had made him feel unwelcome at the university.

Meanwhile, other lecturers saw potential in these students. For instance, speaking about a PhD student, one lecturer remarked: 'her spoken English is still a little ... behind both in reading and writing, but this has nothing to do with her intelligence and capacity as a student', and noted that the student had produced a very original research proposal. Similarly, some lecturers hired students as tutors. It is thus safe to assume that these lecturers believed that these students were able to think critically, even though this ability may not have been exploited in their earlier academic careers.

The more relevant question is what can be done to assist students to make a smooth and successful transition from a descriptive and/or banking approach to knowledge to a critical thinking or problem-posing approach. Embedding this in the self–other discussion, one notices that instead of the 'self' and 'other' seeking dialogue for mutual growth and true self-consciousness, they sometimes terminate their contractual agreements. The moment a student refuses to engage in work, the student–supervisor relationship ends, as does the supervisor's authority over the student. Hence, much as one may consider the student a victim of an unfair system with flagrant power differentials, it appears that supervisors too bear the brunt of students' failures by foregoing their role. In this dry process of risk management, they both lose their voice.

Reflections on Risk

Reflecting on the implications of speech versus writing, speech can be regarded as less risky because, while what is said cannot be unsaid, speech is transient. Writing, on the contrary can be doubly risky – it can be retrieved at any point in the future and by a larger group of unanticipated readers. International students' writings tend to bear the remnants of academic habits that may no longer apply, and consequently, students' identities themselves may be misconstrued by their readers. In fact, what we write, who we are, and how we write ourselves into being, are so enmeshed that texts can commit students to forms of selfhood they may not willingly embrace. Similar to body markings, texts can either inhibit or liberate their creators, depending on whether they reproduce and measure up to an institution's 'divine discourses' or, eventually, challenge them in a productive way. The latter situation requires authority that, according to Ivanic (1998), many student writers do not have.

Applying Derrida's notion of 'aporias' or impasses to the notion of risk, one could say that risk resides in:

> The undecidable is not merely the oscillation or the tension between two decisions; it is the experience of that which, though heterogeneous, foreign to the order of the calculable and the rule, is still obliged – it is of obligation that we must speak – to give itself up to the impossible decision, while taking account of laws and rules. (Derrida, 1992: 24)

The decisions Derrida speaks of could be between two or more equally plausible options, his example being that between 'respect for equity and universal rights' versus respect for the 'always heterogeneous and unique singularity of the unsubsumable example' (Derrida, 1992: 24). This aporia is a moment of stasis, fragile but generative, that opens up myriad options, which can either disrupt or reproduce the status quo and, in this case, an institution's expectations. By formulating risk as a moment or 'impasse' (Derrida, 1992), one moves away from a reductive notion of risk, whereby efforts are made to isolate and diffuse the bomb that risk represents. The idea of risk as an aporia also allows one to choose from a range of options, rather than being forced to opt for either defusing or exacerbating the risk. Risk here can be productive if writers creatively appropriate or challenge the corpus of often-cited texts and generate new knowledge. Conversely, risk can be reproductive if writers unfailingly align themselves with accepted norms of production. For risk to be productive in the context of first-year students or novice researchers using languages and discourses that they are not yet entirely fluent in, enabling sites need to be created in which different voices can be rehearsed and gain purchase before being confidently articulated in the contact zone. As Bakhtin (1982) puts it, voices do not resound in a vacuum, they are inevitably dialogical and their material expression presupposes the idea of a hearer.

While voices may not be intrinsic to the self and may at times be products of cultural conditioning differentially manifested across contexts, they can potentially engender a 'tilting point between self and other' (Thesen, Introduction to this volume). They can allow for dialogue and for consensus to be reached between individuals. Even dissonant voices can be a fertile ground for the beginnings of understanding. They can allow us to perceive 'self' and 'other' as dialectically conjoined.

According to Hegel (1869/1998), initially, the 'self' and the 'other' assert their 'pure' individualism in isolation from the 'other'. In extreme cases, the assertion of self-sufficiency can lead to negating or 'killing' (in a figurative way) everything beyond the contours of the 'self'. Yet, through this, neither the 'self' nor the 'other' is fully satisfied because neither can perceive their identity in relation to the other. Hence, they are far from fully satisfying the quest for selfhood or 'absolute knowledge'. According to Hegel, selfhood, characterised by 'true self-consciousness', can only be attained once a person recognises the 'other' as a necessary part of his or her own 'self'.

In an institutional setting, and perhaps especially in universities aspiring to an Afropolitan or similar kind of identity, the fruitful assertion of 'other' or minority voices necessitates their recognition by the official gatekeepers. It also requires the acceptance of 'self' by the minorities themselves, and a recognition that there are situations in which minorities enact their own gatekeeping practices, and become responsible for their own bondage. What the self–other dialectic signals is the nature of our vulnerability to our own being and other beings, hence calling for risk to be transcended first within one's own being, where both 'self' and 'other' reside, and then beyond ourselves.

Unfortunately, by classifying minorities (in this case international students) as 'others', some individuals consider these minorities as a potential threat to their institutions' reputations (Haugh, 2008). This leaves the minorities with only one option for success in the new context: to reproduce (without question) the institution's dominant academic–literacy practices, and hence risk deleting their own beings. In this case, the self assimilates the other, but effaces itself in the process. In the process, students do not achieve self-consciousness but a form of 'other' consciousness.

For example, instead of working harder to make himself understood, the limited English fluency of one of the students interviewed led him to delete any information that his supervisor could not comprehend. Thus, students may begin to view themselves as incapable of negotiating with their supervisors about the meanings they wish to express, a situation in which power becomes binary, or even unidirectional rather than relational. The consequences for students are likely to include the loss of voice, passive assimilation to the new discourses and inhibition of the capacity to think critically – all of which threaten their academic identities.

All these factors are likely to make international students see risk in a negative or unproductive light, as was the case for the participants in our studies. This trend may well be more marked in postgraduate programmes given their relatively higher demand for knowledge production, but it seems likely that they originate in the very first years of students' academic journeys.

Conclusion

Although processes of internationalisation play out unevenly in different institutions, the progressive opening of the borders between traditions of scholarship (both inside Africa, and between Africa and the rest of the world), does offer some hope:

Emmanuel: So, can our experiences at these universities move us towards having our African representatives too on board in the making and appraising of world knowledge?

Aditi: I suppose to some extent. We are at an interesting transitional phase, where new researchers are being given more leeway to be creative, experimental. I wonder if it's across the board. What do you think?

Emmanuel: I also think that the experience has made me assume the identity of a novice researcher – someone who can now contribute (maybe a little) to the world of knowledge. And there is hope for a great shift.

Aditi: That's true.

Emmanuel: It has instilled in me a habit of questioning and critically analysing things.

Aditi: Yes. I agree. I think the critical outlook that the universities encourage us to adopt, allow us more room to explore and negotiate existing academic possibilities. And stretch them.

Emmanuel: True. It also increases our self-confidence. Then we feel that we have something worth saying.

Aditi: Yes, and it makes us more receptive to and accepting of others. I think its culturally diverse environment also has a role to play there. I just hope that in future, there are more solid structures for international students at the universities, especially with the increasing cohort.

Emmanuel: True. It enriches and extends our vision.
Aditi: If not the centre, we [UCT, Wits] can be role models.

The Role of International Students in the Dialogue

On the whole, the process of shaping new academic identities in the contact zone relies on successful transactions of ways of doing between 'self' and 'other'. While universities need to be well disposed to welcome a diverse cohort of international students, the latter also need to be encouraged to step out of their comfort zone and to learn from the 'other'. For instance, *nou base's* assertion of independence rings hollow since it does little to mitigate the impact of the actual risks of moving into the contact zone. For true 'self-consciousness' to triumph on university campuses, international students, such as those in these studies, have no choice but to deliberate with other students, faculty members, and so on, to negotiate legitimate grounds for selfhood. The emerging being is then not merely a mimic who gets assimilated unquestioningly, but, as Bhabha (1994) suggests, a 'hybrid' who has successfully learnt to explore relevant resources from different contexts. Such students will have their voices heard by the others in a hybrid 'third space' where the disparaging norms of the mainstream would probably not hold.

In writing this chapter, we have learnt a lot from each other, from our research and from the writing process itself. In addition to allowing us to learn about each other's culture, history and educational systems, the process of sharing our experiences and our research processes has helped to deepen our understandings of the issues that we have written about. We now have a richer understanding of the commonalities and differences in the experiences of international students at certain South African universities. Our conversations and the emails we exchanged gave us a more nuanced view of the Afropolitan phenomenon and of how it manifests itself in the lives of international students, over and above the visions of our universities.

As international students, we understand how difficult it is to adapt to new and different academic contexts and discourses. We have gained more insight into the writing difficulties that (particularly international) students and novice researchers experience, and have reflected on some of the ways in which these can be addressed. This is crucial for both of us as prospective researchers and university lecturers who, in different ways and contexts, will be dealing with our own and other university students' writing in the future. At a personal level, the writing of this chapter has enabled us to create a kind of 'community of practice' (Wenger, 1998) and we hope to continue working together in our professional career.

We are of the opinion that any written work is neither the critic's nor the author's own, but ultimately belongs to the public reading it (Wimsatt & Beardsley, 1954: 5). In the process of appropriating a piece, readers may rewrite it in their own way. So, while authors may well assume that they transfer their vision to other minds through the sheer power of words, in the end, they have little control over how their work will unravel in the public sphere. Thus, we expect our readers to understand our experiences and stories in various ways, but we hope that all of these will provide them with insights into the challenges of being an international student at an Afropolitan university.

Notes

(1) For the purposes of this chapter, this term refers to peer groups formed around students' national identities.
(2) The participants in Aditi's master's research were students from Mauritius, studying towards undergraduate degrees in various fields at UCT, while the participants in Emmanuel's were postgraduate students from Rwanda, who were registered at the School of Education at Wits. For her PhD, Aditi has worked with students from the broader southern African region.
(3) Installation address by Dr Max Price, University of Cape Town, 19 August 2008, accessed 10 May 2012. www.uct.ac.za/downloads/uct.ac.za/about/management/vcinstallation/installation_address.pdf
(4) See, accessed 10 May 2012. www.uct.ac.za/about/intro/
(5) This is also from Price's installation address, see note 3.

References

Bakhtin, M. (1982) *The Dialogic Imagination: Four Essays*. Texas: University of Texas Press.
Bhabha, H. (1994) *The Location of Culture*. New York: Routledge.
Bourdieu, P. (1991) *Language and Symbolic Power*. Cambridge: Polity Press.
Cadman, K. (2005) 'Divine discourse': Plagiarism, hybridity and epistemological racism. In S. May, M. Franken and R. Barnard (eds) *LED: Refereed Proceedings of the Inaugural International Conference on Language, Education and Diversity* (CDRom). Hamilton, NZ: University of Waikato Press.
Canagarajah, S. (2004) Subversive identities, pedagogical safe houses. In B. Norton and K. Toohey (eds) *Critical Pedagogies and Languages of Learning*. Cambridge: Cambridge University Press.
Derrida, J. (1992) Force of law: The 'mystical foundation of authority'. In D. Cornell (ed.) *Deconstruction and the Possibility of Justice*. London: Routledge.
Freire, P. (1968) *Pedagogy of the Oppressed*. New York: Seabury Press.
Gee, J.P. (1996) *Social Linguistics and Literacies: Ideology in Discourse*. London: Falmer Press.
Gee, J.P. (2001) Literacy, discourse, and linguistics: Introduction and what is literacy? In E. Cushman, E.R. Kintgen, B.M. Kroll and M. Rose (eds) *Literacy: A Critical Sourcebook*. Boston: Bedford/St. Martin's.

Haugh, M. (2008) The discursive negotiation of international student identities. *Discourse: Studies in the Cultural Politics of Education* 29 (2), 207–222.
Hegel, W.G.F. (1869/1998) *Phenomenology of Spirit*. Delhi: Motilal Banarsidass.
Ivanic, R. (1998) *Writing and Identity: The Discoursal Construction of Identity in Academic Writing*. Amsterdam: John Benjamins.
Jones, C., Turner, J. and Street, B. (1999) *Students Writing in the University: Cultural and Epistemological Issues*. Amsterdam: John Benjamins.
Kraak, A. (2004) Discursive tensions in South African higher education, 1990–2002. *Journal of Studies in International Education* 8 (3), 244–281, accessed 25 July 2009. www.jsi.sagepub.com/cgi/reprint/8/3/244
Kutz, E., Groden, S.Q. and Zamel, V. (1993) *The Discovery of Competence: Teaching and Learning with Diverse Student Writers*. Portsmouth: Boynton/Cook Heinemann.
McLellan, C. (2008) Speaking of internationalisation: An analysis policy of discourses on internationalisation in higher education in post-apartheid South Africa. *Journal of Studies in International Education* 12 (2), 131–147, accessed 25 July 2009. www.jsi.sagepub.com/cgi/reprint/12/2/131
Montaigne, M. de (1923) *The Complete Works of Michel de Montaigne*. London: Naverre Society.
Mthembu, T. (2004) Creating a niche in internationalization for (South) African higher education institutions. *Journal of Studies in International Education* 8 (3), 282–296, accessed 4 May 2012. www.jsi.sagepub.com/cgi/reprint/8/3/282
Pahl, K. and Rowsell, J. (2005) *Literacy and Education: Understanding the New Literacy Studies in the Classroom*. London: Paul Chapman.
Pratt, M. L. (1991) Arts of the contact zone. *Profession* 91, 33–40, accessed 10 May 2012. ww.jstor.org/stable/pdfplus/25595469.pdf?acceptTC = true
Rose, M. (ed.) (1985) *When a Writer Can't Write: Studies in Writer's Block and other Composing-process Problems*. London: Guilford Press.
Rouhani, S. (2007) Internationalisation of South African higher education in the post-Apartheid era. *Journal of Studies in International Education* 11 (3–4), 470–485, accessed 25 May 2009. www.jsi.sagepub.com/cgi/reprint/11/3-4/470
Sheridan, D., Street, B. and Bloome, D. (2000) *Writing Ourselves: Mass Observation and Literacy Practices*. Cresskill: Hampton Press.
Todd, L. (1997) Supervising overseas postgraduate students: Problem or opportunity? In D. McNamara and R. Harris (eds) *Overseas Students in Higher Education: Issues in Teaching and Learning*. London: Routledge.
UCT (University of Cape Town) (2012) Policy on Internationalisation, accessed 10 May 2012. www.uct.ac.za/downloads/uct.ac.za/about/iapo/internat_pol.doc
Wenger, E. (1998) *Communities of Practice: Learning, Meaning, and Identity*. Cambridge: Cambridge University Press.
Wimsatt, W.K. and Beardsley, M.C. (1954) The intentional fallacy. In W.K. Wimsat (ed.) *The Verbal Icon: Studies in the Meaning of Poetry*. Kentucky: University of Kentucky Press.
Zamel, V. (1993) Questioning academic discourse. *College ESL* 3 (1), 28–39.

Part 3
Pedagogies that Invite the Edge

5 Rehearsing 'the Postgraduate Condition' in Writers' Circles

Clement Mapfumo Chihota and Lucia Thesen

In this chapter, we look back on a practice we embarked on intuitively when we started multidisciplinary writers' circles some years ago. The circles have evolved and mutated in response to what we have learnt about the complexity of the writing lives of our students and the challenges of thesis completion. Apart from providing enabling spaces for students, particularly those in search of community, the writers' circles have also been a source of our emerging understanding of the importance of risk as central to the conceptual work of our collective project. From early on, we thought of the circles as spaces for the rehearsal of postgraduate identities. We became aware over time that the circles enabled students to work out their attachment to ideas before taking them into more threatening situations in which the stakes are higher. They became spaces for exploring the flux of risk, as students weighed up whether it was worth persevering with a line of thought, an analysis, a term, a method, a style or a site for research, all of which have to be communicated in writing.

It is a challenge to describe an emerging pedagogic practice. We neither want to make simplistic claims to success – our circles are far too unpredictable for this – nor are we ready to embark on a systematic review of what they do. Instead, what we offer here is a sense of what the circles are not, and present the metaphor of a rehearsal as a way to understand the spaces that we create. We give a brief description of how one of our circles operates, and then reflect on some of the generative tensions that emerge from participating in and facilitating these kinds of spaces.

Situating Writers' Circles

One place to begin is by saying what the writers' circles are *not*. Circles are neither a replacement for supervisory relationships nor for generic writing workshops, from which students and supervisors expect clear guidelines for how to write a literature review or a proposal, edit work or manage citations. Instead, the circles offer a space that complements these two pedagogic practices.

Certainly, the supervisory relationship can be fraught with challenges. At worst, it has been described as a '*mad* process in its assignment of a structural role to insecurity' (Frow, 1988: 319, emphasis in original), and at best, as 'cooking up an intellectual feast' (Bartlett & Mercer, 2000: 63–64). However good the relationship with one's supervisor, there are inevitably times of isolation and confusion, which often bog down in a complex tangle of 'random clogged misery',[1] where intense emotions of loss, blame and frustration are quick to surface. High expectations ride on the 'pop-up pedagogy' of writing workshops too – supervisors hope that their students' writing problems will be remedied, while students tend to expect recipes that they will be able to imitate, as if the complexities of thesis writing could be laid out neatly, once and for all. In offering these kinds of workshops too, we find ourselves asking many questions about them. Why is there almost always a drop-off in attendance? Are we providing safety valves for supervisors who are unable or unwilling to take on the challenges of increased student diversity? Are we failing to speak to the disciplinary needs of students? Are we recycling idealised notions of the set forms of academic writing in English? And, with what consequences?

From the beginning, the circles seemed to complement supervisory and workshop practices by offering the much-needed rehearsal spaces where postgraduates could work through their ideas before presenting them to more challenging audiences. The metaphor of a rehearsal thus informs this chapter and serves several purposes. It points to an aspect of practice related to performance – rehearsals are spaces for trying out, for weighing things up in preparation for going public. The word rehearsal also suggests a distinction between the research-writing process and its final product – a distinction well established in undergraduate writing pedagogy. The idea of rehearsal can also be applied to the writing of this piece as 're-search'; that is, we do not report on a formally constituted research process in this chapter, but instead explore a complex practice through multiple rich points in texts generated by this practice. These rich points include texts produced in the circles, comments from participants, descriptions of moments in circles, extracts from a published article and from a discussion recorded in the early days of the practice. The chapter is performative in the sense used by Pelias (2005: 419), in that it features lived experience, seeking the complexities; it 'creates a space where others might see themselves' and asserts that this recognition is often felt in the body. It offers glimpses, fragmentary and partial, as a form of truth that is tuned to paradox and uncertainty. For Pollock (1998: 80–81), performative writing is first of all evocative: it 'favours the generative and ludic capacities of language and language encounters ... [it] does not describe in a narrowly reportorial sense, an objectively verifiable event or process but uses language like paint to create what is self-evidently a *version* of what was, what is, and/or what might be'. It invites the 'generative force' of being between presence and absence, and being between scholarly and creative forms.

In the years since we started writers' circles, interesting work has begun to emerge about the writing group and its place in postgraduate pedagogy, and we are now able to relate practices in writers' circles to similar scholarly work elsewhere. The principle of peer-based writing pedagogy is well established in undergraduate writing scholarship, particularly in the process-writing movement (Elbow, 1998; Murray, 1978), but it is relatively recent in the postgraduate sphere. Boud and Lee (2005) argue for a shift in the discourse from seeing research as training to seeing research as education. The training discourse is saturated with an emphasis on vertical 'provisionism', with strategies for more effective supervision and funding to improve graduation throughput. The shift that Boud and Lee argue for seeks a more horizontal, distributed notion of peer learning. For them, the notion of the peer group is useful in the research-writing field as it is already present at the centre of the research identity: the researcher works collaboratively, 'at the centre of a constellation of others' (Cullen *et al.* cited in Boud & Lee, 2005: 21). The interest in writing pedagogy, and particularly in writing groups, signals a desire for a more nuanced understanding of the challenges of research completion, and the need for a wider range of responses to support postgraduates in their writing. This need is enhanced by the changing context in which geographical and conceptual mobility are rapidly becoming the norm. Thus, Cuthbert *et al.* (2009) emphasise the role of multidisciplinary groups in enhancing the likelihood of getting published, Parker (2009) evaluates the possibilities for community-learning approaches in 'scholarly writing groups', and Aitchison (2009) analyses how the pedagogy of writing groups for doctoral researchers actually works, noting an unintended but crucial shift in disposition: a growing confidence in the value of critique. Collectively, these articles attempt to share the practice and possibilities of this emerging pedagogy. Those who argue for a role for peer-based writing groups (and their possibilities for dispersed authority) caution against any easy claim that peer pedagogy is a 'good thing'. Boud and Lee (2005: 514, 515) warn that 'questions of power and difference are conceptualized only in terms of a reduction in top-down imposition of pedagogic authority'. They note that 'There is a general need to surface assumptions of the "good" in pedagogical discourses such as peer learning and to be vigilant in relation to the dangers of idealizing which accompany horizontalizing moves in pedagogy.' They call for situated and nuanced approaches that do not romanticise peer relationships. This chapter is written partly in response to their call, as we seek out the tensions and paradoxes in the flatter spaces offered by writers' circles. We believe that these practices have a place, but only as one of many kinds of responses to the complexities of what we call 'the postgraduate condition'. There is no single pedagogy that can hold all that is going on. Perhaps, the greatest strength of writers' circles is that they can open up our understanding of the postgraduate condition itself. They can offer a multifaceted lens for what is going on in a time of intense institutional change in internationalising universities.

We now approach the circles via some of the many texts that have been created in the years since they were established. From these shards, we hope to offer glimpses of an emerging practice that is risk-sensitive and has its ear to the ground.

A Brief Description of a Multidisciplinary Writers' Circle

Different kinds of circles have evolved in the six years since their inception. There are discipline-based circles such as monthly gatherings for cohorts of students in the research phase of a taught master's degree. Other 'tailor made' circles meet temporarily for a specific purpose, such as the preparation of conference papers. There is a fortnightly circle for scholarship students from a range of disciplines in their honours year.

For this chapter, we describe the oldest and the most freewheeling of all the circles, our weekly multidisciplinary group. When we initiated the circles, we invited potential participants via posters showing a hand-drawn image of people communicating intensely; the artefacts of writing (laptop, pen and paper) in the image are shown as secondary to the body language of the figures and to the teacups and eats on a table. We waited to see who came. The early trends that emerged still apply. Those who joined the group sought a sense of community. Typically, they have not been through the university's honours programmes and so have not yet learned the institutional ropes. They reflect the changing demographics of a globalising university with its drivers of internationalisation and lifelong learning. Many are international students, usually from sub-Saharan Africa; they are typically older, often women, have careers in service professions and are returning to university. Many are between disciplines, or find themselves in disciplines that are changing rapidly or look different in different places. Some have only recently adopted English as a language of learning. Some do not yet have supervisors, or are seeking opportunities to speak English. Most are in the humanities field. Several are staff members who locate themselves between disciplines, or who find it safer to be vulnerable outside of their own departments.

The circle revolves around an offer from a participant to bring a draft to be read by the group. Over time, we have developed the practice of printing just two pages of a work in progress. These are read in the circle, and responded to 'live' in the moment. One of our ground rules is that there is no homework: no one reads screeds beforehand or feels obliged to respond to a lengthy chapter, although members do sometimes get involved in reading each other's work informally outside of the circles. Students are also invited to bring various kinds of texts – we have listened to poster and conference presentations, looked at transcripts of interviews, respondent's drawings as well as drafts of conventional texts. There is usually a quiet quarter of an hour while the writer's two pages are read, and participants annotate their copies if they have comments. After the critique, the writer collects the drafts. This seems to encourage participants to make their comments constructive. We have also tried 'speed editing' sessions which allow everyone's work to be read and commented on at the same event.

In addition to discussing the draft, there is always a second element – a spotlight on an aspect of skill or theory that has some bearing on writing. There is no particular curriculum for this – the facilitator decides, based on what emerges from the draft or sometimes a suggestion comes from a group member. The focus may relate to aspects of writing such as citation strategies to enhance a writer's voice, writing introductions, structuring a thesis, writing abstracts or different ways of giving feedback. Some of our most generative circles have begun with a discussion of an aspect of theory chosen by one of us as facilitators – Bhabha's 'third space', or Bourdieu's 'habitus' or different definitions of genre, for example – and how these relate to our lives and our research projects. We explore techniques for surfacing meaning such as free writing and drawing, strategies for dealing with 'writer's block' as well as tips on how to manage your supervisor or keep track of your readings. Circle members who are 'techies' share their know-how on the use of bibliographic software. As befits a rehearsal space, these skills spotlights have an oblique relationship to the actual written product of research writing, making it possible to talk and feel one's way around some facets of the writing process in an exploratory mode.

As opposed to the (somewhat parental) supervisory relationship or the guidelines offered by pop-up pedagogies, membership of the circle tends to be nomadic; people move in and out as it suits them. Sometimes students come once or twice then move on; or they disappear on data-gathering trips or go and visit their funders. Some do not attend for months due to clashing teaching commitments. Loose contact is maintained, however, through the university's internal online network. A weekly email is sent to the group, keeping everyone in touch, pointing backwards and forwards, making announcements, sharing resources. These emails also do some conventional pedagogical work of reviewing and anticipating activities in the group. This is typical of messages from us as facilitators:

> Hi all
>
> Thanks to Neo[2] for sharing her conference presentation last week.
> This week (tomorrow!) we will read and engage with Elise's proposal for her PhD on collective identity and the urban agriculture movement in Cape Town. One of the options for her title begins with the phrase: 'I'm a farmer now.' Nice! Looking forward to that.
>
> Since Elise is at proposal stage, and wants some input on her research title, I thought we could all bring our titles and research questions/hypotheses with us to the circle. If you forget, that's fine, you can make them up in the moment! I really struggled with my questions as they kept changing.

At each weekly meeting, a 'participant details' form is handed around and filled in. It includes key words from one's research, what one is busy with that week, and intends to do the following week. These are sometimes revisited, often with wry laughter, as participants see that they have been saying the same thing for several months, or how they misjudged what would be involved in reviewing literature or revisiting a data chapter. In this way, participants acquire a reference group that unofficially monitors their progress. They feel compelled to report on their progress and they witness the progress of their peers.

Students attend for a wide range of reasons. Some, like Clarence, come to 'clear their throats'. Others come for the structure and accountability – something to bind their day. Wandile came a few times, disappeared, then reappeared to invite us all to a presentation after his thesis had been handed in. Fehmi joined to improve his English. Salma came twice, and left, perhaps finding insufficient understanding of her research on the place of Islamic banking in South Africa, but the decision to stop attending may have helped her to find her way to another process.

Generative Tensions in Writers' Circles

This section of the chapter reflects on practices in multidisciplinary circles and links the circles to the wider frame of the postgraduate condition. It also links the tensions in this rehearsal space with our interest in risk as a productive element in research writing.

In 2006, we tape recorded a discussion about how to facilitate circles. The discussion revolved around Clement, who was the central and most experienced person in our evolving pedagogy. Lucia and Ellen (a colleague and circle member who was busy writing her PhD) wanted to catch some of the tacit stuff that was emerging so that we could describe it and share it with others who might be interested. At the time, Clement had (somewhat wryly) coined the term 'the postgraduate condition' that was emerging as we reflected on our practice (Chihota, 2007). In the tape, the discussion focuses on how Clement facilitates: how he establishes an ethos, what that ethos is and on what the facilitator needs to know and do. Clement talks about how facilitation is necessarily shot through with tensions. The first is the tension between the facilitator's disciplinary 'habitus' and the need to engage with the various disciplinary fields in which circle members are located – engineering, the health sciences or philosophy, for example. The second is the tension between the serious and the comic. Clement talks of the need to make space for an 'august' presentation of self, and yet stresses that the index of a thriving writers' circle is the amount of laughter that emanates from the group. Third is the tension between the need to be directive and the need to foster a space in which group members can freely express whatever they have on their minds.

All three tensions are indicative of 'the postgraduate condition' – a pervasive state in which the individual tussles with the structural in a long drawn-out process. We think of the postgraduate condition as akin to the human condition. It is necessarily complex and paradoxical. All we have are moments of engagement through occurrences and utterances that we need to make sense of. In this sense, doing a postgraduate thesis – particularly a doctoral thesis – is a human venture at the centre of which is risk taking. While this 'old-fashioned' view of the thesis now has little place in the changing count-culture of the university with its emphasis on rapid throughput, we feel that the circles made space for this transitioning and predicament-welcoming identity – an identity that is not possible without writing.

Writing must embrace these predicaments because, as we write, we always hover on the edge of commitment.

Central to the predicament is that we do not know, other than at the most instrumental level, where we are going: there is no clear end that can be held on to once and for all. There's a general direction and a contour map (which keeps changing), but no beaten path to follow. In his exploratory piece, Clement began his description of the postgraduate condition in this way:

> Imagine this thing called graduateness. This thing that is often dangled at us from the great heights above. This thing that we leap so high to catch but never quite grasp. This thing painted in quaint colours and made of exotic materials whose texture we can never be sure of. This thing which we sometimes think is made of glass, or of gold or of silver, or of silk or of just plain papier-mâché. Just imagine that one day this thing would slip from the grasp of those who dangle it down at us, yes, imagine it were to fall down, land right there in our midst ... Imagine what we would do with it! Wouldn't we love to kick it around, kick it at each other, roll it on the floor, topple it onto its side, climb on top of it, wear it on our heads, or roll it around our shoulders like a gown? Wouldn't we love to feel its grain and at last, really know all the secrets of its composition? Wouldn't we wish to carry it with us when we went into our toilets, rode in our buses or taxis, visited our shebeens, carry it everywhere and show everyone who asked, what it *really* was? Only then would we truly posses it, demystify it, own it, make it ours, make use of it, and in the end, be unselfconscious when we carried it around and hopefully even get bored and disinterested in it. If only someone could drop it right down to our level, we would surely say, 'Aha, so this is what you really are', then begin to see it in the way we see trees or bucketfuls of water or bottles of coke.
>
> But of course, no one ever drops it. It must be secured by strong bonds 'up there'! It never really comes within our grasp. So what do we do? Imagine us huddling in groups and talking about it, exchanging notes and drawings and pictures and reports on it ... Imagine us creating composite pictures of it out of these bits and bobs, patching up gaps in the picture with whatever materials or colours we have at hand, and stopping from time to time to savour our handiwork. Imagine us also acting on the basis of these approximate images of 'the thing' or acting out our developing understandings of the mobile, ephemeral and ever-changing thing. Imagine a place in the university where people could do things like that! (Chihota, 2007: 131–132)

Writing one's way into being a postgraduate involves many small acts of trying on that identity and slowly building into a composite experience. If the condition is a predicament, then the pedagogy of postgraduate spaces needs to embrace these tensions rather than bury or ignore them. Postgraduate identities tend to be seen as unattainable, high up, shrouded in a complex language and not easily made ordinary. However, attaining this identity is only made doable by making it out of 'bits and bobs', out of what is 'to hand'.

We now briefly discuss each of the three tensions that emerged from our recorded discussion, and show how they typify the lifeworld of a writing circle that invites risk taking into its centre.

On the Edge of a Discipline

As a circle facilitator, one is inevitably outside of one's disciplinary forte, so one needs to listen carefully for the presenter's logic. Similarly, most participants in the circle are outside of their disciplines. We work with what Clement calls 'beyond content':

> In a sense you're aware of your limitations. You need to get the gist without pretending that you can review the content, so you're reviewing the logic, the way it's presented. The postgraduate condition is not just a matter of content – graduateness is beyond content. This is what we're drawing out, that fraction of the participant's knowledge. We want to accentuate that key fraction. (Tape recording, 2006)

This 'fraction' is what Sharon, a town planner who returned to the university to undertake a master's degree, experienced after joining the circle. The degree began with an intensive year and a half of coursework, after which students wrote a short thesis. Sharon attended the circle while writing her thesis. She said little, but listened intently. When asked why she came regularly, although she seemed to have so little to say, she gave the following explanation in an email:

> At one point it was proposed that I move into a special circle dedicated to town and regional planning. I'm glad this didn't happen. When I first arrived at UCT, I thought it would be a good place to meet a huge number of really diverse and interesting people – this didn't really happen. The massive workload meant that I never left the building and I only had time to socialize with people studying the same course – not really the best environment to broaden my horizons. The writers' circle was the only

place where I came into direct contact with motivated and passionate people from other disciplines. It's kind of weird but listening to everyone talking about their work – most of which I didn't really understand – forced me to put my tiny project into perspective, as one in a massive range of possible topics. After working on one project for four months I began to think that my work was *it*, I sort of got tunnel vision and the circle was an opportunity to get tangled up in the passions of other people. It was sort of an escape, and I learned loads of stuff I never would have considered before.

If carefully held, a circle's more open exploratory space can also yield rich dividends within a discipline itself, genuinely making 'new knowledge'. Ellen, who subsequently completed her PhD, coined the term 'stylect' while searching for a term to describe a particular usage of Tsotsitaal, an informal South African urban language. She brought a conceptual dilemma to the group. She had become aware of a particular usage of Tsotsitaal during her field research that no existing sociolinguistic term adequately described. During the discussion, one of the circle members suggested the term 'stylect'. The term stuck. Ellen took it back into discussion with her supervisor, and into her writing, where it took on the form of 'new knowledge'. In her thesis and subsequent articles, Ellen acknowledged the circle's contribution.

Part of this outsider relationship to the discipline is how, as a facilitator, one finds a role that complements that of the supervisor. Clement advises:

> One thing you never do [when facilitating a writers' circle] is seem to be undermining the authority of the student's supervisor. You need to constantly remind yourself that you are not meant to act as a wedge between the student and the supervisor. Rather, you work behind the students, pushing them closer to their supervisors. You are often invisible to the supervisor. In short, you mustn't ever collude. (Tape recording, 2006)

Lucia and Ellen ask how to react when students express frustration with their supervisors:

> You have to allow them to talk, but constantly remind them of the ethos of the circles. Our awareness of the postgraduate condition warrants that we listen attentively and sympathetically to members' frustrations and emotions. Having listened, we don't pretend there are any easy solutions. We also need to allow other group members to offer advice. It should be clear that we have our own limitations. We don't possess any weapons which we can fire back in defence of a member. We don't get into fights.

Rather, we strengthen our members. We try to help them to become more creative and resilient so that they find a way past any presenting obstacles. (Tape recording, 2006)

The backstories discussed in writers' circles are often not heard in the official spaces provided by supervision. Students often seem to feel that, as postgraduates, they should be able to deal with the challenges they confront. They are uncomfortable admitting that they feel lost.

Not (Only) Writing, but Laughing (or How Do I Laugh in Writing?)

The above-quoted excerpt touches on the importance of creating space for emotions without taking sides or being directive. In the recorded discussion there are frequent references to laughter. When we started circles, Clement's circles were richly laced with laughter from the beginning. When Lucia started facilitating a circle, she remembers feeling that something was wrong: it was far too earnest. Over time, her circles started to take on a similar quality, with frequent laughter punctuating the proceedings. In our recorded discussion, we talk about the moments in the circles that feel good – moments of critique, when everyone has read something and is richly engaged; 'warm-up' activities that have worked brilliantly, times when a writer realises that there is an implicit contradiction that has been teased out through discussion, or when group members share a newly discovered resource. But some of our richest moments of collective edification (or transcendence?) are those moments when we laugh together. There have been times when colleagues have complained that we are too noisy, that these are laughing circles rather than writing circles. Clement emphasises that

> Laughter is an index of how well it's worked and how likely people are to come back. If they're not laughing, watch out!

How do we make sense of this laughter in what is a serious practice? In discussing the challenges of facilitating circles, Lucia asks whether there is a danger of perpetuating the postgraduate condition by talking about it. Clement replies:

> We are aware of it, but not as an academic topic to be rigorously unpacked or a generalised pain to be countered with analgesics. We are in the zone of tensions all the time. What members experience privately is part of a

generalised condition. But we don't want to dwell on it, otherwise it would become huge and overwhelming and we might as well just fall flat on the ground and be crushed.

We struggle for the right word to describe this wallowing, which we are aware of but which – if allowed to dominate our consciousness – may turn into a sort of hypochondria. Ellen remembers a writer' circle session in which we had been sharing strategies for managing 'writer's block', and we did drawings to show how we thought about ourselves at that point in our writing processes. Figure 5.1 shows Ellen's drawing. It is comical. She huddles in terror behind a chair, hiding from a laptop that has grown crocodile teeth and has a battery lead rearing up from it like a snake. Her popping eyes turn our serious pursuits into the stuff of a child's nightmare, but her humour pricks the power of the nightmare and provides symbols that refract her fear and avoidance.

Weeks later, Ellen remembers her drawing and how she felt:

We're having fun and laughing but this also makes me feel depressed. Are we actually enjoying this?

Perhaps, in inviting this moment and acknowledging it, one is able to move through and on.[3] Other participants' drawings were much more serious, but no less emotional. Several showed some sort of left to right vector suggesting a journey unfolding from a problematic 'given' to a more

Figure 5.1 Ellen's sketch: A reflection on writer's block

hopeful 'new'. In his later work, Bakhtin reflects on laughter, and on the importance of the body in struggles over meaning in the context of a medieval carnival. Discussing 'peoples' ambivalent laughter', Bakhtin shows how laughter expresses an 'inversion of power structures, the parodic debunking of all that a particular society takes seriously, including and in particular all that it fears'. Laughter is always ambivalent, argues Bakhtin, 'it asserts and denies; it buries and revives' (Bakhtin, 1968: 12).

In most contemporary institutions, the easy public movement between the sacred and the parodic has been split. The procedural, bureaucratic 'provisionism' that Boud and Lee (2005) speak of, which increasingly shapes much of our activity and institutional strategy in the postgraduate research terrain, drives a wedge between the sacred and the profane and, in the process, raises the emotional stakes. Hargreaves (2001, 2004) writes of the 'emotional geographies' of teaching and learning, showing how an economy of emotions functions in educational institutions. As we move through the schooling process from primary school to a PhD, emotions are increasingly set aside as rationality officially takes over. The increased emphasis on throughput and accountability measures in higher education has the potential to heighten difficult emotions for both students and their teachers. Douglas's (1992) work on purity and danger shows how the interplay between emotions of disgust and distinction work in establishing failure for school students who are 'other'. These emotions also play a strong role in shaping how risk is experienced and made sense of. As Steinberg (2008) shows, in her analysis of emotions around assessment practices in schools, there is a contradiction between the informal, lived emotional experience in the private sphere and what is signalled in public. This contradiction is strongly evident in the postgraduate sphere too. It requires intense emotional work to retrieve positive emotions that enable postgraduates to find agency in their research journeys.

Although, the link between risk and emotion in the postgraduate writing is only hinted at in this chapter, writers' circles provide a canvas for students to manifest emotions linked to the postgraduate condition, and offer spaces for them to work with these emotions in various ways.

A Curriculum in Perpetual Motion

The third tension is the challenge of facilitating the pedagogy of the circles in an organic way, and of working with a curriculum that is in perpetual motion. Our curriculum was loosely defined and allowed to mutate in response to the numerous pressures and surfaces of the postgraduate condition. It was shaped by (or continually adjusted on the basis of) what we, as facilitators, observed, perceived, felt, heard and so on as we engaged with postgraduate students. The following description of a moment in a writers' circle, Lucia tries to convey this organic pedagogy, the dilemmas of framing an ongoing practice which responds to the flux of the 'brought alongs' of those who attend, and where they are in their research processes.

> Today Jo has offered to bring 'something' from her data. We are a cosy group by this stage, mainly women. I have been conscious that we are perhaps a little too cosy. Patrice is no longer coming. Why? Should I send him an email to ask if he's OK? There are PhDs, masters, at different stages, different disciplines. Elizabeth is close to finishing her study of carers of terminally ill cancer patients in urban Kenya. She and Jo are disciplinary worlds apart, but are both using versions of phenomenology. They share readings, talk about Heidegger; we joke about 'authenticity'. We have shared the ups and downs of Jo's PhD on preparing nurses in intensive care units to talk about their experiences related to the deaths of patients under their care. The link between her life and her research topic is sharp at this point. She is returning to the circle after her mother's recent death, and has brought a cake to share with us.
>
> She walks into the room shyly, cake in hand, holds back as she sees two new circle members in the room. They are both men. Fehmi is a historian with a special interest in the Ottoman Empire in Africa. He has strong views on history, believing that if there is still disagreement about past events, those events are not yet really history. Last week we read a translation of an article he is writing on typology and knowledge paradigms in the Ottoman Empire. I have been struggling with how to offer constructive critique and am worried that I misunderstand him and might be steering talk away from what he really wants to say. Langa is also new in the group. He is close to finishing his PhD on land and democracy in the rural Eastern Cape. He is an activist and ex-teacher with a commitment to participatory knowledge-making processes. I know that he sees history very differently from Fehmi. I have a moment of anxiety: how will I knit this changing group together yet again? I ask Adam to describe what we do: 'Everyone gives and everyone gets.' he says. 'There's no "homework"; bring two pages.' We go round the circle, introducing ourselves quickly and putting a name to our projects.
>
> Jo clears her throat. She tells us that she has not yet met with her supervisor. He is keen to make contact but she just isn't ready to bring her work to him. She shows us her students' drawings representing death and dying

in the ICU wards. One is particularly challenging. It shows a child lying on a bed, wrapped head to toe in bandages. The carer, a young male nurse, has drawn a self portrait of himself standing next to the bed, forming a striking vertical line as he seems to look at us, with large tears rolling down his cheeks. Jo explains how the drawing fits into her data, and then reads an interview with the student nurse in which he describes the drawing. The bandages cover burn wounds from a fire in the child's home and the boy's mother seems to have been responsible. He talks about the bond that developed between the boy and himself. Jo reads for about 10 minutes. We hear her questions, and the student nurse's responses. She stumbles as she reads some of his words. 'The responses are a bit incoherent,' she tells us, 'English isn't his first language.' There is silence in the circle. Then the questions begin. What had the boy's mother done? I try to steer the conversation away from a judgement of the mother. There is relief as Langa asks about the interviews. We are now shifting into the stuff of research. How did the formality of the set-up with the young student nurse, and his awareness that Jo was his lecturer, affect what he said? What about language differences? The nurse had had to express complex emotions in English. We talk about how incoherent we, as researchers, sound in interviews. We wonder whether we can treat spoken language in the same way as written language? We talk about the status of the drawings. The talk brings out the best in us: a constructive critique that expresses our rigour and ethical awareness.

Towards the end of our two hours together, Elizabeth mimics our different responses to Jo's introduction of her data. She goes round the room, faces us one by one, acting out disbelief, sorrow, relief, scepticism and scholarly concern in turn. Laughter unites us. A few weeks later, Jo tells us that she has written a draft analysis and shown it to her supervisor. He likes it.

The sketch recreates a circle that was shot through with tensions and possibilities. In a writers' circle, everything is consequential and potentially risky, from the research topic that each person is working with, to the ideas and feelings that they bring with them to the circle.

Final Remarks: Writers' Circles and Risk 'from Below'

These circles may or may not assist with throughput, but they do provide rehearsal spaces in which students explore their tilting points, those see-saw moments where the relationship between the lived world of research and its representation in language is decided. In this sense, they invite an exploration of risk 'from below'. This chapter has also looked at the emerging pedagogy in these circles. It listens for the dilemmas – the sticky moments – and does not rush to smooth over them, to reduce risk. Instead, it has its ear to ground and holds these dilemmas up for consideration in the circle. As facilitators, we have had to be open to the generative tensions in these events. We gently push students back towards their disciplines; we explore the space between seriousness and laughter, and we find ways to keep our curriculum in perpetual motion. At another level, this chapter explores a different way of writing about an emerging practice, not as an empirical piece of research, with a preordained structure, but as a performative act of bringing something elusive into being through writing. On all three levels, we hope that this chapter illustrates the potential of risk-taking in the productive sense, as opening up new meanings, rather than closing them for fear of not being heard.

Acknowledgements

We would like to thank Ellen Hurst and Pippin Anderson who were involved with our writers' circles from the beginning. Special thanks to Ellen, who helped us reflect on our emerging practice, and features strongly in this account.

Notes

(1) Nan Yeld, Dean of the University of Cape Town's Centre for Higher Education Development, used this memorable phrase when motivating for new forms of postgraduate writing support.
(2) Names of circle participants have been changed.
(3) Activities such as these point to the importance of the experiments with form that a writers' circle offers. Our experiments drew on different genres (including narrative, commentary, satirical cartooning, free writing) inviting modes of speech, image and a reconfigured writing – not the CBS (clarity, brevity, sincerity) of academic writing in English but of forms that blurred the distinction between process and the conventional notion of a research product.

References

Aitchison, C. (2009) Writing groups for doctoral education. *Studies in Higher Education* 34 (8), 905–916.
Bakhtin, M. (1968) *Rabelais and His World*. Cambridge, MA: MIT Press.
Bartlett, A. and Mercer, G. (2000) Reconceptualising discourses of power in postgraduate supervision. *Teaching in Higher Education* 5 (2), 195–204.
Boud, D. and Lee, A. (2005) 'Peer learning' as pedagogic discourse for research education. *Studies in Higher Education* 30 (5), 501–516.

Chihota, C. (2007) 'The games people play': Taking on postgraduate identities in the context of writer circles. *Journal of Applied Linguistics* 4 (1), 131–136.

Cuthbert, D., Spark, C. and Burke, E. (2009) Disciplining writing: The case for multidisciplinary writing groups to support writing for publication by higher degree by research candidates in the humanities, arts and social sciences. *Higher Education Research and Development* 28 (2), 137–149.

Douglas, M. (1992) *Purity and Danger: An Analysis of the Concepts of Pollution and Taboo*. London: Routledge.

Elbow, P. (1998) *Writing with Power: Techniques for Mastering the Writing Process*. London: Oxford University Press.

Frow, J. (1988) Discipline and discipleship. *Textual Practice* 2 (3), 307–323.

Hargreaves, A. (2001) Emotional geographies of teaching. *Teacher's College Record* 103 (6), 1056–1080.

Hargreaves, A. (2004) Distinction and disgust: The emotional politics of school failure. *International Journal of Leadership in Education* 7 (1), 27–41.

Murray, D. (1978) Write before writing. *College Composition and Communication* 29 (4), 375–381.

Parker, R. (2009) A learning community approach to doctoral education in the social sciences. *Teaching in Higher Education* 14 (1), 43–54.

Pelias, R. (2005) Performative writing as scholarship: An apology, an argument, an anecdote. *Cultural Studies* <=> *Critical Methodologies* 5, 415–424.

Pollock, D. (1998) Performing writing. In P. Phelan and J. Lane (eds) *The Ends of Performance*. New York: New York University Press.

Steinberg, C. (2008) Assessment as an 'emotional practice'. *English Teaching: Practice and Critique* 7 (3), 42–64.

6 Genre: A Pigeonhole or a Pigeon? Case Studies of the Dilemmas Posed by the Writing of Academic Research Proposals

Moragh Paxton

A quick Google search offers copious references to genres as pigeonholes, be they related to music, literature or art. A pigeonhole, as a metaphor for genre, implies that a particular work must conform to a precise, inflexible form or fail to fit a designated space. My question is whether genre may, in fact, bear a closer resemblance to a pigeon, in that it is not fixed or static but vibrant and full of life.[1] In relation to academic work, the pigeonhole metaphor may also imply a focus on linguistic structure and form as distinct from function, as per the Saussurean tradition (de Saussure, 1959). However, when genre is conceived of as a pigeon, the focus tends to fall instead on form within a social context (Hymes, 1974) or, in other words, on the communicative, semiotic function of the form. In this sense, a genre, while still corresponding to certain norms, is enriched by being fashioned and textured by the identity of each new creator, and inevitably echoes aspects of the creator's persona, and their social, historical and cultural context. In writing, this fashioning and shaping is often described as the writer's voice.

Understanding voice, and the way it gets inserted into the conventions and genres of academia – the pigeon in relation to the pigeonhole – is central to my research. I am concerned with the following questions: how do writers understand genre and are there risks related to these notions of genre? How do supervisors or writing teachers mediate these risks? For instance, if the genre is understood as a narrow academic (English) pigeonhole, a container for meaning, what does this mean for a writer's voice? What is lost when a writer's voice is restricted?

In this chapter, I focus on one particular genre – the academic research proposal in the health sciences – and present two case studies of postgraduate proposal writing in a mixed-mode master's course.[2] The course tends to attract mature students who have a wealth of diverse experiences working as doctors, nurses and public-health workers in various parts of sub-Saharan Africa. Working with these students, and assisting them with their research writing, I have found myself mediating between them and their supervisors. I have documented these experiences to reveal some of the risks and potentials in the three-way relationship between student, supervisor and writing specialist during the postgraduate research journey, and I point to some of the genre-related risks that students are exposed to as they make choices about what to write and what to eliminate.

A further interest is to understand the ways in which form affects function (meaning) when texts travel from one context to another (Blommaert, 2005, 2010). Theories of genre and voice are used to present case studies based on the research proposals of two students. The case studies bring to the surface many of the tensions inherent in the genre of the scientific research proposal, and illustrate the difficulties the students can face in trying to weave their experiences into what are perceived as the genre's narrow constraints while positioning themselves effectively in the academic process. This raises questions about the ways in which the academic research proposal, as a genre, may constrain the way participants from different contexts think and write, thus impacting on voice. The case studies illustrate the potential productivity of a writer's voice. If we accept and attempt to understand hybridity in the writing of these students, we may learn much about the diverse experiences they bring, thus opening up a potentially rich source of new knowledge for the academy.

As Cadman (2005) indicates, academic English is riddled with taken-for-granted practices, conventions and traditions, and those of us who work in academia tend to forget that the language structure of academic English may demonstrate very particular ways of processing knowledge. We forget too that these are not sacred; there are other ways of developing and expressing knowledge.

Key Concepts

Genre

The sociolinguistic concept of genre has important links to knowledge and knowledge making because, as genre theorists would argue, genres provide us with 'frames' for constructing knowledge. Understanding the form allows us to shape and communicate our thoughts. Educators, such as Cope and Kalantzis (1993), Hasan and Williams (1996) and Bawarshi and Reiff (2010), have taken up genre theory, and emphasised the need to focus on the explicit teaching of genres as an important step in learning and making meaning.

To this end, genre theorists have done important work in analysing and describing genres, and have encouraged teachers to think more carefully about how to make genres more explicit when teaching students from diverse backgrounds (Bawarshi & Reiff, 2010; Cope & Kalantzis, 1993; Halliday & Martin, 1993; Hasan & Williams, 1996; Kress, 1999; Paxton, 2011). However, as Janks (2010), Luke (1996) and others have pointed out, reifying the features of certain genres and sticking too rigidly to form in the teaching of genre may inhibit possibilities for creativity and transformation.

Swales (2004: 64) argues that defining genres may not be useful – both because of their doubtful truth value for 'all possible worlds and all possible times', and because 'the easy adoption of definitions can prevent us from seeing newly explored or newly emergent genres for what they really are'. Swales prefers to characterise genres in metaphorical terms so that the metaphor that is used sheds its own light on our understandings. One powerful metaphor that he borrows from Bazerman (1997, cited in Swales 2004: 63) is that of genre as a *frame* for creating meaning:

> Genres are not just forms. Genres are forms of life, ways of being. They are frames for social action. They are environments for learning. They are locations within which meaning is constructed. Genres shape the thoughts we form and the communications by which we interact. *Genres are the familiar places we go to create intelligible communicative actions with each other and the guideposts we use to explore the familiar.* (emphasis added)

In this definition, it is possible that Bazerman has done exactly what Swales is arguing against, and defined genre too closely. The notion of genre, as suggested by the phrases 'familiar places we go' to 'explore the familiar' in the last sentence of the definition, seems to indicate that genres are universally known and common to all. But the risk lies in whose 'familiar places' these are. The students, supervisors and writing tutors in a three-way relationship may each go to different 'familiar places'. As Blommaert (2005) points out, writers may have different experiences and come from different contexts from their readers. Blommaert critiques the tendency to assume sharedness and equality in the analysis of communication, arguing that the notion of sharedness is often based on intuitive generalisations of communication patterns prevalent in one's own (often first-world) society. Blommaert is concerned that, in the conditions of globalisation, texts do not move easily from one context to another. He illustrates the ways in which texts produced in third-world countries tend to be misinterpreted when they are transported to first-world contexts because readers project locally valid functions onto the writings of people who have moved from one context to another. He highlights examples of texts that have travelled from one geographical place to another, often from the periphery[3] of the world system (such as sub-Saharan Africa) to the core (e.g. Europe or North America). Blommaert notes that this problem simply mirrors the much larger problem suggested by theorists such as Wallerstein (cited in Blommaert 2005) and Connell (2007), that social theory has been created and produced in the global north, is based on reflections of first-world societies, and often fails to take into account the very different contexts of education on the periphery.

In the case studies described in this chapter, the texts move from workplace contexts in Malawi and Zambia to an academic institution at the southern tip of Africa, illustrating that north and south are relative concepts and, in this case, global power differentials are reproduced regionally, just on a smaller scale.

Voice

As the metaphor in the title of this chapter indicates, genre could be seen as a vehicle for the expression of voice – the pigeon not the pigeonhole. Therefore, it seems important to be clear about what we mean by the concept of voice, and to consider the multiple and complex discussions of the concept that proliferate in theories of writing.

Bakhtin (1981, 1986) has highlighted the 'double-voicedness' (intertextuality) of writing, noting that writing is always 'interanimated' by other voices. Voices are a set of discourses that the writer brings to the act of writing, they are part of his or her social and historical formation, and a writer's voice can be considered as his or her unique combination of these discoursal resources. Bakhtin says that writers make these voices their own by assimilating, reworking and re-accentuating them (1986). This notion has been further theorised by Ivanic (1997: 32) and Clark and Ivanic (1998), who argue that writing is an act of identity in which people align themselves with 'socio-culturally shaped subject positions'. By doing this, they reproduce or challenge dominant practices and discourses and the values and beliefs they embody. In her work with English-speaking adult learners in the United Kingdom, Ivanic finds that academic writing sometimes presents a conflict for students because the self that is inscribed in academic discourse feels alien to them, and they feel that they lose voice.

A variety of theorists have noted that writers are constrained in establishing a voice when their resources do not match the functions they want to accomplish (Hymes, 1996; Ivanic, 1997; Maryns & Blommaert, 2001; Wertsch, 1991). Blommaert (2005: 68), however, has placed notions of voice in a more global context by using illustrations of texts from different parts of Africa to argue that voice is 'uptake' or 'the ways in which people manage to make themselves understood or fail to do so'. He argues that voice is 'the capacity to accomplish desired functions through language' and that in order for a writer's identity to be established, it has to be recognised by others. Globalisation has led to increased mobility of text and this has made the problem far more complex.

Resources

To have voice, people have to use the linguistic and communicative resources at their disposal and use them in clearly defined contexts. If the resources do not match the context, then people do not make sense. Blommaert (2005) defines communicative resources as codes, language varieties and styles, and reminds us that those who have different resources often find that they have unequal resources because access to particular resources is embedded in power and inequality. Resources are organised in hierarchies – so, for instance, certain dialect varieties are perceived to be inferior while standard dialects are accorded value as superior. Differential access to forms (genres, styles, language varieties, codes), and to contextual spaces (spaces where particular forms conventionally receive specific functions) leads to differing capacities to map form to function (or to interpret what is being communicated). Whenever the resources people possess do not match the tasks they are supposed to accomplish, they risk being attributed functions other than those intended, in other words, the resources acquired fail to fulfil the required function and speakers lose voice.

The dilemma and risk for me, as a writing tutor, is how to balance Bakhtin's notion of voice as hybridised and interanimated with Blommaert's notion of voice as 'uptake'. An acceptance of hybridity in the voices of our students has the potential to reveal much about the identity and values of the writers, and about the potential for hybridity to act as a resource for the making of new knowledge. However, as Blommaert argues, in order for the writer's identity to be established, voice has to be recognised. If the writer's resources fail to fulfil the required function and voice is misconstrued, it tends to be silenced. The challenge for us, as teachers of writing, is how to avoid the silencing of these voices, and sources of knowledge, as the writers are pressed to conform to academic writing conventions.

Research Methodology

The academic literacies department of the university at which I teach has increasingly been drawn into work at the postgraduate level. We run workshops on the writing of research proposals, literature reviews and so on. In 2007, I facilitated a workshop for master's students but, because the two-hour workshop allowed us to touch only briefly on issues such as academic referencing and coherence, I offered some ongoing online help to the students in relation to their writing. I subsequently assisted some of the students over a three-year period, and it is from this group of students that case studies discussed in this chapter are drawn.

Concurrently, with providing assistance to the students with their writing, I set out to understand the role of voice in knowledge making, and the relationship between form and function in the writing of academic research proposals. I have thus been involved with the students both as writing teacher and as researcher. In my research, I adopted an ethnographic approach, involving sustained engagement over the three-year period in the two students' writing worlds. The students were engaged in dialogue around their texts allowing them to act as 'expert witnesses' (Herrington & Curtis, 2000) in interpreting their texts. In addition, I collected and analysed a range of data types, including observation of the students during their classes, online literacy-history interviews, students' writing, such as course-work assignments and the drafts and redrafts of their research proposals.

Where possible, analyses of student writing was enhanced by using the supervisors' written feedback to students on their research proposals. This enabled me to identify the research methods and procedures generally used to produce knowledge in the health sciences, as well as the specific writing practices that are valued in that field. Interviews with supervisors formed a further source of data and assisted in understanding what the supervisors value in student writing, what they see as the barriers and affordances to success in this discipline, and whether they believe that knowledge in this area has the potential to change as a result of the epistemologies and experiences that some of these students bring. This enabled the development of 'holistic understandings' (Lillis, 2008: 362) and ensured 'thick description' (Geertz, 1973 cited in Lillis, 2008: 367) of the data.

Context

The university where this study was undertaken is striving to increase its postgraduate throughput rates and to enhance its research profile as a leading research university in South Africa and Africa. It has a mission to reach out to other countries in Africa, and is beginning to look for ways to cater to the needs of (mostly) foreign-language students from Africa. However, although the university describes itself as 'Afropolitan',[4] established first-world academic literacy practices and genres remain entrenched.

The Course and the Students

As mentioned, the course from which the case studies are drawn is a mixed-mode master's course for district health managers in southern Africa. Students attend face-to-face sessions at the university for two weeks at the beginning and two weeks at the end of the first year; they complete a coursework component and are then expected to write a research proposal and proceed with a mini dissertation. The course focuses on maternal and child health care, and draws on a very diverse group of doctors, nurses and public health workers from different countries in southern Africa, many of whom are leaders in their professional fields. Students are required to have an undergraduate degree (or 'equivalent' qualification) in the health sciences but, because the course is designed for mature health workers who are pursuing a career in district health management, most students have been away from academic study for some time. A number of the students are second-language English speakers, and even those who regard themselves as first-language English speakers find that academic discourse is not necessarily the one they feel most comfortable using. A conflict of discourses is not uncommon, and the fact that academic discourse is alien to these students was brought home to me during a writing workshop held at the start of the first face-to-face session. The course convenor asked them to respond in writing to a newspaper article on HIV and circumcision, and to explain whether or not they supported the promotion of male circumcision as an HIV-prevention method. No genre had been specified for the assignment and students resorted to 'familiar places' – a range of diverse genres. Some preferred the more professional approach, such as a letter to the Minister of Health, whereas others used genres that may have been familiar from school such as short essays. I was struck by the impact of orality and the use of rich metaphor in these early pieces of writing. For instance, one student introduced her piece as follows:

> South Africa should not wait to see what shaved the guinea fowl – a lot of people are dying of HIV/AIDS.[5]

Although the students were required to write in a range of different genres through their coursework assignments, the research proposal seems to have presented particular challenges because it is an unfamiliar and rather contradictory form. It is therefore in the development of research proposals that I have often been called upon to support students with their writing.

The Research Proposal Genre

Although there are a number of university websites, books and other guides to writing a research proposal (Murray, 2006; Punch, 2000; Vithal & Jansen, 1997), there are surprisingly few articles that focus on the dilemmas involved in proposal writing, and the contradictions inherent in the genre. What makes research proposal writing particularly complex, is the dual and conflicting roles it carries as both gatekeeper and formative pedagogical tool – roles that led Cadman (2002: 85) to describe the proposal as a 'contested site in postgraduate genre pedagogy'.

On the one hand, the research proposal is seen as introducing students to a research culture and, in some cases, to the discourses of a particular discipline. This is where students get a sense of the differences between highly structured undergraduate or postgraduate coursework curriculae, and the more open and negotiable world of the research dissertation. The writing of the research proposal provides an opportunity for students to map out their research journey and identify possible pitfalls. In this sense, it is a formative document where students are given a chance to demonstrate that they have learned the conventions of the discourse.

On the other hand, the research proposal can be used as a gatekeeper or an assessment tool for filtering out students who may not be regarded as 'good postgraduate research material'. It is a semi-legal document showing that the student has obtained ethics permission and fulfilled the necessary requirements to continue with postgraduate studies. Students who cannot write a successful research proposal may not be allowed to continue with their studies. Yet, what makes some proposals succeed and others not is often unclear and, in my experience, supervisors have difficulty both in articulating what they are looking for in a research proposal, and in defining the criteria they use to assess them.

Cadman (2002: 84) surveyed supervisors to understand the criteria that they were using to assess research proposals, and found that they often assessed proposals, not in terms of the text features but rather, 'in terms of the student who had written it, constructed either as the discoursally instantiated writer/persona, or even as the embodied student as subject'. She describes this as 'evaluated "readings" of students' (Cadman, 2002: 100). The process of judging a research proposal in terms of whether the researcher is likely to be able to successfully complete the research project is challenging, particularly in 21st-century higher-education contexts, where a greater diversity of students makes for more demanding teaching and assessment processes. However, if the criteria for assessment are not clearly signalled, the task of student writers (and that of the writing teachers assisting them) in tailoring their knowledge to the constraints of the genre is that much more complex.

Risk and its Links to Genre and Voice in the Two Case Studies

In this section, I explore the notion of risk more explicitly and look at the ways in which genre and voice are often linked to risk. The role I played as a writing tutor and researcher, a third element in the supervisor–student relationship, seems to have created a space in which I could more openly explore risk in relation to the processes of text production and reception.

Serina

Serina is a midwife with extensive local experience as head of the busiest labour ward in Malawi (there are, on average, 12,000 deliveries a year). She spent more than a year working on her proposal and was then advised by her supervisors that she would not be allowed to continue with her master's but would be awarded a postgraduate diploma instead. Her supervisors believed that a number of problems put her at risk of not completing the dissertation. In my discussions with them it seemed that they regarded her writing as the chief obstacle: they were concerned that her writing was full of grammatical errors and that there was extensive 'plagiarism' in her literature review. The second obstacle was that 'there may be no scientific milieu, no scientific supervision' in the hospital in Malawi where Serina would have collected her data. This could well be a problem in the work contexts of many of the students who enrol for this master's course.

However, is it not precisely these 'non-scientific milieus' that we, in academia, need to learn from? For instance, how does one reduce childbirth-related mortality rates in labour wards with very large patient loads and limited resources? Surely, students who have first-hand experience in these contexts have an important contribution to make to medical knowledge. Similarly, could the medical principles that are taught in our university lecture halls and textbooks not do with reforming and updating, based on what we can learn from these students and their work environments?

Serina expressed her disappointment and unhappiness to her supervisors and the course convenor, pointing out that she already had a postgraduate diploma. She argued that she had an interesting and useful study investigating the use of the partograph – a chart that monitors the progress of women in labour and alerts medical staff to possible problems. This tool, if used appropriately, has the potential to improve the quality of maternity services and reduce maternal and infant mortality. Serina also explained how much work she had already put into revising and rewriting her proposal (she and I had corresponded extensively, via 34 emails, as she worked on various drafts of her proposal and she had made considerable improvements). Ultimately, Serina was allowed to reregister for the master's degree. With the help of the course convenor, she redesigned her study to make it more manageable and achievable.

Serina's case illustrates risk on many levels. Although she was not aware of them, there were tremendous risks for her as she ventured into postgraduate studies, using research genres and methods that seemed rather alien, and attempting to meet standards that were not entirely clear to her. There were risks for me as a writing consultant and a disciplinary outsider, playing the role of intermediary between the student and the supervisor, and attempting to establish from supervisors what their expectations were for the writing of the research proposal. There were further risks in ensuring that I focus on writing only and not on content, and thus avoid trespasssing on supervisor territory – where does the one begin and the other end?

It is interesting to note, that as a writing tutor, I had very little status in the hierarchy of course lecturers and supervisors, but as soon as I took on the role of researcher with ethics approval, I became a risk for supervisors. The balance of power shifted, particularly when it came to decisions around gate-keeping; had Serina been excluded at this point, I might have reported on it in my research writing. It is possible that the space I occupied in the decision-making processes may have had some influence on Serina being allowed to return to the university to complete her master's degree.

Serina's case also illustrates the risks involved for her supervisors as they strive to give substance to the university's Afropolitan vision, and to expand course offerings to postgraduate students from other parts of Africa. This involves collaborating with and understanding complex medical contexts situated some distance from them both spatially and experientially; it means trying to make sense of 'non-scientific milieus' and learning from them. But, as is shown both in this case and in the one that follows, embracing risk has the potential to open up new possibilities and new learning.

Idrina

Idrina holds a senior position in the Zambian health services. For her research project she wished to conduct an investigation into how mothers perceive the quality of care in Lusaka's health facilities following a perinatal death. In her role in the Zambian health services she is an experienced writer but when her writing moves from a professional (the 'familiar place') to an academic context, very different values are attributed to it. The first draft of her proposal elicited extensive comments from her supervisor on what is expected in a research proposal in the health sciences, and emphasised the importance of the impersonal academic voice and scientific tone. An early draft of her research proposal read rather like a narrative of her experiences and findings over two decades of working in the Zambian health services. However, her strong personal voice, well respected in the context in which she usually works and writes, failed to produce uptake in the context of an academic institution as is illustrated by comments from her supervisor in response to the following excerpt in Idrina's draft:

> In obstetrics care, the purpose is to deliver *a healthy and happy baby* and efforts are directed towards the safety of the mother–infant dyad. *Pregnancy loss* is an apparent failure in the system. It seems that this intense loss tends to make everyone uncomfortable. (emphasis added)

The supervisor responded to the two phrases italicised in the paragraph above. In response to the phrase *'a healthy and happy baby'*, the supervisor commented, 'Be cautious of using emotive phrasing in academic writing.' In relation to *'pregnancy loss'*, she suggested that Idrina should use a more 'scientific term' when writing a research proposal.

The emphasis on 'scientific tone', for Idrina's supervisor, seemed to include an avoidance of the use of the first person. For instance, Idrina described American and British research studies that have documented poorly managed care of mothers suffering perinatal loss (such as removal of the baby before the grieving mother is allowed to see or hold it, and placing of the mother in the same medical ward as mothers of live babies). She then went on to observe, 'Some of these are still common in most of *our* African settings' (emphasis added). In her response, the supervisor signalled that the use of the first person was not acceptable, 'If you can't find a reference you may say "It is the experience of the author that in Lusaka ..."'

Kneebone (2002) warns medical practitioners against an uncritical adherence to a traditional scientific mode of thinking and writing. He argues that scientific writing is not nearly as objective as writers of scientific articles would like to believe, and that, in fact, all writing serves the purposes of the writer. The researcher/writer is in a position of power, selecting which issues to present and which to ignore, as well as the manner in which to present them. Therefore, avoiding the use of the first person can be construed as hiding behind an aura of neutrality and failing to own up to the political and personal nature of one's writing. In this case, the supervisor was concerned, not only about the use of the first person, but also about Idrina's frequent references to her own experiences, and her failure to support her observations with evidence from the literature. Idrina's difficulty, however, was that very little research has been done on the issue of care following perinatal death in specifically African settings. Idrina, her supervisor and I were involved in a three-way conversation where these issues were discussed and compromises reached.

There are also indications in Idrina's draft proposal that her linguistic resources were not quite up to the challenge of communicating adequately in an academic context. As Blommaert (2005) indicates, particular resources often fail to perform certain functions when they are moved from one environment to another. This is illustrated in Idrina's excerpt below:

> The difficulty in curbing neonatal mortality is that most neonatal deaths in African countries are unaccounted for and undocumented because most of the deliveries happen at home. This means there is very little attention from health services towards the neonates at this period. Even more dangerous is that *most parents are not willing to take neonates to health facilities* because of long distances to the facility and lack transport to reach and access care. This further compounded by the uncertainty of finding a skilled health provider to administer appropriate care for the mother and baby. Resulting in most *mothers confining neonates in the house* at a critical time when medical attention is needed. (emphasis added)

In response to this passage, Idrina's supervisor commented that the phrase *'most parents are not willing to take neonates to health facilities'* is a strong value judgement and not backed by evidence. Furthermore, she considered the tone of the phrase *'mothers confining neonates in the house'* as 'blaming of mothers' – something she correctly assumed Idrina did not want to do.

My analysis of this passage is that Idrina did not set out to blame or judge mothers, but rather that the resources she had at her disposal are not quite adequate to express what she wished to say – she struggled to find words to fit the situation she was describing.

Idrina's strongly emotive tone was possibly very appropriate in her role as health professional, where she had to write health reports and other official documents urgently persuading colleagues and superiors that action was needed. But the message she received from the feedback on her proposal was that her 'journalistic' tone did not function in the literature review of her academic research proposal.

> *Idrina's text:* For anyone who has been through this experience or seen someone else go through it, there is no doubt that childbirth is a life-changing event. Immediate and effective professional care during and after labour and delivery can make the difference between life and death for both women and their newborns, as complications are largely unpredictable and may rapidly become life-threatening (Graham W, Bell, J, Bullough CH, 2001). Unfortunately, as wonderful and joyful experience as it may be for many, for others it can also be a difficult period, bringing with it new problems as well as potential for suffering.

> *Supervisor feedback*: Please note your emotive style of writing is not appropriate for an academic piece. It is very readable and powerful but the tone is better suited to journalism. I suggest you save the emotive tone for your results section, based on your data collected from the women [you will interview]. Also it is very valid to draw on your own personal perspectives when discussing methodology, analysis, findings and conclusions. In the literature review you need to actually review what others have published and not what your beliefs and experiences are.

The supervisor's feedback contains frequent requests for more references to support the knowledge and experience that Idrina draws on: 'try to find examples from the literature of health workers behaving like this'. As the supervisor indicated, claims need to be backed by evidence from the research.

In the second paragraph of the excerpt below, Idrina is clearly referring to a very personal and painful experience:

> Apparently in Zambia, perinatal loss tends to make everyone uncomfortable and unsure about how to relate with the bereaved person. To worsen the situation, the professional caregivers in this case, the midwives, seem inadequately prepared to deal with perinatal mortality (WHO 2005). Furthermore, the obstetric infrastructure does not make provision for the privacy needs of mothers experiencing this kind of loss.
>
> From personal experience of losing a full term baby a few hours after delivery at a district hospital in Zambia, all mothers are placed in the same postnatal ward as those mothers who have delivered healthy babies. This situation is worsened by some traditional beliefs that prevent the bereaved mother from displaying any emotions publicly. I can only assume that most health providers subscribe to these traditional practices making it difficult for them to demonstrate appropriate compassion or even give psychological and emotional support.

Reading this passage, I realised that Idrina had chosen this particular topic for her research project for very personal reasons. I therefore suggested she write about why she had chosen the research project in the form of a two- or three-page personal narrative, uninhibited by the constraints of academic genre. She then wrote what her supervisor described as a 'deeply moving and powerful testimony' about the way she was treated after losing her baby during childbirth. Idrina described how, after a difficult delivery, her baby was rushed away from her to be put on oxygen,

> Meanwhile in the same postnatal ward were other women who had successfully delivered and were chatting away discussing their various experiences and feeding their babies. I could hear the happy mothers attend their crying babies while I painfully and anxiously awaited the return of my baby from the special unit.

Eventually, her husband, a medical doctor in the same hospital who had been checking on the baby's progress, came to break the news that her baby had died.

> Being in the same room with other happy mothers, I had to contain this new development in my own way. The nurse attending to me only said she was sorry and left me on my own ... I wished I had been given an

opportunity to hold and cuddle my baby upon delivery but things for me were happening so painfully quick. Traditionally, in Zambia, women are advised not to cry for a baby who has died at birth and visitors are advised not to greet you by shaking hands. This added to my emotional pain as I felt stigmatized and ostracized by all this. The following day since my vital signs had normalized my husband and I requested for a discharge. The only hospital condition for discharge was to make sure that the baby is buried. Again, in keeping with tradition, the burial was carried out without my being present. This was yet another tortuous experience for me. I cried within me at the realization that my baby was to be buried at a place I would never ever get to know. Meanwhile there was no emotional or psychosocial support from the hospital to help me go through the period of grief. No postnatal appointment was given to make a follow up to the incident. Upon discharge I had to deal with the grieving process in my own way.

In this personal narrative, Idrina projects a strong and authoritative writer's voice, and the very emotional story of her own experience seems crucial to readers developing a better understanding of the need for care for mothers when their babies are lost in childbirth. The story also provides insights into sociocultural practices associated with neonatal death in Zambia. Thus, experience can be seen as the *source* of knowledge-making, yet traditionally the scientific disciplines have allowed little space for the expression of personal experiences. As Cooper indicates in her contribution to this volume, claims that scientific knowledge should be untainted by everyday experience have been critiqued because they have led to exclusion of knowledge generated beyond the core of the world system, and this has been to the detriment of our collective knowledge archive. Feminist theorists such as Michelson (1998: 217) argue that 'Western knowledge practices have denied the relationship of knowledge to the body and thus lost sight of knowledge as a product of bodily and emotionally grounded human life.' Rather than being an obstacle to learning, our emotional experience allows pain and discomfort to teach us about ourselves and about others.

I had indicated that Idrina should write this narrative as a self-reflective writing exercise for herself, but she decided to include it in the next draft of her proposal and her supervisor felt that while it was not appropriate for her research proposal, it should be saved and included in her dissertation. From this and other feedback (see above), it seems that, even in the hard sciences, genres are shifting. The supervisor was willing to embrace some degree of risk in suggesting that the genre of the research dissertation might include a personal narrative such as this in order to open up spaces for student experience to be heard. The role of the writing specialist or third party in this case study was also interesting, and the case points to ways in which, as writing specialists, we can avoid silencing voices and help to enhance genre shifts. In encouraging Idrina to risk writing a personal narrative, I gave her an opportunity to try out a different genre. Through this, she found an appropriate place for the personal to be validated. In addition, the research enabled me as a researcher to witness and track her writing processes. Functions change, students are agents in their own learning, and they can be assisted in finding ways to have their voices heard. The exercise of writing her personal narrative seemed to help Idrina to articulate more clearly why she came to undertake this particular study. The narrative is an example of what Kamler and Thomson (2006) refer to as 'writing along the way' in preparation for dissertation writing, and which they believe builds reflexivity in a writer. Idrina was shown that there were appropriate and authoritative ways in which she could reshape and include her personal experience in the introduction to her proposal. She was also shown how she could situate the personal in the social and institutional practices by drawing on international research to support her experience that traditional beliefs prevent bereaved mothers from displaying emotion in public. This would assist in making her claim more convincing. Thus, by positioning the self appropriately and effectively in the writing of a proposal, one may be better able to gradually shift the pigeonholes that make up the conventions of academia.

Conclusion

What students do with the supervisor's feedback is crucial. Following feedback to the letter can mean that students make themselves invisible, flattening their texts to fit a narrow pigeonhole. The alternative is to risk ways of writing that avoid the erasure of their knowledge and experience.

As illustrated in the two case studies, epistemologies that are rooted in experience risk being erased through gatekeeping exercises that make students feel they have to conform too rigidly to narrow genres. It is quite complex to unpack what exactly is deleted in students' attempts to comply with the requirements of specific genres, but Idrina's case serves as an example of how important her own experience of perinatal death was as a potential source of knowledge for carers, and of how easily this knowledge might have been lost. Idrina's case indicates that encouraging students to explore other genres (such as the personal narrative) in the scaffolding or supporting of a writing process may help to bring information to the surface that would otherwise be excised, avoided or silenced. In addition, the research described in this chapter has enabled me as the researcher to investigate conditions of uptake (or the lack thereof) in ways we often do not see because the research proposal is rejected or some of the material it contains is deleted.

Idrina's story also illustrates that a good three-way relationship between writer, supervisor and writing advisor may mean that we can shift a genre so that it allows for more flexibility. While acknowledging the inevitable risks involved in attempting to break from traditional patterns, it is vital that academia heeds Cadman's (2005) call to consider new ways of developing and expressing research knowledge in English, so as to promote wider acceptance of hybrid academic discourses in international research communities and give recognition to the diversity of scholars. For this to be achieved, it is important that those of us who play the role of writing specialists and purveyors of genre show an openness to a variety of established and new genres and develop criteria for evaluating them as they evolve.

Notes

(1) I would like to thank Professor Brenda Cooper for introducing me to this metaphor; it is borrowed from Fowler (1982: 37) who refers to genre in literature as being 'much less of a pigeonhole than a pigeon'.
(2) A mixed-mode course is one that offers both distance and face-to-face teaching.
(3) Note that the term 'periphery' as used here implies marginality, and not necessarily a geographic location.
(4) The university's Afropolitan vision is to play a significant role as one of Africa's leading institutions and to embrace its African identity more meaningfully.
(5) This idiom means to land oneself in great trouble due to negligence, disrespect or rudeness; it can also refer to disagreements and buying time.

References

Bakhtin, M.M. (1981) Discourse in the novel. In M. Holquist (ed.) *The Dialogic Imagination: Four Essays by M. Bakhtin* (trans. C. Emerson and M. Holquist). Austin, TX: University of Texas Press.
Bakhtin, M.M. (1986) The problem of speech genres. In C. Emerson and M. Holquist (eds) *Speech Genres and Other Late Essays* (trans. V. W. McGee). Austin, TX: University of Texas Press.
Bawarshi, A.S. and Reiff, M.J. (2010) *Genre: An Introduction to History, Theory, Research, and Pedagogy*. West Lafayette, IN: Parlor Press.
Bazerman, C. (1997) The life of genre: The life in the classroom. In W. Bishop and H. Ostrum (eds) *Genre and Writing*. Portsmouth, NH: Boynton/Cook.
Blommaert, J. (2005) *Discourse: A Critical Introduction*. Cambridge: Cambridge University Press.
Blommaert, J. (2010) *The Sociolinguistics of Globalisation*. Cambridge: Cambridge University Press.
Cadman, K. (2002) English for academic possibilities: The research proposal as a contested site in postgraduate genre pedagogy. *Journal of English for Academic Purposes* 1 (2), 85–104.

Cadman, K. (2005) 'Divine discourse': Plagiarism, hybridity and epistemological racism. In S. May, M. Franken and R. Barnard (eds) *LED: Refereed Proceedings of the Inaugural International Conference on Language, Education and Diversity 2003*. Hamilton, NZ: University of Waikato Press (CDRom).
Clark, R. and Ivanic, R. (1998) *The Politics of Writing*. London: Routledge.
Connell, R. (2007) *Southern Theory: The Global Dynamics of Knowledge in Social Science*. Cambridge: Polity Press.
Cope, B. and Kalantzis, M. (eds) (1993) *The Powers of Literacy: A Genre Approach to Teaching Writing*. London: The Falmer Press.
De Saussure, F. (1959) *Course in General Linguistics* (trans. Wade Baskin). New York: McGraw-Hill.
Fowler, A. (1982) *Kinds of Literature: An Introduction to the Theory of Genres and Modes*. Oxford: Clarendon Press
Geertz, C. (1973) *The Interpretation of Cultures*. London: Hutchinson.
Halliday, M. and Martin, J. (1993) *Writing Science: Literacy and Discursive Power*. London: The Falmer Press.
Hasan, R. and Williams, G. (eds) (1996) *Literacy in Society*. London: Longman.
Herrington, A.J. and Curtis, M. (2000) *Persons in Process: Four Stories of Writing and Personal Development in College*. Urbana, IL: National Council of Teachers of English.
Hymes, D. (1974) *Foundations in Sociolinguistics: An Ethnographic Approach*. Philadelphia: University of Pennsylvania Press.
Hymes, D. (1996) *Ethnography, Linguistics, Narrative Inequality: Towards an Understanding of Voice*. London: Taylor & Francis.
Ivanic, R. (1997) *Writing and Identity: The Discoursal Construction of Identity in Academic Writing*. Amsterdam: John Benjamins.
Janks, H. (2010) *Literacy and Power*. London: Routledge.
Kamler, B. and Thomson, P. (2006) *Helping Doctoral Students Write: Pedagogies for Supervision*. London: Routledge.
Kneebone, R. (2002) Total internal reflection: An essay on paradigms. *Medical Education* 36 (6), 514–518.
Kress, G. (1999) Genre and the changing contexts for English Language arts. *Language Arts* 32 (2), 185–196.
Lillis, T. (2008) Ethnography as method, methodology, and 'deep theorizing': Closing the gap between text and context in academic writing research. *Written Communication* 25 (3), 353–387.
Luke, A. (1996) Genres of power? Literacy education and the production of capital. In R. Hasan and G. Williams (eds) *Literacy in Society*. London: Longman.
Maryns, K. and Blommaert, J. (2001) Stylistic and thematic shifting as a narrative resource: Assessing asylum seekers' repertoires. *Multilingua* 20 (1), 61–84.
Michelson, E. (1998) Re-membering: The return of the body to experiential learning. *Studies in Continuing Education* 20 (2), 217–233.
Murray, R. (2006) *How to Write a Thesis*. Maidenhead: Open University Press.
Paxton, M. (2011) How do we play the genre game in preparing students at the advanced undergraduate level for research writing? *Teaching in Higher Education* 16 (1), 53–64.
Punch, K. (2000) *Developing Effective Research Proposals*. London: Sage.
Swales, J. (2004) *Research Genres: Exploration and Applications*. Cambridge: Cambridge University Press.
Vithal, R. and Jansen, J.D. (1997) *Designing Your First Research Proposal*. Cape Town: Juta.
Wertsch, J. (1991) *Voices of the Mind*. Cambridge, MA: Harvard University Press.

7 Of House and Home: Reflections on Knowing and Writing for a 'Southern' Postgraduate Pedagogy

Kate Cadman

> The university will have to find other modes. This is another mode ... This is the way to write an essay now. I'll teach you. I teach you how. I teach you now. The university is going to enter into new modes of writing. The university is going to have to now. The university is expanding but it's not sure. The university is confused now. Which way will we go? What will we teach now? The docile body of the institutionalised subject. The educational response. The task to offer. I'll do it. I'll do it all ...
> Ania Walwicz, No, no, no: The reluctant debutante

Introducing and Jangling

About four years ago, after more than 15 years of fairly traditional work in the applied linguistics discipline known as advanced academic literacy (Sengupta, 2005), I took a professional risk and wrote a confronting, auto-ethnographic PhD thesis. In doing this, I challenged both my disciplinary and institutional positions, as auto-ethnography was a new research methodology that was not well considered in my science-oriented university. In my opening chapter, I explain defensively why I chose this genre as my doctoral contribution to scholarship. Citing eminent philosophers and analysts, I explicate the 'narrative turn in the social sciences' to advance the argument that auto-ethnographic narrative is a fundamental guiding principle through which we come to ascribe meanings and values to the events and actions of our lives, making it an especially valid, and validated, methodology for the kind of analysis I was conducting (Cadman, 2006: 5–6). The final paragraph of this introduction reads:

> So – in order to sustain vitality in the restless consciousness that explains me to myself, and in full awareness of the geographical and historical conditions of this project, I join with Linda Blanton (2003: 156) to say, OK then, '... let the little girl tell her story'. (Cadman, 2006: 11)

Now, in choosing again to take an auto-ethnographic approach to analysing pressing issues for research education in a globalising, 'developing' academy, I find myself in a very different frame of mind. In fact, I am quite problematically jangled. What forcibly strikes me about this previous writing is the confidence, the realisation of *authority*, through which the author, 'Cadman, 2006', can be heard to speak. Notwithstanding the deliberately flouted academic register in 'So' and 'OK then', allied with the explicit construction of personal subjectivity and voice, here are the unmistakable hallmarks of dominant scholarly writing: argument grounded in the abstract analyses of 'western' theorists; an assumption of the universal application of the developed understandings; heavily nominalised prose; direct and conventionally acknowledged quotation from a contemporary writer in the same political as well as disciplinary methodology. Clearly, the discursive authority of this author's argument emerges from the control in which these writing strategies are yoked together with a few powerful, strategically selected, transgressive phrases to forge a new relationship with a scholarly audience, one which challenges many of the conventions of global academic English but which self-consciously exploits its recognised historical values.

If, as it seems, I have developed this ability to realise the notion of 'expert' in my own academic writing, it seems perverse that I have become so troubled and confused about my writing in recent years. Paradoxically, it seems that the more skilled and accepted I am as a scholar, the more I lose confidence in the scholarly writing I can do. Right here, right now, I don't know how to start, how to 'tone' the contribution that I can legitimately make to this project. The sticking point for me is how to craft a voice of authority that does not effectively re-enact all the obscenities that have been articulately attached to conventional academic writing by fully fledged members of this very academy, and which I myself will explicate in this chapter. My overt desire is straightforward: I want a further scholarly inquiry into how Anglo-Celtic academic knowing and writing exert a colonising violence on epistemic and discursive practices; I want to provoke serious reconsideration of alternative structures for generating and representing knowledges, together with their implications for the pedagogies that teach them. And yet, I am caught in a web of insights that is likely to bring to the fore my conscious complicity in this violence, and lead me to an unproductive confusion. This is, I know, old ground for exponents of fictocriticism (such as Walwicz, 1997: 337), who share my challenge and my extreme unease: 'The university is going to enter into new modes of writing. The university is going to have to now ... The university is confused now. Which way will we go? What will we teach now?' However, as I will show, the fictocritics' discursive location within the academy is very different from the one I wish to speak for here.

And this brings me to the most deep-rooted cause of my personal anxiety, to which I will return – how to proceed with such a project as this in the face of my understanding of what has been seriously denounced as the 'violence of representation' (Spivak, 1988, 1990)? I know, with a feeling of deep insecurity, that I can never adequately represent the postgraduate writers whose interests I want to prioritise here. Yet I will try, aiming to engage with the pointed advice that has been offered to those of us who seriously want to mitigate the silencing and extinguishing effects of authority in traditional academic discourses.

First, we must be prepared to explicitly acknowledge, in our texts and in our methodologies, that all knowledge is contingent, that all expression of it is produced to contextual specification by embodied writers with their own learning histories. What is known must have a location, a genesis and an agent; to write today as though this is not the case is to become a cog in the grinding machinery of neo-colonial invasion. So, as Spivak demands, the way to mitigate the effects of today's prevailing 'epistemic violence' is by 'working critically through one's beliefs, prejudices and assumptions and understanding how they arose and became naturalised' (Spivak, 1990: 121). Writing, such as mine here, then, must exploit its potential for exploring *self-representation*; who we are matters, when we are the ones exerting our power to represent the positions of others. In an often-quoted passage, Armstrong and Tennenhouse stress the violence deeply inherent in such an enterprise:

> As American academics at this moment in history we feel it is somehow dishonest to speak of power and violence as something that belongs to the police or the military, something that belongs to and is practised by someone somewhere else. For clearly, the subtler modalities of modern culture, usually classified as non-political, keep most of us in line, just as they designate appropriate 'others' as the objects of violence. (Armstrong & Tennenhouse, 1989: 4)

Traditional, so-called 'author-evacuated', academic writing (Geertz, 1988) is just such a subtly destructive modality of culture, which keeps its writers 'in line' by denying them the chance that I am taking here, to interrogate their own epistemic practices. For this reason, I want to write myself into the analysis which follows, to contextualise and humanise the process by which these interpretations came into the light, to embody my voice of authority in this discussion, however partial, incomplete and subject to coercion we know such a representation must be. This, at least, will be a way for me to attempt to reconcile the means of my contribution with its end.

And yet, I am conscious of multiple risks in doing this. For me, here, there are few precedents so the discursive steps are relatively unmapped. I have doubts about the reception of such writing in a public domain dominated by global academic and economic structures. And, not least, unless I balance my self-disclosure with enough appropriate markers to traditional discourse norms, I may compromise my ability to be taken seriously as a scholar by those whose opinions I respect and value today. These risks inevitably constrain the choices I will make now, and those I make on a regular basis in my teaching. Clearly, in this context, I cannot ignore historically respected forms in my own writing. Nor, much more significantly, do I advocate dangerous, groundbreaking practices for my own research students – it is not appropriate today for novice researchers to spearhead the risk taking that I believe is required. Yet, it is only by embracing some of these risks that I can ethically locate myself as a writer and teacher, and seriously urge their reconsideration by powerful actors within the global academy.

Reflexing

My background and life history have acutely influenced the considerations I have come to as an academic-English writing teacher, and I have explored these relationships in detail in previous auto-ethnographic analysis (Cadman, 2008). The aspect I would like to stress here is what I now see as a deeply internalised blindness, a happily willing surrender to William Blake's 'mind forg'd manacles'[1] in relation to my gender, social class and, significantly, to my attitude to written English, that sucked me into hegemonic aspirations and set lasting goals for the structures of my life.

I was born into a north-of-England, dialect-speaking family. My father was a Yorkshire bricklayer by trade, and my mother a piece-working factory hand. We lived in rented, terraced housing, with no bathroom and a shared outside lavatory. Despite this environment's obvious privations, it was irrepressibly language-rich – we all routinely read, exchanged, quipped and recited delicious-sounding phrases; we prided ourselves on dialogues thick with puns and double-entendres; we revelled in Yorkshire idioms, expressions and humour. It wasn't long, however, before my rigorous girls' grammar-school education, with its heavy emphasis on the three Rs and compulsory Latin, fractured my innocence. I was easily indoctrinated into the belief that there was another English, a 'public' language that alone conferred institutional respect and power, an English to which my 'home' language (vocabulary, syntax, idioms, accent) was grossly inferior. I came to see that this superior English was everywhere, underpinning the belief system of my education; it was lauded even by communities like mine, which it explicitly despised. My conversion was total; I wanted to be just like the writers of my English grammar textbooks and get into their world.

And so, as a northern working-class girl, it was through language that I was 'interpellated', as Althusser (1971) defines it, 'hailed' unconsciously as a subject into the ideologies of the southern English cultured classes. In a feminist, post-structural analysis, Elizabeth St. Pierre (2000: 502) traces how subjectivities are produced socially through these language relations: 'we take up or resist certain subject positions that are already available in discursive formations operating within cultures and are obliged to work within the confines of those positions'. In this way, as St. Pierre (2000: 503) points out, citing Judith Butler, 'the "I" who would select between [positions] is always already constituted by them'. In other words, I am 'always-already a subject', in Althusser's (1971: 119) terms, waiting to be hailed.

I still wonder at the extent of my collusion in this process, and in the ideological values that degraded me and those I loved. Stuart Hall explains: 'They had the power to make us see and experience *ourselves* as Other' (1990: 226, Hall's emphasis); thus, our desires become fixed on those targets that are discursively accessible to us. Gunew explains a similar process for Australian migrants:

> English was employed as a technology that structured the cultural terrain so that the self-defining gaze was always mediated by a cultural legacy which rendered one's immediate context alien and unworthy. (Gunew, 2001: 741)

Perhaps, it was this internalised conviction of unworthiness that sustained my hegemonic belief in the superiority of academic English for so long. Ironically, in the early 1960 s as an undergraduate student of English at the University of Birmingham, I attended groundbreaking lectures by working-class cultural theorists such as Richard Hoggart (1957) and Raymond Williams (1965). They argued that the rise of this 'Standard English' acted as a key process in the production of patterns of social dominance, marginalisation, and injustice, through which we were educated to become 'ashamed of the speech of [our] fathers' (Williams, 1965: 247), as I did. Remarkably, even in this exciting and highly esteemed intellectual context, I was unable to hear these arguments. Indoctrinated as I was, I became an enthusiastic, 'old-fashioned' teacher of English and continued zealously to spread the Standard English word to other unfortunates like myself for more than 20 years. I unreflectively wielded power and rules based on the dominant coded forms of written Standard English – I became a 'language boss', as Lakoff (1990) splendidly defines them,[2] and I experienced no contradiction between this invisible belief system, my marginal place within it and that of other disrespected varieties of English.

Today, I see these experiences as clear instances of regularising social formation, yet I still find it hard to understand how I acquiesced so thoroughly in my positioning. It was only much later that, quite serendipitously it seems to me now, I found myself asking about the possibilities for agency that mimicry of language-use can open up. Homi Bhabha famously identifies an unstable 'third space' that is generated when identities are negotiated across cultures and languages. He describes this as

> [a] liminal space, in-between the designations of identity ... an interstitial passage between fixed identifications [that] opens up the possibility of a cultural hybridity that entertains difference without an assumed or implied hierarchy. (Bhabha, 1994: 4)

Others also have confidence in this interstitial 'third space', in which social meanings and realities are seen to be *mutually* constituted in the colonial contact. Notions of 'transformation' and 'writing back' have extended and emphasised the creative openings offered through manipulation of the powerful versions of language (Ashcroft, 2001; Ashcroft *et al.*, 1989). Ashcroft presents an illuminating discussion of inter*pol*ation (as distinct from inter*pel*lation), which he defines as

> the access such 'interpellated' subjects have to counter-discursive agency ... the capacity to interpose, to intervene, to interject a wide range of counter-discursive tactics into the dominant discourse without asserting a unified anti-imperial intention, or a separate oppositional purity. (Ashcroft, 2001: 47)

For Ashcroft (2001: 14), 'language is the key to this interpolation, the key to its transformative potential, for it is in language that the colonial discourse is engaged at its most strategic point'.[3]

In my professional investigations, I eventually came to the point of productively interrogating these creative tensions in my own teaching practice, when I met the face-slapping challenge that forced me to crystallise my position. Feminist scholar Audre Lorde (1984: 112) allows no quarter in her famous call to arms when she declares, unequivocally, and in italics, that

> 'the master's tools will never dismantle the master's house'. (Lorde, 1984: 112)

Instantly, I was thrown into the confusion with which I opened this chapter, and my comfortable world of scholarly debate was invaded by an unbidden rush of fracturing, personal, interrogatory demands: Is this *true*, for me? *Is* it necessarily so, when the 'tool' in question is a powerful, elite variety of English? Isn't that what I am doing now in my own scholarship, with my own academic language proficiency? What exactly *are* the possibilities for agency in the processes of interpolation? In short, how confident am I of inter*pol*ated outcomes in the global academy for which I teach?

The answer is that, finally, I am not. Despite my scholarly interrogation of the interstices and 'third spaces' inherent in social formation, my own growth to subjectivity leaves me in fear of that colonising 'lens' which colours all while it 'imperially thinks it is a window onto the really real' (Scheurich, 1997: 174). For me, the dangers and distortions of this lens are never entirely extinguished by its productive potential, and so my bedrock position rests with Lorde:

> For the master's tools will never dismantle the master's house. They may allow us to temporarily beat him at his own game but they will never enable us to bring about genuine change. And this fact is only threatening to those women [and men] who still define the master's house as their only source of support. (Lorde, 1984: 112)

Indeed, around me I am not seeing the dominant disciplinary discourses that I teach being used effectively to 'dismantle' the invisible frameworks that sustain white, elite knowledges. In my observation they continue to build the kinds of structures for which they are designed. My diverse postgraduate research students, and I, are not free agents; conflicting interests inevitably intervene to influence our educational goals. To me it is not realistic to think that these academic language tools can exist in any *conventional* form outside the norms of the colonising, self-sustaining academy and its operations. They are so powerful and so inherently a part of this house's imaginary that even to see them, to pick them up and learn to use them, is to have already closed off possibilities for other, more locally apposite and significant knowledges. Even to wield them destructively is still to act within the mores of the house, and to reify its worldview.[4] In the all-consuming ontological and epistemological assumptions of metropolitan research, and equally in its discourses, there is no assumption of dialogue with other knowledges and language forms, nor does any such assumption inspire its teaching. In my own life I am aware that, even as I have grown to 'master' some of the knowledges and discourses of this house and can speak powerfully to its occupants, with all the economic and social privileges that brings, I can no longer command the deeply integrated knowledge and language that sustain the worldview of my north-country community,[5] nor appreciate the *wealth* of the social understandings that inform their lives.[6]

And so, largely as a result of my own life trajectory, I feel that if I want to 'bring about genuine change' in postgraduate research education in the way envisaged by Lorde, I must do more than 'educate' my students; I must also be prepared to work towards a radical redesign of the global academy that is such an immensely powerful wing of the 'master's house'. The main purpose of this chapter, then, is an attempt to begin this process. I will first aim to authorise my central argument by referring to relevant trends in metropolitan, Indigenous and periphery scholarship, with particular reference to Africa, in order to demonstrate the powerfully colonising effects of so-called northern ways of knowing and writing.[7] I will then explore some of my own periphery students' understandings of these issues, before suggesting some alternative criteria by which knowing and research writing might be viewed differently for southern scholars and southern contexts, in a deliberately 'ecological' and dialogic global academy.

It is important, however, for me to stress again that I am not advocating transgressive practices for today's novice researchers – the conditions are not yet in place which would allow this to be viewed positively. Nevertheless, it is my strong conviction that it is the responsibility of those of us involved in developing 'southern' pedagogies to consider seriously what inter*pol*ation might look like for southern postgraduate students, in order that we might open up 'third spaces' for their futures. My primary purpose in this discussion is to ask the powerful educators of the northern academy to enter new dialogues around its historically resilient practices, especially its assessment criteria, its ways of engaging with research texts from southern contexts, and the assumptions underpinning its research pedagogies. I am aware that, in doing this I am now advocating, and taking, serious epistemological, discoursal, and institutional risks which for many years I did not consider.[8]

Authorising

Working towards these goals, it is important for me to show explicitly how theorists in the conventionally critical tradition influenced my thinking. Not only have their analyses thrown light onto my intellectual darkness but, in so doing, they have provided me with the emotional resources to create a credible discursive representation of my 'self' here. Significantly, I know that, in this context, my arguments will lack due gravity and 'worthiness' unless they are yoked to those of appropriate northern thinkers. Before I do that, however, I need to remind myself that first and foremost I draw on experience of more than a decade's teaching of postgraduate writing in humanities and social sciences, and especially on my collegiate relationships in those multicultural and multilingual contexts. It is primarily in relation to my own teaching that I have begun to develop some perspectives on theoretical notions of 'knowledge', 'academic discourse' and the 'postgraduate condition', which are at the heart of the teaching of postgraduate writing in English.

Knowing

It was in working with periphery students on the writing of their formal research proposals that confirm their entry into a metropolitan higher-degree research program that I transformed my own pedagogic approach. Through this teaching, I became acutely aware of the interdependent relationships that exist among three key criteria: the expectations of the written 'proposal' genre as disciplinary discourse; the positioning of the student writer, both in and out of the document; and, the kinds of knowledge that it is possible to seek and develop through metropolitan research-degree training (see Cadman, 2002). In this context, I experienced first hand a range of problematic situations for international doctoral students, in which the expectations of northern research culture unquestioningly assumed imperialistic, dominant knowledge paradigms within social science disciplines. The following instances provide a small snapshot from a much bigger picture: a headmaster from a remote island school trying to justify the focus of his project from within English-language scholarship; a colonel in a repressive regime's army distraught at the instruction that the appropriate research direction dictated by the field required a project based on critical social theory; a professor of education from a rural centre in Asia struggling with advice to explore the relevance of communicative English language teaching in his institution; a Middle-Eastern professional studying institutions in her own environment advised that material written in her own language could be only peripheral to her study. Examples like these gave me glimpses into real-life research-shaping practices, and my colleagues working with science students shared similar experiences. These are the day-to-day enactments of epistemic colonisation, which have been described as issuing from 'a disembodied epistemology that assumes the locus of enunciation of the master as the universal one' (Mignolo, 2000 cited in Cadman, 2005b: 6).

The intellectual quests at work in such processes are clearly characterised by their lack of self-reflexivity, by their unwillingness, perhaps their inability, to engage with their genesis, to confront what they *don't* know in dialogue with what they know, to consider their own partiality and incompleteness in terms of universal 'truth'. Scholars such as Santos (1995, 1999) and his colleagues (Santos *et al.*, 2007: xxxiii) emphasise the vast destructive global consequences, especially for social justice, when this aim of 'reducing the understandings of the world to the logic of Western epistemology' remains unchallenged. As these authors show, the effects are catastrophic:

> The epistemological privilege granted to modern science from the seventeenth century onwards, which made possible the technological revolutions that consolidated Western supremacy, was also instrumental in suppressing other, non-scientific forms of knowledges, and at the same time, the subaltern social groups whose social practices were informed by such knowledges. (Santos *et al.*, 2007: xix)

In some cases, this suppression of knowledge is clearly seen as a form of epistemicide, the 'other side of genocide' (Santos *et al.*, 2007: xix; see also Santos, 1995). In an edited collection, *Another Knowledge is Possible*, Santos (2007) powerfully demonstrates the ways in which these suppressions have driven a conceptual wedge between the north and the south, extending in practice to current political and institutional structures, which determine social futures through the global machinery of aid and development:

> Having been stripped of experience, the South can regain it only through the accumulated experience of the North, exported under the form of the 'transfer of scientific knowledge and technology'. International agencies still operate on the premise that the South has problems and the North has solutions to them. (Santos *et al.*, 2007: xxxviii; see also Tikly, 2004)

The all-consuming impact of these operations is beautifully demonstrated in relation to science and biodiversity by Egziabher (2007). It is also strongly argued by Preece (2006, 2009) from her work in African education, where the often hidden, neo-colonial agenda of northern capitalism has crippling and ongoing effects on Indigenous ways of knowing.

I have also been greatly influenced by Connell (2007), who makes this same point in relation to academic scholarship in an illuminating study of the processes desperately needed now for the production of what she calls southern theory. Connell describes in detail how northernness is effected as 'knowing', and how the forceful interplay of global mechanisms creates a 'geopolitical logic' which 'relies exclusively on the metropole for [its] tools and assumptions and therefore...closes off the possibility of social science working as a shared learning process, a dialogue at the level of theory' (Connell, 2007: 68). I had previously actively embraced Scheurich's (1997) confronting challenge that this geopolitical logic enacts a white racism that infects all our scholarly knowing and doing, so that, despite our interpolitive or 'third space' opportunities, all our northern conceptions, indeed all that we are capable of imagining, in some way refers directly or indirectly to the dominant set of 'white' social formations we have experienced (see Cadman, 2005b). For Scheurich and his colleagues, this is the taken-for-granted practice of 'epistemological racism':

> we researchers in education avoid White racism by believing or presuming that it somehow does not infect our research assumptions, questions, epistemologies, and methodologies, that somehow we in the university have a special immunity that protects us... [W]e appear to hope that if we avoid it, ignore it, don't look at it, it will quietly go away. It won't. (Scheurich & Young, 1998: 27)

And so I came to understand that the practices sustaining the impregnable operations of the master's house exclude outsiders and suppress their ways of knowing.

Through my teaching experience I met these same arguments repeatedly expressed by Indigenous students, as Scheurich and Young themselves point out, and by academics of colour within the centres of academic power. In Australasia, scholars in critical race and whiteness studies have initiated incisive dialogues around the operations of 'white' privilege and control over available ways of knowing for both Indigenous and non-Indigenous communities (Moreton-Robinson, 2004; Nakata, 2006; Rigney, 2001; Smith, 1999). 'Research' is described as a dirty word for most Indigenous people, inextricably linked as it is to Eurocentric imperialism and colonialism (Smith, 1999; Umulliko, 2006). Other Indigenous writers such as Battiste (2000, 2008) and Steinhauer (2002) in Canada, Porsanger (2004) in northern Europe and Bataille (2001), Warrior (1999), Mihesua (1998) and their colleagues in the United States, are working explicitly and with an uncompromising intellectual energy to 'resist cooptation and to challenge the dominant conventions of our disciplines ... [towards] a reordering of the power structure and an Indigenizing of the academy' (Mihesua & Wilson, 2004: 14). Warrior (1999) and Rigney (2001) (in Australia) have argued that what they and their contemporaries are seeking is 'the freedom to break out of the strictures of Western academic conventions' and, critically, to 'seek out their own ground of intellectual engagement' (Rigney, 2001: 9).

With similar goals, scholars in periphery contexts have identified what Diawara (2000: 362) has called the 'sterile excess' that characterises 'theories of modernisation and/or westernisation of the world'. For Africa, there is articulate conviction that the distorting effects of colonisation have resulted in epistemological eradications, erasures, misrepresentations and acts of axiological violence which northern models of analysis have failed to redress (Ahluwalia, 2001; Odora-Hoppers, 2002; Sitas, 2006). According to Diawara (2000: 363), although recent post-structural initiatives are turning their gaze back to analyse the multiple ways in which 'western observers and strategists mistook [their] purely local phenomena for universally valid ones', even these studies serve only to continue the tradition of northern metropolitan epistemic privilege and so remain sterile.

Writing

In my earlier thinking about racist epistemologies in the Anglo-Celtic academy, I made the association between 'knowing whitely', which colours all before it, and its 'natural corollary', *'writing* whitely' (Cadman, 2005b: 6–7). The racism implied in these terms operates through the authoritative speaking positions we take up discursively, which serve to silence those whose world-understandings are not articulated in the same way. bell hooks (1990: 242) presents a confrontational account of how metropolitan research appropriates alternative knowledges and reworks them discursively for its own ends:

> No need to hear your voice when I can talk about you better than you can speak about yourself. No need to hear your voice. Only tell me about your pain. I want to know your story. And then I will tell it back to you in a new way. Tell it back to you in such a way that it has become mine, my own. Re-writing you I write myself anew. I am still author, authority. I am still colonizer, the speaking subject, and you are now at the centre of my talk. (hooks, 1990: 242)

Even as I flinch and try to engage with the implications of hooks' accusations here, I know that I have reproduced these processes exactly in my own research and writing.

Academic Violence

Scheurich (1997) suggests that, however racist and 'white' these processes may be, they are, most often, unconsciously 'civilisational' rather than the result of deliberately motivated intention on the part of individuals. Nevertheless, this does not necessarily absolve them from the charge of violent patriarchal epistemicide, as Peter Elbow (1991) clearly shows in an early fine-grained analysis of 'academic discourse'. Almost as an aside, Elbow quotes a metropolitan professor of physics as saying,

> Scientific communication is faceless and passionless by design. Data and conclusions stand bare and unadorned, so they can be evaluated for what they are without prejudice or emotion. This kind of impersonal communication has helped science achieve the status of public knowledge, a coinage of truth with international currency. (Raymo, 1989 cited in Elbow, 1991: 142)

In my experience, this quest for universal 'truth', 'coined' in prose, shores up the fundamental belief system that inspires metropolitan academic research. Elbow shows how values indoctrination occurs through a set of specific 'social and authority relations' that students are taught through the conventions of disciplinary academic discourses:

- A version of reality – through the expectation of explicitness and straightforward organisation
- A set of social and authority relations – how to talk to each other as professionals in such a way as to exclude ordinary people
- Techniques for self-concealment – an anxiety often revealed by a flat, monotone, author-evacuated style, more passives, more formal language, more technical vocabulary
- An element of display – linguistic strategies for impressing readers who have more knowledge and more authority, including appropriately chosen and presented citations and footnotes. (Elbow, 1991: 146–148)

In presenting these discursive techniques, neither does Elbow engage with their obviously violent social impacts, nor does he see such impacts as reasons to problematise the teaching of the dominant discourses.

Post-academic Challenge

By contrast, recent writing specialists in the academic discipline of creative writing have taken a much more politically motivated position. They argue that in mastering academic discourses as theoretical tools of disciplinary representation, researchers learn to adopt and then reproduce the destructive processes and power relations which govern what it is possible to know and how it is possible to express it. This is the epistemic space opened up by 'fictocriticism', and other strategic ways of claiming an 'I'-voice, out of which to speak critically and with authority. However, in an insightful interrogation of the issues involved in this trend to self-representation, Flavell (2006) demonstrates that simply situating oneself in one's critical writing may realign, but rarely effectively refigures, the authorial appropriation of others' experiences and voices. She argues that this strategy is most often a superficial rhetorical one, which does not in any way problematise the assumptions of texts and their production, and so remains complicit with the violent operations of 'his master's voice' in the metropole. Flavell concludes that 'mere identification with the margin is not nearly enough... We need texts that more completely surrender their authority – embracing a loss of self and meaning... Academics must take risks with the self' (Flavell, 2006: 285).

The intersection between this fictocritical call to arms, my own self-representation in this chapter, and my institutional work with diverse academic discourses, is brought to its most strategic point here. What is inescapable for me, however, is that, as Flavell (2006: 257) briefly says, 'To have the choice of self-disclosure – that is, either to refute the neutral, universal voice of academic writing or continue speaking in that way – one must be in a central position in the first place' – that is, be able to command and transform the *academic*, to construct an authoritative speaking position that is *post-academic*. And today, most of the world's postgraduate research students are not.

Engaging the *Pre-Academic*

This is the real challenge for those of us teaching research-writing skills in the global academy. Our task is to ask how we position ourselves, reflexively and ideologically, in relation to draft writing which patently reveals itself as *pre-academic*, in other words that *fails* to effect the required 'standards' of disciplinary discourse, as distinct from self-consciously subverting them. A driving question has become increasingly relevant for me: to what extent does students' mastery of the target discourses have to be the goal of international research education? Indeed, *should* such student mastery still be the dominant focus of a teacher's pedagogic expertise and the primary measure of her success? The answers are by no means self-evident to me; my own complicity in the extinguishing and marginalising of periphery knowledges demands a deeper interrogation of my role in the pedagogic process.

Northern scholars in the critical tradition have actively engaged with these issues in relation to conventional features of academic discourse. Canagarajah, for example, in *A Geopolitics of Academic Writing*, makes a strong case for reconsideration and reform in 'English style and written discourse' (Canagarajah, 2002a: 269), and discusses the rhetorical structures of different academic genres without the prevailing assumption that western English language conventions are stable and should remain inviolate. Elsewhere he extends this analysis, and calls for teachers to develop a 'fundamentally different orientation' to the teaching of English grammar in writing, advocating moves from 'error' to 'choice', from 'correction' to 'negotiation' and so on (Canagarajah, 2002b: 51–52). For me, these suggestions don't go far enough. Canagarajah, like other advocates of this kind, remains within a discourse which privileges 'knowledge of grammar rules' (Canagarajah, 2002b: 52). His explicit position on 'negotiating grammar' is as follows:

> Students also learn that in certain special cases they may try out a peculiar structure for [their own culturally] unique purposes. But they should indicate to the audience that they are using this with full awareness of the established grammar system. (Canagarajah, 2002b: 56)

Paradoxically, what is demanded here is that students for whom English is an additional language develop a greater and more complex facility with English than that required by most first-language writers – a mastery comparable to that of the fictocritics.[9] The risks of accepting divergent forms are obvious here, as conceded by German scholar Ulrich Ammon (2000: 114): 'Doing away with standards altogether would certainly be no viable option since it would endanger successful communication.' This position seems to be the prevailing one, even among critical linguists, perhaps because the risks of opening the floodgates to globally escalating hybridisation of English grammatical forms strike fear in those who are its masters.

In complex ways, then, in relation to both the design and the communication of research in the periphery, neo-colonial operations clearly underpin the epistemological and discoursal conventions of most of the world's postgraduate education. Research education plays out in the 'master's house' in an ontological politics, based on the assumption that ways of classifying, ordering and describing the world are definitive, universally applicable, and grounded in the historical values of the 'metropolitan north'.

Triangulating

My own students have experienced this all too often. Trained as I am in dominant modes of social science research, I am conscious that what is missing from my discussion at this point are the voices of the postgraduate students at the heart of this matter. In my previous writing and publication experience I have been required to confirm the 'trustworthiness' of my scholarly arguments by engaging in a process of 'triangulation' through which I would increase the objectivity, and therefore the value, of my contribution (Denzin, 1970/2006).[10] Thus, it is especially appropriate for me to include further, 'primary' evidence drawn from discussions with southern postgraduate students I have taught, to provide readers with a touchstone for my contextual understandings and reasons to believe me. I have not developed my political, professional or personal beliefs in a vacuum; my students live, and can describe their own experiences and views. For me to represent them here (within the forms and ethical conditions that are prescribed) will strengthen my reception in this 'master's house', even as it paradoxically deepens my complicity in the violence of representation I am exposing.

I have discussed all the issues raised here with four African students with whom I have worked individually on their drafting of research proposals and thesis chapters at my own Australian research-intensive university. These students were all mature, experienced professionals enrolled in PhD programs in humanities or social science disciplines, having arrived in Australia for the first, or in one case the second, time not long before I met them. When asked (via a series of interviews) to identify what they felt were the most pressing challenges for them in constructing a research proposal, they all immediately stressed the relationship between the epistemological assumptions that were taken for granted in their disciplines and the writing of the proposal document that would successfully justify their research. One student explained her own situation insightfully:

> Perhaps for me the epistemology and finding an appropriate theoretical framework has been the most challenging in my research process. My earlier education had not prepared me to question the philosophy behind knowledge... I will give an example. I spent a considerable time reading on feminism as a possible theoretical framework on which to base the arguments of my thesis. But ... the whole premise on which feminism was based and is understood in a western framework is different from my own personal worldview... a lot of writing is based on what I believe was the dominant framework in the west in which men as a breadwinner and as a result women were fighting for their emancipation and rights to

work and be recognised. However from my African background, women have always worked and they held very important place in society ... in many cultures women were the primary business women, [and] they worked in the farms alongside with their partners and thus they were the primary producers of resources for the family. (Interview 3)

As a result of this tension, this student finally abandoned feminism as a theoretical framework; with her supervisor's guidance she used gender as 'an organising principle' in her thesis but neither to inform the purpose behind the research nor as a tool for analysis.

Another student, I'll call him Thomas, made a direct link between the length of his proposal draft and his own epistemological understanding. The university mandates a 5000-word limit and Thomas could not reduce the arguments he was making to this number of words. He was repeatedly advised that he was going in too many directions, that he needed to pull his analysis back to key western theorists in the discipline and streamline his thinking. He explained that for him this wasn't possible; in his view,

They are all connected, you can't cut one thing off from another. I see the intersections clearly but they don't see it. I see all the connections but they don't see them ... I have to cut across people's experiences and different disciplinary understandings ... so it needs a lot of patience for me. (Interview 5)

One of Thomas's supervisors was extremely understanding and supportive, and took what Thomas understood was quite a 'risky' stance on his behalf, allowing him to 'do it my way' but with a proviso: 'They told me I always have to explain it ... If I do something, I must explain why I do that this way' (Interview 5). His final proposal was much longer than the prescribed limit and was accepted. Thomas laughed as he told me that, at his formal departmental proposal seminar, a senior academic asked abruptly, 'But where is Foucault?'; Thomas knew he would be okay though, because his supervisor publicly explained on his behalf why it wasn't necessary for Foucault to be referenced (Interview 5).

As I came to learn through examples like these, it is through human interaction, through the teaching/learning relationships that are developed in research education, that these students gain positive experience of becoming researchers, or not (see Cadman, 2005a). Whatever the skills training deemed to be required, finally it is through the attitudes taken by metropolitan scholars in their handling of epistemological and discoursal diversity that individual students can or cannot find openings for dialogues that allow them to contribute to international research conversations. All of the students I refer to here emphasised how important it was to them to feel 'at home' in their disciplinary environments. For them this meant 'safe', that they 'fit in', despite their cultural, language and physical differences, and that they could be accepted for what they were. They all expressed the importance of 'social chit-chat', of taking food or coffee with supervisors and other students, of smiles, of basic human interaction; three of them specifically mentioned the significance of welcoming greetings, pointing out that 'for me it is very important – just nodding your head is not enough' (Interviews 1, 4, 6), one explaining:

> In Africa a lot of time is spent on developing relationships within the working environment. When you come into work you greet everyone – I think the saying is, 'you find out how they are, how their wives and children are, and how the animals are'. There is a lot of time spent talking about everything, especially current affairs. I think here it would be seen as over-sharing – it is just not done. (Interview 1)

Further, what they felt was central in this was that their contribution to the research community was respected and valued, so, as one expressed it, 'it can only become home if your work is made useful, if you can contribute and feel part of the community – that's what makes it become home' (Interview 4).

For these students, these were the conditions that were needed to facilitate their ability to negotiate entry into this 'master's house' as a fertile learning environment. They all initially experienced some perceived problems in writing, whether in relation to their different ways of constructing rhetorical arguments, to unintentional plagiarism, or to their perceived lack of command of traditional grammar or scholarly referencing techniques. Significantly, two did not find flexible, creative approaches to their difference within their disciplinary contexts, and their voices were gradually silenced. In several cases, the students naturally talked in terms of what Bhabha (1992) has called, the 'unhomely' banalities of everyday life: 'I hated being there – I felt out of place and in the way'; 'I didn't belong'; 'If I died in my office it would be three days before anyone found me'; 'They never saw any merit in my thesis' (Interviews 4, 6, 7 and 8). Bhabha explains: 'it is precisely in these banalities that the unhomely stirs, as the violence of a racialised society falls most enduringly in the details of life: where you can sit, or not; where you can live, or not; what you can learn, or not...' (Bhabha, 1992: 149–150). One student summed it up as follows: 'No, I'm not sorry to be going home – there's no smoko here' (Interview 7).

Risking

My goal in this chapter so far has been to lay a clear foundation for understanding the specific ways in which northern institutional contexts of study and the research paradigms, methodologies and discourses of the metropolitan academy work together to marginalise other knowledges and silence other voices. It is my belief that we need to acknowledge and interrogate these processes if we seriously hope to mitigate our complicity in the 'inter*pell*ations' that we effect, and open up 'inter*pol*ative' spaces for students. In my view, however, there is also much more that we can do. The globalisation we are all experiencing is accelerating and we are presented with a critical moment for strategic redesign, for thinking beyond the norms we are used to, to consider new possibilities in line with the inclusive and emancipatory values that we hold. On this point, it is interesting to note that Lorde's (1984) metaphorical challenge (cited earlier) does not refer to *demolishing* the master's house, but to *dismantling* it, and herein lies space for action. 'Dismantling' involves carefully evaluating the usefulness of component elements; it demands a coherent belief in the new (as yet unformed), different (and by definition, unfamiliar) 'house' we are imagining – this global academy *can* work differently, if we want it to. Appadurai similarly challenges our courage; he argues that the 'world-generating optic' of our research operations leaves us 'confined to our own first-order, necessarily parochial, world pictures' (Appadurai, 2001: 9), and asks,

> Are we prepared to move beyond a model of internationalising academic research that is mainly concerned with improving how others practice our precepts? Is there something for us to learn from colleagues in other national and cultural settings...? [Are] we serious about building a genuinely international and democratic community of researchers...? (Appadurai, 2001: 15–16)

If those of us at home in 'the master's house' want to say a resounding 'yes' to this, we must be willing to risk the radical steps that are demanded for transforming our day-to-day academic protocols in terms of both their methodological processes and their discursive products.

Towards an 'Ecology of Knowledges'

Global scholarly knowledge is largely disseminated in the books and journal articles that are generated through universities and publishing houses which have a financial investment in their products. In *Geopolitics,* Canagarajah

(2002a) engages in detail with the operations of this machinery of publication (see also Canagarajah, 2003). I have advocated various institutional strategies, such as working to give credibility and financial support to periphery research projects and widening institutional acceptance of race-based journals and publications such as those celebrated in the *African Journals Online* collection, as appropriate vehicles for securing tenure and promotion.

It seems clear to me that, before such initiatives will be seriously taken up and implemented, a shift is needed at a deeply conceptual, 'civilisational' level. Those of us engaged in the operations of the global academy need to radically reconceptualise the fundamental purpose behind research communication, indeed behind research itself. As Santos *et al.* (2007: xlix) convincingly demonstrate, we need first to imagine, and then adopt, an 'ecology of knowledges', a 'new epistemological stance from which to [create] a new type of relationship between scientific knowledge and other knowledges'. This stance presupposes scholarly research as a seeking for one way of knowing among many, simply one way of understanding phenomena among all the diverse, accumulating knowings of humankind. Thus, research grows from a global desire to share local human insight, not a competitive drive to define the known. Such a goal can only be achieved, however, through a dogged and uncompromising reorientation of existing practices, effected through 'the construction of a scientific community under conditions and according to rules largely outside the conventional models' (Santos, 2007: xvi). Connell (2007: 227) expresses similar zeal for opening up the relations between knowledges, and argues for a 'retooling' of the mechanisms of the academy as the key to 'a mutual learning process on a planetary scale'.

How we, then, might work in practice though our 'insider' situations in research education to facilitate the creation of these 'new rules' and 'retooling' strategies raises some radical questions for new ways of thinking about the knowing and writing that we teach, and how we might imagine them differently.

'Interpolating' Methodologies

At this point, I am again aware of my hesitation about my authority to speak on this point, to share here the idiosyncratic position that I have come to out of my own experience. Canagarajah (2005: 746) has argued that periphery scholars do not 'want their own perspectives to be the dominant principles in the field or ... different standards and norms applied to study the realities in their regions'. But I am now at a point where I, as a metropolitan insider, tentatively want to consider in what circumstances periphery perspectives *might* legitimately be given dominant status, and how 'different standards and norms' might look, for the generation of southern knowledge. In addition to Connell's clear and detailed first steps towards 'southern theory' (Connell, 2007: 212–216), southern scholars themselves have put forward specific suggestions. The concept of 'race-based' epistemology has been advanced by Collins, through which black women's knowledge may be validated and, as Collins argues, 'serve as one specific social location for examining points of connection among multiple epistemologies' (Collins, 2000: 270). Elsewhere, Indigenous scholars are actively debating the potential for an Indigenous research methodology, interrogating the implications of Smith's (1999) claim that 'decolonising' does not mean rejecting metropolitan methodologies but working *with* rather than *against* the prevailing epistemological paradigms, explicitly for Indigenous interests (see e.g. Rigney, 1999, 2006; Steinhauer, 2002). In this way, historically othered ways of knowing can be written back into academic dialogues with 'rhetorical sovereignty' (Lyons, 2000).

In periphery contexts, the same issues are evident in active intellectual debate, especially in education. In Africa, for example, there have been ongoing evaluations of the possibility of identifying a unifying 'African philosophy' out of the diversity of experience that is Africa's colonial history (Bell, 2002). Proponents have argued that such a philosophy has to avoid the traps of ethnocentrism and 'unscientific' essentialising (Houndonji, 2002); rather, it must 'contest the dominance of Eurocentric philosophy by engaging and contesting it – even using its own tools such as rigorous rational analysis – to challenge the power relations that underpin and are expressed through Eurocentric discourse' (Parker, 2003: 32). Others seek rather to stress what is left out, rendered invisible, when primarily metropolitan assumptions inform the philosophical ground of African research methodology (Tikly, 2004).

In relation to the conduct of research, Carroll (2008) shows convincingly how 'an Afrikan worldview' can be identified, and that it has at least two vital contributions to make to global ways of knowing. First, in epistemological and axiological terms, African knowledge-making 'is grounded in cooperation and collective responsibility; corporateness and interdependence', which is 'in contradistinction to the European axiology which is founded on competition and individual rights; separateness and independence' (Carroll, 2008: 10). This axiological framework has historically been articulated through the deep-rooted ethical notion of ubuntu, translated as 'I am because we are, and since we are, therefore, I am' (Mbiti, 1992), thus expressing the primacy of responsibility to the well-being of others and to the common good, ahead of the interests of the individual. And I, from a vastly different social context, seem instinctively to resonate with this principle; in my own childhood it was a lived ethic within my marginalised family and community, an unspoken, though much more significant, marker of respect and admiration than wealth. However, the dangers of uncritically celebrating this principle in Africa today have been well articulated, especially for the complex, gendered distribution of power and labour in AIDS-torn communities (Mangena, 2009). As Morrell and Swart concisely point out,

> By concentrating on racial and ethnic oppression primarily as a result of external forces, the internal forces of gender oppression have been concealed or ignored. In this sense, there is a real danger of focuses on *ubuntu* simply reflecting or reinforcing patriarchal discourses. (Morrell & Swart, 2005: 99)

Despite these dangers, Drucilla Cornell draws on analytical data to support the continued relevance of ubuntu in Africa today. Defining ubuntu as 'a coming into being ... a modality of existence and interactive ethic in which who we can become is inevitably intertwined, not with some static entity called community, but with actual day-to-day interactions with each other' (Cornell, 2005: 3), Cornell and her colleagues thus stress the interpolative space for activism within its ideals (see also Cornell & Van Marle, 2005). For Cornell, the principle of ubuntu is vitally necessary to stem what Paget Henry described as the 'Calibanization of Africans' by colonial, European race-logic (2000, cited in Cornell, 2008: 9). Cornell argues strongly that, today, philosophical recognition of ubuntu, as deeply embedded in the cultural heritage of the majority of people, is 'crucial to the restoration of Caliban's reasoning' (Cornell, 2008: 9), and thus to Africa's future.[11]

Carroll (2008: 14) goes on to identify a second potential African contribution to global scholarship, in terms of cosmology, ontology and spirituality. He emphasises an African understanding that 'all things in the universe are interconnected and interdependent'. This means that

> whether apprehensible logically or illogically ... at the fundamental level of all existence is a spiritual energy/force manifesting itself on all levels of human reality [which] grounds one's investigation of the Africana experience in the most basic level of reality, which is spirit. (Carroll, 2008: 15; see also Wilson, 1995)

As Carroll points out, northern research methodologies take no account of an ontological assumption of spirituality, and thus vast worldview differences 'influence the nature of your research methodology...[and] the nature of your hypotheses and models that you attempt to interrogate through your research project' (Carroll, 2008: 10).

From my own fluctuating positions across the range of territories involved here, I can see some real possibilities for the reorientation of criteria for methodological rigour in southern research design. New criteria could explicitly aim to address prevailing epistemological erasures, and so actively resist the metropole's reappropriation of periphery research processes and products. For equitable as well as transformational, explicitly 'ecological', outcomes, southern methodologies could, for example, take account of the following:

- *Dialogue-engagement* – a requirement to engage in some way with northern scholarship, whether by contesting, subverting, extending, bypassing, or even joining, established global trends on the target topic (Preece, 2009).
- *Analytical focus on the local* – privileging local content and issues of local relevance, while simultaneously aiming to contribute to global theory (Connell, 2007; Preece, 2006).
- *Writing back to historical oppression* – explicit acknowledgement of histories of oppression with their relevance to the growth of understanding.
- *Context-driven creativity in methodology and methods* – engagement with and creative extension of metropolitan paradigms and methodologies (see Seale, 1999); new contextual methodologies devised, explained and justified; detailed discursive construction of the researcher(s) and the research context in relation to specific issues being researched.
- *Ontological connectedness* – inclusion of relevant interdisciplinary and intercontextual analyses, with explanation of the logics of their connection (see Dixon, 1971, 1976, cited in Carroll, 2008: 14).
- *Responsibility to others* – specific accounts of the research goal and its process as enactments of goodwill for the advancement of fellow humans – possibly articulating a dynamic, interactive ethic similar to that of ubuntu as defined by the Ubuntu Project (Cornell & Van Marle, 2005)[12] – perhaps incorporating a scholarly assessment of the social value of the research outcome, first within its own community (as in Serpell, 2007), and then in relation to global understandings.
- *Teleological justification* – explicit grounding of the research purpose in spiritual fulfilment, with the moral and ethical frameworks that support it – the commitment to 'do no harm' (McCandless *et al.*, 2007: 131).

These criteria, or others like them, emerge naturally from any serious intention to integrate diverse ways of knowing into currently dominant methodological and institutional assessment frameworks, as a legitimate striving for that 'race-equity validity' that northerners like Scheurich and Young (1998: 29) are also seeking. Thus, by opening negotiations around how 'rigour' might be realised in new ways in specific disciplinary and institutional contexts, postgraduate education could provide a 'third space' location for transforming assessment criteria in institutional policy and pedagogic practice, not as *mandates* for any learner's research directions but as formal, optional specifications which could be negotiated in specific pedagogic contexts.

Reading and Writing the *Extra-Academic*

The communication of research is at the heart of its purpose and its life, and such diverse and, for us, unfamiliar ways of knowing as those suggested above, will naturally find written form in equally diverse and unfamiliar genres and English language structures. Such new, context-specific ways of writing will need new ways of reading. If we in the dominant disciplinary reading positions seek genuine change in Lorde's (1984) terms as mentioned above, important questions for us will focus on the extent to which conventional English language structures are necessary, if at all, for interpreting and understanding knowledge and theory emanating from periphery local communities. If communication and interrogation of rigorously developed insights are to be the 'true' goals of research, it becomes an open question whether traditional forms of rhetorical organisation, critical 'voice' construction, even adherence to basic grammar rules, are finally required.

In our long-standing work with postgraduates for whom English is an additional language, my colleagues and I have become adept at approaching periphery students' draft writing, not as remedial and *'pre-academic'* but rather as *'extra-academic'* expressions of alternatively informed research. This involves our reading *through* language to an available meaning, seeking, as we read, to understand the content, ideas and contextually derived insights that the writer is trying to convey. Such a reading demands that we do not focus immediately on a text's rhetorical or grammatical difference from the norm, but read for the research 'story' that is being told. In other words, we read the 'English' discourse as a negotiation of ideas without the monolingual framing that usually accompanies it. And so often with texts like these, the learning, redrafting and 'correcting' that are deemed to be required by our disciplinary gatekeepers constitute little more than an artificial exercise to satisfy metropolitan assessing or examining readers (see Cadman, 2005b). For me, it is only by learning to respect such texts as *extra-academic* demonstrations of research skill that we can engage in open dialogue with their research goals and assumptions. Thus, we need to become readers for clarity, comprehensibility and contextual relevance, and open up non-conventional texts for their communicative potential, rather than evaluating their contributions through their conformity to the structures we are used to.

In practice, these issues come to the fore most starkly in the teaching of the three fundamental aspects of academic discourse: the rhetorical logic of the disciplinary argument; the development of a critical 'voice' in scholarly attribution; and command of the standardised mechanics of English grammar.

With respect to the first of these, it is clear that if we create methodological guidelines for fulfilling criteria for 'southern' knowing, as I have suggested above, a raft of diverse logics would naturally result. A new range of genre moves and steps would need to be creatively negotiated to achieve a new variety of logical purposes, perhaps including some among the following:

- *Introductory background* sections might bring contexts and communities to life in ways traditionally seen as irrelevant;
- *Research justification* might take forms other than establishing gaps in northern scholarship (see Cadman, 2005b) or abstracting new theoretical interpretations of social situations;
- *Data discussion* might follow a logic dictated by subjective emotional intelligence or communal agency rather than by thematic categories exclusively coherent with metropolitan scholarship;
- *Methodology and methods* sections would necessarily involve a detailed account of the principles of belief, community values, practices and events that led to knowing in this specific context, that is, fully demonstrating the 'means' to knowledge gained rather than adhering to pre-validated concepts of 'methodological' rigour or 'method' steps (see Seale, 1999);
- There may be no *conclusion* as such, but somewhere the research account would need to explain explicitly why this research knowledge is important, why it matters to the people from whom it emerged, including the researcher,[13] in addition to its significance to the world.

With respect to the second aspect, in such mutable discourses the self-location of the author through a hybridised English-language 'voice' would be a central construct. The realisation of an authorial 'persona' might then take a variety of forms so, as readers, we would no longer limit ourselves to reading for mastery of traditional *academic* or experimentally *post-academic* discourses, but rather for a scholar's *extra-academic* self-realisation. Thus, we may learn to appreciate alternative ways in which a researcher-writer might create and situate themselves in their research context, described, perhaps, through their life history, or their role in a community, their technical expertise in a specific context, or their creative production of newly imagined, conceptual forms. In such cases, a writer's self-representation would explicitly demonstrate the grounds for their authorial position, much as I have tried to do here, and construct a speaking position in relation to, rather than in mimicry of, that of their desired readers.

In negotiating such relationships, readers may no longer feel the need to demand the ridiculous and sterile conventions of metropolitan bibliographical referencing, but may look for writers to provide adequate, simple and pragmatic information that is relevant and useful for readers. Most significantly, in discourses designed expressly to increase community well-being and develop communal knowledge, the currently dominant definition of plagiarism in critical analysis would almost certainly prove an anachronism. Literally, billions of world users of English are today engaging actively in knowledge- and theory-building, informed by worldviews that do not afford status to individuals as the 'owners' of words and ideas. As a result of this globalisation of education and technology, unintentional reworking of ideas and words is rapidly expanding (Cadman, 2005b), and will become increasingly accepted practice as it becomes formally disjoined from theft, fraud and corruption. If we in today's power positions are prepared to create the conditions which foster these movements, and open pedagogic spaces for them, periphery writers will become free to weave global learning into their research stories in their own diverse ways, through other more relevant demonstrations of integrity.

Thirdly, then, if we are willing to risk embracing such diverse discourses, similarly radical shifts will be needed in our reading and response to unconventional English grammar. For myself, I do not have that fear of the descent into Babelisation and chaos that others have expressed at the thought of striving for mutual intelligibility rather than standard accuracy in writing (see Maurais, 2003: 28–29). Ammon (2000: 114) has pointed out that in relation to thesis assessment, in Europe, as in Australia, 'quality judgment of texts [is made] according to the language in which they are written', to the extreme disadvantage of writers for whom English is an additional language. Personally, I am comfortable reading research stories written in hybridised grammatical structures, and intervening pedagogically only when communication breaks down. I can easily imagine formal documents written in what Bhatt (2005) has celebrated as those 'gloriously impure' local Englishes; I already have first-hand examples of their acceptance in international journals and local institutional contexts.[14] And my own experience of internationally successful transnational theses suggests that it is not uncommon in periphery contexts for assessors to focus their attention beyond form,[15] as Pennycook (2000: 115) suggests by his question: '[I]s international intelligibility always a negotiation of possibilities with no obvious standard?'

A final question then becomes: is it feasible to implement the kinds of changes I am suggesting here into northern institutional policies and practices? For myself, I think the risks would be well worth it. In Australia, for instance, the last five years have seen a marked change in the range of possible formats for PhD and Masters' theses as a result of the drive to attract a wider range of students and to increase enrolments.[16] Disciplinary research contributions have thus been significantly re-formed to accommodate changing economic imperatives, and it seems to me that other latent transformations are waiting to happen. The iron may be hot enough for striking now to achieve other, explicitly equitable and emancipatory outcomes. Whether we are positioned in northern or southern research contexts, we may be approaching a critical moment to begin negotiations for local action to redesign institutional and disciplinary assessment documents, and the intellectual processes that lead to them. As Walwicz (1997) shows in the work quoted in the epigraph to this chapter (and which was presented and published in scholarly contexts with marked success), northern universities increasingly have to find ways to accommodate new voices and new forms of argument; they are indeed 'confused now' but are active in working through that confusion. North and south, we need to work together to come up with creative, emancipatory alternatives to existing violent epistemological and discourse structures, and, when the time is ripe, to mobilise the political will and professional expertise to integrate them into our pedagogies.

Concluding: Towards a Southern Postgraduate Pedagogy

In this chapter, I have traced my own growth to subjectivity and detailed my intellectual journey to making my home – living, working and researching – in 'the master's house'. It was primarily through the English language that I was bonded and gained entrance: its invisible, colonising technologies, embedded as they were in the 'white' structured formations of my schooling and society, were deeply inscribed in my identity. My own ways of knowing (and expressing that knowledge) were imperceptibly and irrevocably transfigured, and because I saw the world through that all-colouring lens so completely, and for so long, the traps of that process are now as apparent for me as its liberations. Gunew shows how colonised subjects are inevitably bound up with their masters in these colonising mechanisms of mutual constitution, so that in learning and teaching contexts, '[t]he ideological baggage carried by curricula and texts serve[s] to camouflage the imperial process' (Gunew, 2001: 735). I have presented my own story here to suggest why it is that I now experience a profound dissatisfaction with traditional modes of researching and writing, which effect the alienating and silencing of vital, active intellectual communities, and why I am actively seeking directions for emancipation and change.

Such an ideological goal requires that we interrupt and redesign the colonising machinery of global scholarship at every level of its operations. Through our involvement in international journals, community programs, institutional policy-making, educational leadership and especially, in our postgraduate pedagogies, we will need to work dialogically to make formal as well as informal changes to transform our own local conditions. And we, not our students, will need to take the risks that will be involved. As Charmaine Perkins has argued, *'identifying* with the oppressed' is not enough – 'although many such individuals feel genuine concern, very few it seems are prepared to do anything about it, least of all to give up any of the perks that come with traditional power structures' (Perkins, 1997 in Flavell, 2006: 278–279, Perkins' italics). The risky work begins with those of us in more powerful positions being willing to interrogate our privilege and the forms it takes, to reflect on our intellectual and emotional positions in relation to the professional acts we are required to fulfil, and to work with others to establish the understanding that knowledge can never be universal – *all* knowing is contingent, requiring its own contextual validation and expression in a diverse range of language forms.

In research education, such commitment demands, above all, a morally robust pedagogy which is no longer instrumental in continuing the 'transfer of knowledge' goals that permeate the metropolitan discourse of international education. Rather, as I have argued strongly elsewhere (Cadman, 2005b), research education needs to *problematise* its still-privileged methodologies and discourses, even as it creates opportunities for postgraduate students to learn them. Above all, it needs to privilege 'connecting' with students as learning individuals. Diversity of student backgrounds demands diversity of learning conditions, of curricula, of teaching and learning styles, and of the very assumptions that inform the knowing and writing practices that are salient and equitable for postgraduates today. Students need to be made to feel at home as they enter the complex interactions required for them to negotiate around existing disciplinary practices, and to work with us to create new ones. Effective teaching then becomes focused on helping each student to develop the skills to communicate their own research position, their present location on an intellectual journey of their own designing, in negotiation with the kind of academic leadership and success they want. To this end, postgraduate research education is not just about students commanding the 'masters' strategic methodological, scientific or linguistic techniques. Rather, it is as much about how they can learn to identify their personal investment in their own, possibly transgressive, epistemological, linguistic and life goals, and to evaluate the feasibility of achieving those goals in today's epistemologically 'white', but expanding, global academy.

Thus, the risks for a truly 'southern' postgraduate pedagogy are substantial because they demand strategic, and dangerous, challenge to the prevailing mores of the international academy. If we are to contribute seriously to the global knowledge ecology that our planet and its people vitally need, today's scholars of power will need to act against the grain of existing Eurocentric notions of reason, and create new openings for ownership both of the content of research contributions, and the form of their written expression. Without such openings, the future for all our communities is potentially more devastating than the past; as Egziabher so powerfully declares: '[Those] who oppose us should be treated as enemies worse than their colonizing ancestors' (Egziabher, 2007: 433).

Notes

(1) Blake's famously powerful image of 'mind forg'd manacles' is from the poem 'London', line 8.
(2) 'Simply put, a language boss is anyone who finds it necessary to tell others how to talk; feels some words, pronunciations, or constructions are "bad", "ungrammatical" "degenerate", "illogical" or "corrupt" (or any of several other terms of abuse); and fears that the prevalence of such errors presages not just a decline in the culture's linguistic prowess, but also its cognitive ability and probably its political freedom' (Lakoff, 1990: 284). I have described elsewhere how I turned into a language boss (see Cadman, 2008).
(3) For a discussion of language interpolation in a local context see Bhatt (2005: 37), who challenges the eco-linguists' 'expert' view that English is guilty of 'linguicide', and argues that 'discourses of globalisation tend to under-represent the power of the local to appropriate dominant codes and discourses', especially in the case of Indian Englishes.
(4) With undeniable global effect in the field of cultural studies, periphery voices are among the centre's leaders (Appadurai, Bhabha, Fanon, Hall, Spivak spring to mind). These scholars have exploited the north's own value systems and 'temporarily beat [the master] at his own game'. Nevertheless, for me this kind of work remains deeply constitutive of the excluding and marginalising operations of the metropole,

especially in the structures of its English (for an entertaining critique of the 'pretentiously opaque' language paradox of post-structuralism, see Eagleton, 1999).

(5) I understand that this is also the shared experience of many Aboriginal people in Australia who have been immersed in mainstream northern education systems (May O'Brien, pers. comm.; see also O'Brien, 2002; Marika, 2000).

(6) At the end of Willy Russel's (1980) famous play, *Educating Rita*, written precisely on this topic, when Rita is asked what she has gained through her metropolitan education, she replies, 'I ha[ve] the choice ... I'll choose.' To me, however, this is a banal and uninterrogated response. In fact, as the play starkly demonstrates, Rita cannot 'choose' to know the world as she previously did; eventually, through her prescribed educational development, she evaluates significance very differently from her community and no longer respects their value systems. Above all, she has lost the capacity to dialogue with them, and has even become uncomfortable in their company.

(7) In this discussion, I have adopted the north/south terminology of the United Nations, and so refer to the dominant Anglo-Celtic global academy as 'northern' and 'metropolitan' in line with the work of Connell (2007) and Santos (2007).

(8) And I'm not alone in noting the risks involved in disclosing the force of my own interpellation. In a fascinating MA thesis analysing the 'neocolonising global conditions' of development, Ling (2004: 22) declares, 'The magnetic pull I felt to join this "first world cultural expansion" by ab/using my experience ... simply to further a "career" in development work that fits its dominant framework, has been enormously alluring I can shamefully admit now. I was also influenced by powerful forces of socialisation.'

(9) Elsewhere, Canagarajah critiques the writing of certain periphery scholars for being 'not ... written/structured coherently' and having 'convoluted syntax' (Canagarajah, 2000: 301), suggesting the expression of a relatively conservative position.

(10) On two occasions, I have been required by international journal reviewers in a social science field to 'generate more data' and to 'interview supervisors'. Their explicit justification was that this would 'give more substance to the conclusions', as well as making the arguments 'clearer and stronger than the earlier version'.

(11) McCandless et al. (2007) provide an effective example of this principle used as a methodological criterion for justifying a research project and its outcome in their Peace Research for Africa project.

(12) From an analysis of interviews with young South Africans in the Ubuntu Project, Cornell (2005: 4) emphasises the potential for critique within the concept of ubuntu: 'If we only become a person through other persons, even something that would usually be conceived as an attribute of an individual such as intelligence, is instead refined through the modality of being with others that both enhances and supports creativity and critical thinking'.

(13) In my own context, a successfully negotiated variation occurred when a colleague and a faculty supervisor concurred in helping a dedicated Muslim student to write his religious value system and acknowledgement of God explicitly into his PhD thesis. A long, contextualising chapter was specially designed to allow him to 'remain true to [his] values and beliefs while dancing to different cultural steps' (Ingleton *et al.*, 1996: 7). Examiners in his applied science discipline praised his work, highlighting, among other things, its originality and individuality.

(14) I have collected examples of many internationally published Asian journal articles that use English in unconventional ways, mostly without compromising the communication of meaning (see e.g. Patanakan & Kidokoro, 2005; Zhou & Hu, 2005).

(15) I have records of many instances where Australian supervisors were quite satisfied with a final draft thesis but required it to be subjected to detailed editing, often expensively, purely to overcome the examination hurdle. Furthermore, in prestigious Japanese universities I have found several examples of successful PhD theses in Education written in English by students from Myanmar under the supervision of Japanese supervisors and assessed by examiners from a range of South East Asian countries. These theses are written in noticeably unconventional English in terms of all the three aspects I refer to here, argument, self-representation and technical structures of standard academic English.

(16) In addition to the conventional thesis format accepted by the University of Adelaide, we have seen the emergence of formats such as the 'thesis by publication', the 'thesis by a combination of the conventional with publication', and the 'thesis by creative work'. The latter may include an exhibition, musical composition or performance, a literary work or a film, and an exegesis or critical essay (University of Adelaide, 2010).

References

Ahluwalia, P. (2001) *Politics and Postcolonial Theory: African inflections*. London: Routledge.

Althusser, L. (1971) *Lenin and Philosophy and Other Essays* (B. Brewster, trans.). New York: New Left Books.

Ammon, U. (2000) Towards more fairness in international English: Linguistic rights of non-native speakers? In R. Phillipson (ed.) *Rights to Language: Equity, Power and Education. Celebrating the 60th Birthday of Tove Skuttnab-Kangas*. Mahwah, NJ: Lawrence Erlbaum.

Appadurai, A. (2001) Grassroots globalization and the research imagination. In A. Appadurai (ed.) *Globalization*. Durham, NC: Duke University Press.

Armstrong, N. and Tennenhouse, L. (1989) *The Violence of Representation: Literature and the History of Violence*. London: Routledge.

Ashcroft, B. (2001) *Post-Colonial Transformation*. New York: Routledge.

Ashcroft, B., Griffiths, G. and Tiffin, H. (eds) (1989) *The Empire Writes Back: Theory and Practice in Post-colonial Literatures*. London: Routledge.

Bataille, G. (ed.) (2001) *Native American Representations: First Encounters, Distorted Images, and Literary Appropriations*. London: University of Nebraska Press.

Battiste, M. (ed.) (2000) *Reclaiming Indigenous Voice and Vision*. Vancouver, BC: University of British Columbia Press.

Battiste, M. (2008) The decolonization of Aboriginal education: Dialogue, reflection, and action in Canada. In P.R. Dasen and A. Akkari (eds) *Educational Theories and Practices from the Majority World*. New Delhi: Sage.

Bell, R. (2002) *Understanding African Philosophy: A Cross-cultural Approach to Classical and Contemporary Issues*. New York: Routledge.

Bhabha, H. (1992) The World and the Home. *Social Text* No. 31/32, Third World and Post-Colonial Issues (1992), pp. 141–153.

Bhabha, H. (1994) *The Location of Culture*. London: Routledge.

Bhatt, R.M. (2005) Expert discourses, local practices and hybridity: The case of Indian Englishes. In S. Canagarajah (ed.) *Reclaiming the Local in Language Policy and Practice*. Mahwah, NJ: Lawrence Erlbaum.

Cadman, K. (2002) English for academic possibilities: The research proposal as a contested site in postgraduate genre pedagogy. *Journal of English for Academic Purposes* 1 (2), 85–104.

Cadman, K. (2005a) Towards a pedagogy of connection in international research education: A REAL story. *Journal of English for Academic Purposes (Special Edition on Advanced Academic Literacy)* 4 (4), 353–367.
Cadman, K. (2005b) 'Divine discourse': Plagiarism, hybridity and epistemological racism. In S. May, M. Franken and R. Barnard (eds) *LED: Refereed Proceedings of the Inaugural International Conference on Language, Education and Diversity* (CDRom). Hamilton, NZ: University of Waikato Press.
Cadman, K. (2006) Trans/forming 'the King's English' in global research education; A teacher's tales. PhD thesis, University of Adelaide, SA.
Cadman, K. (2008) From correcting to connecting: A personal story of changing priorities in EAL teaching. *TESOL in Context* 17 (2), 29–37.
Canagarajah, S. (2000) Review of *The native speaker: Multiple perspectives*, by R. Singh (ed.) 1999. *English for Specific Purposes* 19, 300–301.
Canagarajah, S. (2002a) *A Geopolitics of Academic Writing*. Pittsburgh: University of Pittsburgh Press.
Canagarajah, S. (2002b) *Critical Academic Writing and Multilingual Students*. Ann Arbor, MI: University of Michigan Press.
Canagarajah, S. (2003) A somewhat legitimate and very peripheral participation. In C.P. Casanave and S. Vandrick (eds) *Writing for Scholarly Publication: Behind the Scenes in Language Education*. Mahwah, NJ: Lawrence Erlbaum.
Canagarajah, S. (2005) Conclusion. *TESOL Quarterly* 39 (4), 745–753.
Carroll, K.K. (2008) Afrikana studies and research methodology: Revisiting the centrality of the Afrikan worldview. *Journal of Pan African Studies* 2 (2), 4–27.
Collins, P.H. (2000) *Black Feminist Thought: Knowledge, Consciousness, and the Politics of Empowerment* (2nd edition). New York: Routledge.
Connell, R. (2007) *Southern Theory: The Global Dynamics of Knowledge in Social Science*. Sydney, NSW: Allen & Unwin.
Cornell, D. (2005) Exploring ubuntu – tentative reflections. In F. Herrschaft (ed.) *Felicia Herrschaft Publications*, accessed 15 January 2012. www.fehe.org/index.php?id=281
Cornell, D. (2008, 10 September) Ubuntu, pluralism and the responsibility of legal academics to the new South Africa. Inaugural lecture, Department of Private Law, Faculty of Law, University of Cape Town.
Cornell, D. and van Marle, K. (2005) Exploring ubuntu – tentative reflections. *African Human Rights Law Journal* 5 (2), 195–220, accessed 15 January 2012. www.chr.up.ac.za/images/files/publications/ahrlj/ahrlj_vol05_no2_2005.pdf
Denzin, N. (ed.) (1970/2006) *Sociological Methods: A Sourcebook* (5th edn). New Brunswick, NJ: Transaction.
Diawara, M. (2000) Globalisation, development politics and local knowledge. *International Sociology* 15 (2), 361–371.
Eagleton, T. (1999) Review of *A critique of post-colonial reason: Toward a history of the vanishing present* by Gayatri Chakravorty Spivak. 1999. *London Review of Books* 21 (10), 3–6.
Egziabher T.B.G. (2007) People-based globalisation. In B.S. Santos (ed) *Another Knowledge is Possible: Beyond Northern Epistemologies*. London: Verso.
Elbow, P. (1991) Reflections on academic discourse: How it relates to freshmen and colleagues. *College English* 53 (2), 135–155.
Flavell, H. (2006) Writing-between: Australian and Canadian ficto-criticism. PhD thesis, Murdoch University, Perth, WA.
Geertz, C. (1988) *Works and Lives: The Anthropologist as Author*. Stanford, CA: Stanford University Press.

Gunew, S. (2001) Technologies of the self: Corporeal affects of English. *The South Atlantic Quarterly* 100 (3), 729–747.

Hall, S. (1990) Cultural identity and diaspora. In J. Rutherford (ed.) *Identity: Community, Culture, Difference*. London: Lawrence & Wishart.

Hoggart, R. (1957) *The Uses of Literacy*. London: Chatto & Windus.

Hooks, B. (1990) Marginality as a site of resistance. In R. Fergusson, M. Gever, T.T. Minh-Ha and C. West (eds) *Out there: Marginalization and Contemporary Cultures*. Cambridge, MA: MIT.

Houndonji, P. (2002) *The Struggle for Meaning: Reflections on Philosophy, Culture, and Democracy in South Africa*. Athens, OH: Ohio University Press.

Ingleton, C., McGowan, U. and Brine, J. (1996, 18–19 April) The dance of the PhD: Steps with international students. Paper presented at the International conference on Quality in Postgraduate Research: Is it happening? Adelaide, South Australia.

Lakoff, R.T. (1990) *Talking Power: The Politics of Language*. New York: Basic Books.

Ling, M.L. (2004) Methodology of decolonizing gender and international development: A view from China. MA thesis, Faculty of Graduate Studies, University of British Columbia, Vancouver.

Lorde, A. (1984) *Sister Outsider*. Berkeley, CA: The Crossing Press.

Lyons, S.R. (2000) What do American Indians want from writing? *College Composition and Communication* 51 (3), 447–468.

Mangena, F. (2009) The search for an African feminist ethic: A Zimbabwean perspective. *Journal of International Women's Studies* 11 (2), 18–30, accessed 03 March 2011. www.bridgew.edu/soas/jiws/Nov09v2/Fainos.pdf

Marika, R. (2000) Valuing Yolnu knowledge in the Australian education system. *TESOL in Context* 10 (2), 45–52.

Maurais, J. (2003) Towards a new global linguistic order? In J. Maurais and M.A. Morris (eds) *Languages in a Globalising World*. Cambridge, UK: Cambridge University Press.

Mbiti, J.S. (1992) *African Religions and Philosophy* (2nd edn). London: Heinemann.

McCandless, E., Bangura, A.K., King, M.E. and Sall, E. (eds) (2007) *Peace Research for Africa: Critical Essays on Methodology*. Addis Ababa, Ethiopia: University for Peace, Africa Program.

Mihesua, D.A. (ed.) (1998) *Natives and Academics: Researching and Writing About American Indians*. Lincoln, NE: University of Nebraska Press.

Mihesua, D.A. and Wilson, A.C. (2004) *Indigenising the Academy: Transforming Scholarship and Empowering Communities*. Lincoln, NE: University of Nebraska Press.

Morrell, R. and Swart, S. (2005) Men in the third world: Postcolonial perspectives on masculinity. In M. Kimmel, J. Hearn and R. Connell (eds) *Handbook of Studies on Men and Masculinities*. Thousand Oaks, CA: Sage.

Moreton-Robinson, A. (2004) Whiteness, epistemology and Indigenous representation. In A. Moreton-Robinson (ed.) *Whitening Race: Essays in Social and Cultural Criticism*. Canberra, ACT: Aboriginal Studies Press.

Nakata, M. (2006) Australian Indigenous studies: A question of discipline. *The Australian Journal of Anthropology* 17 (3), 265–275.

O'Brien, M. (2002) First-hand experiences of a learner from a diverse culture. *TESOL in Context* 12 (2), 3–8, accessed 17 March 2012. www.tesol.org.au/esl/docs/O'Brien.pdf

Odora-Hoppers, C. (2002) *Indigenous Knowledge and the Integration of Knowledge Systems*. Cape Town: New Africa.

Parker, B. (2003) Back on the chain gang: Some difficulties in developing a (South) African philosophy of education. *Journal of Education* 30, 23–40.

Patanakan, M. and Kidokoro, T. (2005) Local government initiative on community building approach: Case study of Phitsanulok Municipality, Thailand. Proceedings of the 8th International Conference of the Asian Planning Schools Association (11–14 September). Online document: www.lingfeiqi.cn/uploads/soft/201103/6_14143726.pdf

Pennycook, A. (2000) Disinventing standard English, Review of *Standard English: Widening the debate* by T. Bex and R. Watts (eds) 1999. *English Language and Linguistics* 7 (4), 115–124.

Porsanger, J. (2004) An essay about Indigenous methodology. *Nordlit,* 15 (Special issue on Northern Minorities), 105–120, accessed 10 November 2010. www.ub.uit.no/munin/bitstream/10037/906/1/article.pdf

Preece, J. (2006) Lifelong learning and development: A perspective from the South. *Compare: A Journal of Comparative and International Education* 39 (5), 585–599.

Preece, J. (2009) Beyond the learning society: The learning world? *International Journal of Lifelong Education* 25 (3), 307–320.

Rigney, L.I. (1999) Internationalisation of an indigenous anti-colonial cultural critique of research methodologies: A guide to 'indigenist research methodology' and its principles. *WICAZO SA Review: Journal of Native American Studies* 14 (2), 109–122.

Rigney, L. (2001) A first perspective of indigenous Australian participation in science: Framing indigenous research towards indigenous Australian intellectual sovereignty. *Kaurna Higher Education Journal* 7, 1–13.

Rigney, L.I. (2006) Indigenist research and Aboriginal Australia. In J. Kunnie and N.I. Goduka (eds) *Indigenous People's Wisdoms and Power: Affirming our Knowledges Through Narrative.* London: Ashgate.

Santos, B.S. (1995) *Toward a New Common Sense: Law, Science and Politics in the Paradigmatic Transition.* New York: Routledge.

Santos, B.S. (1999) On oppositional postmodernism. In R. Munck and D. O'Hearn (eds) *Critical Development Theory.* London: Zed.

Santos, B.S. (2007) *Another Knowledge is Possible: Beyond Northern Epistemologies.* London: Verso.

Santos, B.S., Nunes, J.A. and Meneses, M.P. (2007) Introduction: Opening up the canon of knowledge and recognition of difference. In B.S. Santos (ed.) *Another Knowledge is Possible: Beyond Northern Epistemologies.* London: Verso.

Scheurich, J.J. (1997) *Research Method in the Postmodern.* London: Falmer Press.

Scheurich, J.J. and Young, M.D. (1998) Rejoinder: In the United States, in both our souls and our sciences, we are avoiding white racism. *Educational Researcher* 27 (9), 27–32.

Seale, C. (1999) Quality in qualitative research. *Qualitative Inquiry* 5 (4), 465–478.

Sengupta, S. (2005) Editorial. *Journal of English for Academic Purposes* (Special Edition on Advanced Academic Literacy) 4 (4), 353–367.

Serpell, R. (2007) Bridging between orthodox western higher education practices and an African sociocultural context. *Comparative Education* 43 (1), 23–51.

Sitas, A. (2006) The African renaissance challenge and sociological reclamations in the south. *Current Sociology* 54 (3), 357–380.

Smith, L.T. (1999) *Decolonising Methodologies: Research and Indigenous Peoples.* London: Zed Books.

Spivak, G.C. (1988) 'Can the subaltern speak?' In C. Nelson and L. Grossberg (eds) *Marxism and the Interpretation of Culture.* Basingstoke, UK: Macmillan.

Spivak, G.C. (1990) The intervention interview, with T. Threadgold and F. Bartowski. In G. Spivak (ed.) *The Postcolonial Critic: Interviews, Strategies, Dialogues.* New York: Routledge.

Steinhauer, E. (2002) Thoughts on an Indigenous research methodology. *Canadian Journal of Native Education* 26 (2), 69–81.
St. Pierre, E. (2000) Poststructural feminism in education: An overview. *Qualitative Studies in Education* 13 (5), 477–515.
Tikly, L. (2004) Education and the new imperialism. *Comparative Education* 40 (2), 173–198.
Umulliko (Indigenous Higher Education Research Centre) (2006) Indigenous research methodology? University of Newcastle, New South Wales, Australia, accessed 14 October 2010. www.newcastle.edu.au/centre/umulliko/indigenousresearchmethodology/index.html
University of Adelaide (2010) *Research Student Handbook 2011*. Online document: www.adelaide.edu.au/graduatecentre/handbook/
Walwicz, A. (1997) No, no, no: The reluctant debutante. *Meanjin* 56, 334–337.
Warrior, R. (1999) The Native American scholar: Towards a new Intellectual agenda. *WICAZO Review: Journal of Native American Studies* 14 (2), 46–55.
Williams, R. (1965) *The Long Revolution*. Harmondsworth: Penguin.
Wilson, S. (1995) Honoring spiritual knowledge. *Canadian Journal of Native Education* 21 (Supp.), 61–69.
Zhou, Y. and Hu, M. (2005) E-commerce ethics problem and countermeasure of China on the basis of systematic thinking. Proceedings of the 7th International Conference on Electronic Commerce (15–17 August). Online document: www.dl.acm.org/citation.cfm?doid=1089551.1089683

Part 4
Reading the World in Students' Writing

8 'Error' or Ghost Text? Reading, Ethnopoetics and Knowledge Making

Mary Scott

Bourdieu (1994: 94) asks, 'Can anyone read anything at all without wondering what it is that reading means?' His primary purpose is to draw attention to the social conditions pertaining to where, what and how readers read. In this chapter, I suggest that the 'where', 'what' and 'how' of reading are always multilayered and intertwined on the cusp of the actual and the ideological. At the level of the actual, the 'where' is a physical location, the postgraduate college in London at which I am a teacher–researcher, and the 'what' are final drafts of students' master's degree assignments. At the ideological level, however, 'where' extends to the norm-laden environment of regulation and expectation whereby 'what' is read and 'how' it is read are subject to the criteria used to assess students' writing in a particular field of study. In this chapter, that field is education and the related social sciences.

This multilayered approach to reading raises questions of risk for the teacher who is also a researcher. As a teacher my concern is to help student writers avoid the risk of failure; that is I am anxious to help them conform to the expected norms of academic writing. However, as a researcher I have come increasingly to question those norms and to search for ways of reading student writing differently. This involves my taking the risk of challenging conventional expectations by focusing on those aspects of a student's text which represent a lack of conformity in small but significant ways to given assessment criteria. Reading differently has also led me to perceive where students' attempts to play it safe by following the conventions of academic writing are interrupted or complicated by what cannot be contained by the expected norms.

Working within this framework for reading and risk, I ground this chapter's specific concerns in the context of the increasing mobility of students across countries, languages and fields of study. For example, according to the January 2012 registry statistics of the college where I teach, students from 100 countries (excluding the United Kingdom) were enrolled in various courses. If one includes the students from the United Kingdom, hundreds of different languages and dialects are represented among the student body. In addition, the interdisciplinarity of the education and related social-science faculties, combined with the modularisation of master's degree courses, often requires students to traverse disciplines that are new to them.

In responding to the diversity that is a corollary of this level of student mobility, universities in the United Kingdom have attempted to reduce the risk of student failure by initially focusing mainly on 'non-native speakers of English from outside the UK'. For example, since the 1970s, when the British Association of Lecturers in English for Academic Purposes drew attention to this group of students, a number of presessional and insessional courses have been developed. These courses have a range of titles that reflect course designers' or institutions' different priorities, such as English for Academic Purposes, Academic Writing, Academic Literacy, Academic and Professional Literacies or Academic Communication. Under the widening participation agenda that arose in the early 1990s, the college where I teach opened insessional courses in academic writing to students who wish, or are advised by teachers, to enrol. This is an increasing trend across the United Kingdom. The main objective of presessional and insessional courses tends to be to increase the students' resources for knowledge making in English. Teachers who run the courses usually seek to achieve this by focusing on the language forms, generic structures and discursive conventions which they consider likely to contribute to the success of students' assignments and dissertations. Take, for example, the following course overviews that appear on the website of the Institute of Education – London:

Grammar for Academic Writing

Overview: This course will focus on the language forms used in academic writing. It will explore the importance of audience and purpose and will also investigate how grammatical choices are more than just rules, but are a powerful means of enabling our readers to access complex and nuanced meaning in academic writing.

Dissertations 1: Abstracts and Literature Reviews

- To look at the language and organisations commonly used in abstracts and literature review sections of the dissertation

- To consider ways in which research can be described
- To look at strategies for handling the literature and integrating the findings with the literature review[1]

As is typical of English-writing courses, the examples above aim to introduce students to an understanding of the expected normativities (Blommaert, 2011) of academic writing. In courses such as these, teachers tend to place the production of a text in a context that takes into account meaning making, purpose, audience and ways of producing the required parts of a dissertation. The classes are clearly valued by student participants, especially since the tendency to prescription can be mitigated in actual classroom contexts. For example, a teacher of the course on 'Grammar for Academic Writing' has spoken to me of her dialogic style of teaching in which she aims to take account of the diversity of her students' knowledge and prior experience. The verbs 'explore' and 'consider' contained in the course descriptions cited above also suggest a role for the students' voices.

Inevitably though, in view of student numbers and time constraints as well as the institutional positioning of the teachers, many presessional and insessional courses conform to a generic view of students as needy and teachers as suppliers of what is needed. Threaded through the courses is an assessment-focused narrative, in which education tends to be seen as a journey from one measured level to a higher measured level and which culminates in the student being awarded a degree and, with this, an institutional identity. As a subject teacher, I am mindful of this narrative – and of my institutional positioning and responsibilities in relation to it – and there is nothing in the institution's presessional and insessional writing-in-English courses, which I consider irrelevant to a successful master's degree.

My focus as a researcher is different, though. Adopting more of a research role for this chapter, I will seek to redescribe the student journey. The description is derived from my readings of student writing, in which I view the writer of the text as socially and historically shaped. This perspective tends to be made invisible in the assessment of student writing, or, when visible, is regarded as evidence of deficiencies related to particular educational and linguistic histories. It is, however, a perspective that can lend complexity to the implications of student mobility, and include related issues of power. It thus invites a rethinking of issues of pedagogy within a wider framing of education that takes cognisance of the increasing diversity of student histories. It also raises questions around what counts (and what might count) as 'academic writing'. In my conclusion, I suggest briefly how the perspectives of teacher and researcher might be brought together.

'Error' or Ghost Text?

My starting point is Blommaert's (2010: 6) reminder that

> The movement of people across space is ... never a move across empty spaces: They [the spaces] are filled with norms and expectations, conceptions of what counts as proper, normal ... and what does not count as such.

In this chapter, short excerpts from marked student assignments represent conceptions of what 'does not count as proper'. In each excerpt, the teacher–markers sought to draw the student writer's attention to what they saw as breaching one or other of the normativities of academic writing. I loosely group these infringements under the term 'errors' since some kind of textual remedy was called for. However, seeking a term that might both accommodate 'error' as deviation from an established norm in academic writing while extending its implications, I arrived at the word 'style'. I chose this term because of its flexibility of reference. Although it may, for example, be conflated with conformity to particular patterns of grammar and usage (Butler, 2010), it more frequently suggests qualities that I regard as socially contextualised (such as notions of appropriacy or individuality in writing; i.e. implicit normativities, e.g. writing an argument). Comments on style may also resist explicit norm-based description when they mainly reflect the readers' socially formed, biographical expectations. Examples that I have encountered in teacher–markers' comments include the following: 'an elegant style'; 'the writing is pedestrian'; 'a lively piece that held my interest'.

To put it metaphorically, my aim is to read for possible ghost texts in teacher–markers' perceptions of errors of style; that is, to look for what 'errors' hide or make invisible in the text. Although my readings are speculative, I hope that they will draw attention – both theoretical and pedagogical – to ways of reading student writing, that are grounded in an awareness of student mobility across countries and educational systems. Since such mobility is a feature of higher education in many countries, my suggested way of reading may perhaps raise questions and challenges for further discussion.

Seeking a Methodological Frame

The ghost texts I discuss emerge from a reading of the final drafts of master's assignments written by three students. All three students had been educated outside the United Kingdom and were categorised institutionally as 'EU/international' students for whom English was a 'second language'.

A requirement of the assignment was that it includes references to their own countries. In each case, the teacher–marker suggested that the student's text infringed norms of academic style in some small way.

From my positioning as a writing teacher, I attempted to help the students to remedy these perceived errors of style. However, to describe the ghost texts that I saw as being obscured by the normative focus of the original marker of the assignment, I constructed a methodological frame with which to analyse each piece of work. This works as follows:

- I begin by looking for the student writer in the text, an analytical concept that I intend as a contrast to assessment-shaped, ascribed identities (such as an MA candidate).
- I then introduce multimodal semiosis (or multimodal knowledge making) as an alternative to viewing text simply as a set of linguistic/grammatical forms.
- Finally I consider ethnopoetics, which has the potential to link student mobility to the sociocultural–sociopolitical histories suggested by certain textual or 'poetic' features of the ghost texts.

Reading the Student Writer in the Text

In this process, I seek to replace technocratic, assessment-related student identities with an emphasis on the student writer as a 'textualised self'. I owe this description to Bartholomae (1985) and consider it appropriate in its focus on the written product as an integration of text and self. I draw on Kress's (2010) statement that a text represents the writer's (conscious and intuitive) 'interests' at the moment of writing, both in order to extend Bartholomae's description and to include the notion of subjectivity. However, in this situation, subjectivity does not denote a Romantic conception of the writer as engaged in self-expression. I associate it instead with imagination as conceptualised in writing on academic literacies; that is, imagination as socially constructed, rather than as an inner mental capacity (see Kenway & Fahey, 2009).

When linked to imagination in this way, subjectivity can function as a contrast to a conception of identity as static and ascribed (as in the educational narrative I have described) and can accommodate the self's 'interest' (Kress, 2010) as imagined at the moment of writing (and the teacher's 'interest' at the moment of reading).

As I hope to show, this perspective on subjectivity/imagination can also lead to a view of the writer as having been, and still being, ideologically and affectively shaped within a wider context of national and international histories and interconnections (e.g. as suggested by Appadurai, 1996, 2004). It can thus give a different resonance to errors of style in student texts in the context of a university, in which the mobility of students is reflected in a marked diversity in students' linguistic and educational histories.

Knowledge Making as Multimodal Semiosis

I then focus on knowledge making as the social production of signs. Here, I find relevance in Kress's (2010) social-semiotic view of signs as produced by individuals representing particular social relations in specific social contexts. To this I add multimodality. Thus, where Kress sees writing as a separate mode and multimodality as primarily a combination of writing and image, I approach writing itself as multimodal; that is, as multimodal semiosis. When a student text is read from this perspective, the whole text comes into view, not just as words, but as a sign constructed from a set of multimodal resources, which include the handwriting or a selected font, the layout, the choice of surface (determined by a student's access to particular kinds of paper, computers and printers, etc.) as well as the sentence rhythms and sound images (such as alliteration or onomatopoeia). These can all be read as signifiers, and can act as readers' 'prompts' (Kress, 2010), in ways that are very different from the promptings of generally accepted linguistic norms. Consequently there is, as I hope to show, a narrowing of the conventional gap between academic writing and devices used in poetry.

A quote from De Certeau (1984) – in which he criticises the scriptural (or written) economy as oppressive of the oral/poetic aspects of writing (which are nonetheless present) – leads me back to the student in the text, and to issues of power. De Certeau writes as follows:

> The place from which one speaks is outside the scriptural enterprise ... but the voice will insert itself into the text as a mark or trace – a ... ghost in the scriptural economy. (De Certeau, 1984: 155, 158)

Freeing possible ghost voices into voices that might be heard (Blommaert, 2005) by teachers and researchers, is a primary motive for the readings I suggest in analysing the three student texts below.

Ethnopoetics as Methodology

Finally, I widen the methodological frame by turning briefly to ethnopoetics (Hymes, 1996). Ethnopoetics was originally used to describe oral narratives and folk art from 'other' cultures, but I would argue that it is also applicable to written texts and, in this chapter, to a different reading of what the teacher–markers perceived as errors in the selected samples of student writing. While the 'ethno' in ethnopoetics needs further consideration in its relation to conceptions of culture and the cultural, the word 'poetics' can direct attention to the undervalued or ignored textual elements; that is, the ghost texts, that may suggest sociocultural/sociopolitical histories.

Blommaert (2006) uses applied ethnopoetics to signal the meeting in a text of two systems of making meaning. However, for me, an ethnopoetic approach to student writing can primarily serve to highlight what tends to be made invisible by the normativities of academic writing. Using ethnopoetics as a methodology can also address the politics of difference. It can give voice to an individual student as a social individual with a history, rather than as someone who is simply ignorant of how to write in English in acceptable academic style. Ethnopoetics is, therefore, particularly pertinent given the diversity that has resulted from student mobility across countries and educational systems.

Ghost Hunting in Student Texts

Example One: Christina's Text

The text below appeared in an assignment by a student whom I refer to as Christina.[2] The assignment was on the teaching of English in the country that Christina comes from – an EU country which I will refer to as Zeta.[3] Christina wrote:

> [Zetean] teachers do not let the students write an essay at an early age. Of course, only letting students write essays at a later age makes the teachers' task easier. They do not need to do so many corrections. Meanings would be clearer. But is writing made easier for students in that way? I doubt it. Students would get less practice. Does practice make perfect then? Burgess (1973) does not seem to think so. Burgess is sure we would not be able to develop children's writing through practice.

In this instance, the teacher–marker singled out aspects of the text as being too close to speech and therefore as stylistically inappropriate in an academic argument. She highlighted the phrase 'of course', and also the question and answer sequences such as, 'But is writing made easier for students in that way? I doubt it. Students would get less practice. Does practice make perfect then?' I read the teacher's comment as resting on those linguistic descriptions of academic argument which emphasise impersonality and a distanced rationality. A primary example of how this might be achieved textually is the use of nominalisation to achieve lexical density (Halliday, 1989). As a teacher, I would want the student to be helped to convert her everyday way of arguing into an academic argument, and also to appreciate how linguistic conventions can contribute to the kind of knowledge being made.

However, my focus in this chapter is on ghost texts. It is here that Hymes's reference to Basil Bernstein's writing experiment with postal-worker students becomes relevant. Hymes (1996: 185) quotes Bernstein who said of the experiment: 'One day I took a piece of student's continuous text and broke it up into lines. The piece took on a new and vital meaning.'

I use Christina's text to illustrate the potential of this ethnopoetic approach. When separated into lines as shown below, the rearrangement converts the points being made into a dramatisation of thinking and rethinking in progress. Each line has its own space and weight, while the spaces between can be filled with the reader's emphases, meanings and questions.

[Zetean] teachers do not let the students write an essay at an early age.

Of course, only letting students write essays at a later age makes the teachers' task easier.

They do not need to do so many corrections.

Meanings would be clearer.

But is writing made easier for students in that way?

I doubt it.

Students would get less practice.

Does practice make perfect then?

Burgess (1973) does not seem to think so.

Burgess is sure we would not be able to develop children's writing through practice.

I want to focus on the last five lines, which represent different voices – ranging from strong opinion ('I doubt it') with a strongly asserted justification, to the different tone used for the two references to Burgess. My suggested reading is that the move from 'Burgess (1973) does not seem to think so' to 'Burgess is sure' points to the student's struggle to find her agency, her voice, in relation to Burgess whose academic authority is emphasised by the inclusion of the publication date, 1973. This leads me to ask: Should 'does not seem to think so' be taken to refer to an uncertainty in Burgess's statement of his position, or in the student's reading of Burgess, or both? And what of 'Burgess is sure'? Where in this question, and in the excerpt as a whole, is the student writer positioning herself as a teacher from Zeta on a course in London?

It seems relevant that in the main part of the essay, drawing on Burgess, the student treats Zetean classrooms as needing, in a sense, to be transformed into English classrooms in London. Is this the kind of transformation which we UK-based tutors assume to be the primary purpose of mobility across educational systems; that is, that students should take what is offered in the United Kingdom and if possible transport it, as is, to another national context? In my reading, the notion of a one-way journey is complicated by the uncertainties in the voice that emerges in the last five lines of Christina's rearranged text.

Example Two: Jacob's Text

Jacob, a student from a small country off the coast of Africa, which I refer to as Mella, produced a draft of his introduction to an essay on education and international development.[4] Here is a brief excerpt from his first paragraph:

> Development has the meaning lent to it (Rist, cited in Paquette, 1994) ... Development becomes meaningful only if it implies change in technology and an increase in material resources. But development cannot be reduced to material productivity or quantitative growth; it depends to a large extent on how equitably potential benefits of productivity are distributed.

The use of abstract nouns relevant to the field of study, the impersonal sentence constructions, the inclusion of a carefully set out reference, the introduction of a counter argument – these are all familiar aspects of writing as presented in academic-English writing courses, or, to adapt Myers (1990) for my own purposes, in the 'narrative of social science as science'.

However, on being advised to, 'put your own country in the introduction', the student rewrote (and reformatted) the introduction using a more intricate font:

This paper proposes to problematise the relationship between education and national development within the Human Capital and Modernization theories, in [Mella]. Both, the Modernization and Human capital theories, inform development strategies in [Mella]. The Modernization theory postulates that education is a vehicle of national development and economic growth (Fagerlind & Saha, 1987: 15). This confidence in the efficacy of education as the agent of modernisation is reinforced by Human Capital theory, which carries an economic focus within Modernisation theory.

In the first section of this essay I will examine the strengths and weaknesses of the Human Capital theory as an offshoot of the Modernisation theory. The second section uses examples from the [Mellian] *experience of development to demonstrate the positives and negatives of relying on the above theories to draw out development strategies. I draw from the* [Mellian] *experience for two reasons:*

- being myself a [Mellian], it is the situation I can best relate to;
- the [Mellian] economic success story has a reverse side to it that is hardly talked about in official documents.

The teacher–reader considered this a better introduction but commented that the English was 'clumsy'. However, I would suggest that the clumsiness is largely the consequence of small punctuation errors (such as the comma in 'Both, Modernization and Human Capital Theory'), which as a teacher I would simply help the student to correct. However, as a researcher, I would argue that these errors point to a ghost text that can be read as indicating that Jacob, as the writer-in-the-text, continues to attach primary importance to theory. I base this conclusion on the following aspects of his redrafted text:

- Jacob retains the academic conventions used in his first draft; for example, abstract nouns still predominate, such as: 'strengths and weaknesses of the Human Capital theory'; 'the Modernisation theory'; 'development strategies'.
- The comma before 'in Mella' (in 'Modernization theories, in Mella') converts the phrase to the status of an aside.
- The phrase 'Both, the Modernization and Human capital theories,' and the commas it contains, visually places the two theories in their own space in the second sentence, and serves to heighten their importance.

I note in particular, though, the choice of the verb 'talked about' in the reference to 'official' Mellian documents. There is a marked contrast between the phrase 'talked about' and the formal academic register Jacob uses to write about theory in the first draft of his introduction. It is a contrast that, I suggest, implicitly places the Mellian documents in the realm of the less academic, that is, the less theorised.

There is also, perhaps, a specifically sociocultural–sociopolitical way in which Jacob has followed the instruction to put his own country in his text. There was a change of font from the Times New Roman used in his first draft to a more intricate font in his revised version. But, perhaps, the most marked of the changes was the replacement of bullet points with the Sanskrit symbol OM, which stands for the source of all existence.

I would argue that economics, in relation to national histories and international interconnections, may be at work in the text, evident especially in Jacob's emphasis on theory and his use of 'talked about' in his reference to Mellian documents. Coming from a small island, without a well-stocked university library, Jacob may have had his own agenda – related to getting knowledge from a former colonising power and avoiding saying too much about his own country.

So, while Christina seemed uncertain as to how to relate her voice to the voice of a published academic authority when considering English teaching in Zeta, Jacob would, it seems, confidently ascribe authority to the ideas he has received during his course in London, but is hesitant to attribute the same level of authority to his experience of his home country.

Example Three: Myra's Text

I will call the third student Myra, and her country of origin, Kanda. She was also following a postgraduate course in education but her response to her geographic and academic mobility seems different from either Christina's or Jacob's.

In her dissertation proposal Myra described her intended research as follows:

> Education in Kanda is characterised by its banding system – schools are categorised from band one (for the highest achievers) to band five (for the lowest achievers). In the functioning of this categorisation, learners are compared, hierarchised and differentiated in terms of their academic achievement Teachers are directed to bring and keep student performance within the lines of legitimacy (Bernstein, 1972: 173). However, this process of normalisation which leaves many underachievers alienated or excluded in schooling is seldom challenged.

My research precisely charts how the literate culture of schooling is 'naturalised' on the grounds of the learners' difference in their command of English as the medium of instruction and how 'literacy' in schooling signposts learners to distinctive ways of orienting to the world and maps them onto different ways of taking meaning.

Like me, several teacher–readers evaluated this text positively. We noted that Myra skilfully weaves the theoretical into her account of Kandian educational practice in, for example, her references to Bernstein, the Foucauldian echoes in her use of the word 'naturalised', and the use of terms such as 'normalisation'. In fact, her text can be said to be saturated with the educational discourse that is characteristic of a particular ideological perspective.

A small error was also noted, however: one of the teacher–readers placed a squiggly line under 'compared, hierarchised and differentiated' and 'tone this down' was written in the margin of the text. This 'error' of style led me to look for a ghost text. I read Myra's deployment of the three adjoined verbs ('compared, hierarchised and differentiated') as indicating her strength of feeling. I see this as having been visually reinforced by the use of brackets in 'band one (for the highest achievers) to band five (for the lowest achievers)'. I suggest, therefore, that Myra is angered by the hierarchical process of differentiation and discrimination, and is intent on bringing about change in educational practice in her country of origin so that the 'alienated or excluded' might be liberated.

An Overview of Three Ghost Texts and the Questions They Prompt

I have presented three different ghost texts representing three different ways in which I read the student writers' mobility across countries as possibly having shaped their writing. As Blommaert (2005) has observed, individuals write both in and from a place.

While Christina is uncertain of the relevance of her knowledge and experience in Zeta vis-à-vis the authority of the text published in the United Kingdom, Jacob from Mella tends to ascribe an authority to the ideas encountered during his course over and above his own knowledge of his own country. For him, mobility includes acquiring and valuing the theory offered on his London-based course.

Myra, on the contrary, views the theory she is encountering on her course as a weapon that she can use to turn the tables on educational administrators in Kanda. Her 'precise charting' suggests the accuracy of her mappings in contrast to the imperfections of theirs. I would suggest that the intensity of Myra's sense of injustice almost certainly contributed to her understanding of the readings she encountered on her course. Unlike Christina or Jacob, Myra brings her reading and her concerns into a collaborative relationship. But if the norms of academic argument were strictly applied, might she be in danger of substituting assertion for a carefully argued case?

This brings me to a key question, derived from my readings of the ghost texts, namely, What might the instruction to 'refer to your own country' mean textually if one regards the writer in the text as having been shaped by national histories and international inter-relations? Can only the distanced be included under academic writing? Why not a satire? A debate? A poem? I am reminded of Fiona English's (2011) work on 'regenring' (which encourages writers to bend genres including academic essays). However, what I am suggesting focuses primarily on rethinking what 'education' might mean in place of the current emphasis in the United Kingdom on 'performativity', that is, a focus on a narrow range of forms and functions rather than on knowledge making (see Ball, 2003).

Conclusion

In this chapter, I have sought to suggest that perceived lapses in style, when analysed ethnopoetically, might be more appropriately conceived as ghost texts; that is, as texts which are made invisible or ghostly by a readers' focus on the conventions of academic writing. With an ethnopoetic lens, errors might become, not ghosts to be exorcised, but 'fertile facts' (Virginia Woolf, quoted in Gordon, 2006: 366) which might lead us to consider the possible merging of individual, national and international histories and structures of feeling (Williams, 1977).

The chapter has focused on the writing of students from outside the United Kingdom. I would hope, though, that the chapter might provoke a discussion of individual and national histories and interrelations as they affect students in the United Kingdom and in other countries. In fact, I would like to suggest that future research take further the issues around how 'academic writing' is read and does so in a partnership involving students and teachers working on joint projects in several countries.

But what of classroom practice? I have indicated where I shared the teacher–markers' perceptions of error and I have stated that I am not rejecting the norms of academic writing out-of-hand. What I would suggest, though, is that the distinction between teaching and research should be recognised as unhelpful. I do not simply mean that all teaching can be said to involve individual research. What I envisage is a change in the institutional positioning of the able individuals who currently teach courses in academic and professional literacies. In spite of their range of knowledge and experience, these teachers tend to be regarded in many UK universities as providing a 'fixit' service for student writers rather than as individuals with knowledge and experience that could be valuable for academic writing (as well as disciplinary) courses, that are grounded in the need to pay attention to the sociocultural–sociopolitical histories of established norms.

But what I would like to emphasise even more strongly is the importance of the student's voice, that is, of not disabling it but allowing it to be heard in discussions of diversity, in which students' ideas are seen as a resource, and both students and teachers are seen as teacher–researchers exploring the educational possibilities of student mobility across countries, languages and educational systems with all the risks that this entails.

This brings me back to the technocratic educational narrative with which I began, namely, education as a journey from one measured level of achievement to a higher level. In its most decontextualised (i.e. dehistoricised and deterritorialised) mode in the context of formal assessment, the 'risk' of the journey for students (and teachers) tends to be conflated with 'playing it safe' – that is, attempting to conform to stated assessment norms. However, in this chapter I have offered an ethnopoetic reading of student writing which is sensitive to time space and opens up possibilities for risk taking in a generative sense. Consequently, I would hope that my focus on student writing as affectively and ideologically shaped by national and international histories and inter-relations, might encourage teachers to ground their reading of student texts in the larger sociocultural–sociopolitical aims and concerns so often neglected in education when student writing is the topic of discussion.

But finally, who is this 'I' that has read and commented on these small pieces of student writing (Cooper, 1998), and has attempted to make new knowledge for herself as a teacher–researcher? What are my ghost texts? I will not attempt to answer this question here, but in keeping with the paper's emphasis on the poetic and implicit I will end with a quotation from T.S. Eliot. I hope that, recontextualised in this chapter it will work, as poetry, to suggest the importance of ghost texts to knowledge making in reading and writing.

> When I count, there are only you and I together
> But when I look ahead up the white road
> There is always another one walking beside you
> ....
> But who is that on the other side of you?[5]

Notes

(1) Accessed at www.ioe.ac.uk on 31 January 2012.
(2) Text in this section of the chapter draws on my discussion of Christina's work in Scott (2013).
(3) My institution's ethics policy requires that anonymity regarding name and country be respected unless the student requests that these details be revealed.
(4) I have written about this example before (see Scott, 2005), but in this chapter I draw on ethnopoetics to provide a different framing.
(5) T.S. Eliot (1922) *The Wasteland*, lines 360–365, in *Collected Poems 1902–1962*. New York: Harcourt Brace.

References

Appadurai, A. (1996) *Modernity at Large: Cultural Dimensions of Globalization*. Minnesota: University of Minnesota Press.
Appadurai, A. (2004) The capacity to aspire. In V. Rao and M. Walton (eds) *Culture and Public Action*. Stanford, CA: Stanford University Press.
Ball, S. (2003) The teacher's soul and the terrors of performativity. *Journal of Educational Policy* 18 (2), 25–28.
Bartholomae, D. (1985) Inventing the university. In M. Rose (ed.) *When a Writer Can't Write: Studies in Writer's Block and Other Composing-process Problems*. New York: Guilford.
Blommaert, J. (2005) *Discourse*. Oxford: Oxford University Press.
Blommaert, J. (2006) Applied ethnopoetics. *Narrative Inquiry* 16 (1), 181–190.
Blommaert, J. (2010) *The Sociolinguistics of Globalization*. Cambridge: Cambridge University Press.
Blommaert, J. (2011) Normativities (from unpublished notes given to Mary Scott).
Bourdieu, P. (1994) *In Other Words: Essays Towards a Reflexive Sociology*. Cambridge: Polity Press.
Butler, P. (2010) (ed.) *Style in Rhetoric and Composition: A Critical Sourcebook*. Boston, NY: Bedford Books.
Cooper, B. (1998) *Magical Realism in West African Fiction: Seeing With a Third Eye*. London: Routledge.
De Certeau, M. (1984) *The Practice of Everyday Life* (trans. S. Rendall). Berkeley: University of California Press.
English, F. (2011) *Student Writing and Genre: Reconfiguring Academic Knowledge*. London: Continuum.
Gordon, L. (2006) *Virginia Woolf: A Writer's Life* (revised edition). London: Virago.
Halliday, M.A.K. (1989) *Spoken and Written Language* (2nd edn). Oxford: Oxford University Press.
Hymes, D. (1996) *Ethnography, Linguistics, Narrative Inequality: Toward an Understanding of Voice*. London: Taylor & Francis.
Kenway, J. and Fahey, J. (eds) (2009) *Globalizing the Research Imagination*. London: Routledge.
Kress, G. (2010) *Multimodality: A Social Semiotic Approach to Contemporary Communication*. New York: Routledge.
Myers, G. (1990) *Writing Biology: Texts in the Social Construction of Scientific Knowledge*. Madison, WI: University of Wisconsin Press.

Scott, M. (2005) Student writing, assessment and the motivated sign: Finding a theory for the times. *Journal of Assessment and Evaluation in Higher Education* 30 (3), 297–305.
Scott, M. (2013) From error to multimodal semiosis: Reading student writing differently. In M. Böck and N. Pachler (eds) *Multimodality and Social Semiosis: Communication, Meaning-Making and Learning in the Work of Gunther Kress*. New York & London: Routledge.
Williams, R. (1977) *Marxism and Literature*. Oxford: Oxford University Press.

9 'It Was Hardly about Writing': Translations of Experience on Entering Postgraduate Studies

Moeain Arend

This chapter tells a series of stories and shows that storytelling is not neutral; it is an activity at the heart of which lies an attempt at social ordering. Law (1994: 53) argues that while we 'create and recreate our stories we make and remake both the facts of which they tell, and ourselves'. The stories told here could have many possible beginnings and endings, depending on what is incorporated and what is deleted, as well as the position of the storyteller, the characters and the audience.

Story One draws on a section of a short story written by Herman Charles Bosman, and serves to caution readers that when stories do not conform to the conventions of well-known genres, they often order readers in unexpected ways. The advice that Bosman offers in his story sets the scene for stories told later in the chapter. Story Two is about the makers of the recognition of prior learning (RPL) policy at the University of Cape Town (UCT) and Story Three is about Sadia, a student doing her master's in adult education at the same university. Story Two and Story Three tell of the protagonists' attempts at ordering the world around them through their literacies[1] and associated literacy practices. Drawing on actor-network theory (ANT) and on its concept of translation,[2] I attempt to uncover the intentions and effects of both the policy makers' and Sadia's ordering attempts. In doing so, the stories aim to highlight the heroism of their struggles. As Law (1994: 100) notes, the stories that ANT theorists tell tend 'towards the heroic' because agency is an uncertain and risky achievement. In this sense, risk is at the heart of the individual and collective attempts at ordering.

Although subheadings clearly signal the beginning and the end of these three stories, a fourth story 'hovers' over the chapter. Story Four is, in many ways, captured in the chapter's opening lines, and threads through the other stories. It is but one of many possible stories that could be told about the collective struggles of those seeking to understand and ask questions about the postgraduate condition. Considering Bosman's advice in Story One, I had to resist the temptation to sew Story Four into a neat and well-packaged whole – a demand often made of writers in academia. Instead, I attempt to discard some of the ways of writing and theorising that have become 'familiar' to me in order to experiment with others. Needless to say, risk lies at the centre of storytelling as a form of social ordering, and so I tread carefully.

Story One

In a short story titled 'Old Transvaal Story', Herman Charles Bosman unexpectedly breaks with his narrative to offer his readers some advice on the pitfalls of expecting a love story to fit the dominant genre that most of us are familiar with. Some see authors who break away from the known as indulging in undistilled quixotism, while others believe that to risk discarding the known and to explore other ways of storytelling is heroic. Bosman observes:

> Woven on the common pattern of boy-meets-girl, one love story, in respect of its external shape, seems very much the same as another. And it is always at the very moment when you fancy that you have recognised the type of a love story, when you have pigeon-holed it in your mind as belonging to such and such a category – it is at that very moment that you are betrayed; for, lo, there is sudden witchery, and a wand is waved, and it is as though a line of African dancers comes running in suddenly, and you find that a whole number of people are laughing at you from behind the feathers and painted wood of their Congo masks. One must be careful about classifying a love story, tabulating and cataloguing it as belonging to a certain subsection of a particular group – indexing it and labelling it as conforming, in respect of characters and plot and incident, to a well-known and clearly recognised pattern. (Bosman, 1948/2004: 3–4)

Although writers attempt to order, and re-order their social environments, many a time – as shown later in the chapter through the discussion of ANT and the telling of the other stories – the agents we write about possess no innate willingness to 'conform to' or 'obey' a preconceived storyline. Many surprise you just as you attempt to stabilise their identities by pigeonholing them – pigeonholes are but masks that hide the witchery of the competing stories that might contest a neatly written script. In fact, all human beings as agents – storytellers, writers or readers – are 'an effect, an effect of more or less unsuccessful ordering struggles' (Law, 1994: 100).

Attempts at Social Ordering

> ANT is a theory of the site of the social. It sees human and non-human agents, and the interactions between them as potentially having equal weight. Thus, ANT attempts to dissolve the boundaries between human and non-human agents in any social context.

> ANT is not the empty claim that objects do things 'instead' of human actors: it simply says that no science of the social can even begin if the question of who and what participates in the action is not first of all thoroughly explored, even though it might mean letting elements in which, for lack of a better term, we would call *non-humans*. (Latour, 2005: 72, emphasis in original)

Therefore, human and non-human agents ordered through social activity are all seen as actors enabling certain actions within a network of relations. Law (1994: 33) describes humans – and by implication non-human agents – as networks of 'artful arrangements of bits and pieces' and as 'fragile process[es] of network[ed] associated elements'. Therefore, no human or non-human agents can escape being part of a network or multiple networks. Latour (2005) defines an actor network as a heterogeneous network of aligned interests and objects, while Law (1994) refers to networks as metaphors for the way in which meanings, and other effects (including agency), are generated within and by a network of relations between various actors.

Law also argues that all actors may be considered relational effects but cautions that these effects *should not* be considered unified or homogenous. In essence, he claims that actors are effects of more or less unsuccessful attempts at social ordering. An actor is 'a spokesperson, a figurehead, or a more or less opaque "black box" which stands for, conceals, defines, holds in place, mobilizes and draws on, a set of juxtaposed bits and pieces' (Law, 1994: 101). Therefore, Law claims, no real permanent social order exists, only various attempts at social ordering.

Latour (2005: 29) proposes that '[t]he first source of uncertainty' that sociologists should consider is 'that there is no relevant group' that comprises the social and 'no established component that can be used as an incontrovertible starting point'. He critiques the starting points of many social inquiries in which social scientists deem it prudent to identify homogeneous and 'neatly packaged' groupings – a process they claim is necessary under the 'obligation to limit one's scope' or 'the right of a scientist to define one's object' (Latour, 2005: 29). ANT theorists do not see themselves as having a duty to stabilise the social or to offer the reader 'neatly packaged' groupings. Instead, the ANT researchers' maxim is: *Do not attempt to stabilize!* Latour (2005: 30) notes that

> this is a better way for the vocabulary of the actors to be heard loud and clear – and I am not especially worried if it is the social scientists' jargon that is being downplayed. If I had to provide a checklist for what is a good ANT account – this will be an important indicator of quality – are the concepts of the actors allowed to be *stronger* than that of the analysts, or is it the analyst who is doing all the talking? As far as writing reports are concerned, it means a precise but difficult trial: Is the text that comments on the various quotes and documents more, less, or as interesting as the actors' own expressions and behaviours? If you find this test too easy to meet, then ANT is not for you.

Actor-network theorists refer to any attempt at social ordering as *translation*. The process of translation involves four key moments, namely *problematisation, interessement, enrolment* and *mobilisation*.

Clarke (2002) argues that during *problematisation*, actors attempt to invent or displace a particular goal or problem. The actor inventing or displacing a particular goal or problem becomes the network's gatekeeper (or, to use Law's term, the translator). During this moment, gatekeepers or translators make themselves indispensable to the network by defining the problem. They, and other key actors, establish who or what other actors form part of the network, claim to know what their needs are, and work towards convincing them that the roles assigned to them are acceptable (Clarke, 2002).

Clarke notes that *interessement* and *enrolment* must not be seen as consecutive, but rather as moments during which translators attempt to accomplish two goals, namely: to exclude competing interests and definitions that might exist among actors; and to secure alliances among the actors in the network. Enrolment, she argues, is the aim of interessement. Kendall and Wickham (2003) argue that interessement is the act whereby translators strive to stabilise the identity of another actor by stabilising their own links with that actor while weakening the links the actor has with other actors. During enrolment, the actors take on the problematisation of the network as their own, accepting the roles assigned to them during the process of interessement.

When actors are *mobilised* successfully they are metamorphosed or mutated in such a way that they become manageable entities within the network once the translator has successfully achieved the other three moments. Clarke (2002: 117) notes that: '[Actors] that have been successfully translated [and therefore mobilised] are like carefully packaged suitcases which glide smoothly round the airport carousel or stack tidily in the luggage compartments on a train.'

Failures in the translation process create instability in a network and interfere with mobilisation. Clarke (2002) argues that attempts at ordering can be disrupted if alternative problematisations, definitions and perspectives challenge the definitions established by the translators during interessement. She warns that '[m]ore difficult to mobilise are the contested entities which, like carrier bags and chicken hampers and cardboard boxes tied with string, threaten to burst open and spill their messy contents' (Clarke, 2002: 117). Failures in the translation process create opportunities for researchers to bring the original problematisation, identities, roles and assumed interests of actors into the spotlight.

Law (1994) argues that agency and size – in conjunction with non-human agents, social entities, and every other kind of object or artefact – are always the unpredictable effects spewed out by networks and their idiosyncratic forms of interaction. These effects are constituted as objects or artefacts only for as long as the network experiences stability. Actors, in essence, act in a certain way because they embody the ordering effects produced by a network and its modes of interaction. This implies that instabilities in a particular network can be attributed to the effects of competing networks. When instabilities occur, actors' attempts at social ordering become more visible, as do the risks taken at either a collective or individual level. However, it is interesting to note that it is precisely at moments of instability – when the 'well-known and clearly recognised pattern' of a network (or a story) is broken – that individual and collective risk-taking becomes apparent, and opportunities for exploring new ways of 'doing things' open up. In 'Old Transvaal Story' Bosman deliberately creates a moment of instability – incoherence and betrayal – to demonstrate to us that the genre that exists in our individual and collective imagination has translated us into assuming that his story will follow the same pattern. This instability embodies a cautionary tale that attempts at social ordering can often predict only that the effects of these attempts are mostly unpredictable. This is demonstrated in the stories below.

Stories Two and Three

In 2004, UCT's senate adopted an RPL policy to widen access for adult learners who have acquired knowledge outside of formal institutions that can be harnessed into programmes offered by the university (UCT, 2004). The policy also served to concretise the South African government's principle of promoting lifelong learning for all citizens.

In 2007, Sadia was accepted into UCT's Master's in Adult Education programme. Sadia had an undergraduate degree and a postgraduate diploma but she did not have all the usual prerequisites that allow entry into the master's programme. Her acceptance was contingent upon the existence of the RPL policy. The relational effects of this contingency are brought into sharp focus through Story Two and Story Three below.

Story Two

UCT's RPL policy, as a particular form of literacy, is an attempt at social ordering through a process of translation. Law (1994) suggests that heterogeneous technologies, which he claims must be seen as ordering effects, charter a way of ordering distant events from a centre of translation. These technologies, which include policy documents and various other forms of literacies, have the potential to create peripheries and centres. Translators, operating at a distance from the peripheries, often attempt to integrate some of the possibilities stemming from the effects of these heterogeneous technologies in their ordering tactics to ensure a stable network. However, as noted earlier, stability is an uncertain condition, and any attempt at social ordering involves various forms of productive risk taking.

Drawing on the arguments of Kendall and Wickham (2003: 104), I suggest that the policy, although accepted by the university's senate, can be viewed as a 'model of a network yet to be tested'. In essence it is a script that attempts to stabilise the associations between the key actors involved in harnessing prior learning.

If we consider the moment of problematisation discussed earlier, we find that the problem or goal at the centre of the RPL policy was 'to provide an enabling environment in which student access to UCT can be expanded through RPL' (UCT, 2004: 2). As mentioned earlier, during the problematisation phase, the problem or goal established by particular actors defines the network, the actors and the relations that *should* exist between them.

As shown in the following extract, the policy document, as a metaphor for 'a network yet to be tested', makes extensive use of the future tense and various hedging mechanisms to describe the roles and relationships, intentions and obligations that *should* exist between the various actors in the network:

(1) RPL is recognised as an important and legitimate site of teaching practices and research.
(2) In general, RPL activities *will* combine assessment of prior learning with the exploration of the relationship between academic and other cultures of learning and between formal and informal knowledge domains, and *will* typically be linked to the creation of a plan for future learning.
(3) Academics *will* also take the lead in exploring the pedagogical and curricular possibilities opened by and through RPL, and in leading the epistemological debates that arise therefrom.
(4) RPL recognises that the relationship between academic knowledge and the knowledge created in other sites of practice changes with disciplinary context or field of study, and *can* be the subject of healthy contestation. (UCT, 2004: 7, emphases added)

The RPL policy document seems to represent traces of assumed future relational effects that will be fleshed out as key actors harness prior learning within the academy, and as the processes of interessement, enrolment and mobilisation take place. These assumed relational effects include actors (such as academics) being enrolled to explore the potential of RPL by transforming the pedagogies, curricula and epistemologies of the academy as stated in point 3 above. However, in point 4, the translators allude to the conundrum that prior learning poses to the pedagogical practices of the academy when 'knowledge created in other sites of practice' intersects with 'academic knowledge'. We could infer then that the 'healthy contestation' mentioned in point 4 is the *actual* relational effect of risk taking generated by the network. This stands in contrast to *assumed* future relational effects. These actual relational effects may become evident when actors such as Sadia offer alternative problematisations, definitions and perspectives that have the potential to contest the definitions established by the translators involved in the RPL policy. These contestations I discuss later in this chapter.

Story Three

Sadia befriended me at UCT after she gained access to the master's programme through an RPL process. At the time, I was a member of a research project investigating the affordances students brought to their respective postgraduate study programmes, their associated literacies and the barriers they were experiencing. While she was completing the coursework for her degree, Sadia would often visit my office to talk about her and other students' struggles with the theories and literacy demands of the course. She often mentioned how different the theories and the literacy of the lecture room seemed in comparison to her experiences of the RPL process. During the RPL process Sadia, like other students who gained access to the university via RPL, had been asked to compile a portfolio that documented her prior learning experiences – in this case, in the field of adult education. Sadia included various literacies, including academic texts, poetry and sketches, in her portfolio to showcase her meta-understanding of her experiences. On completing her portfolio, she had to present it to the RPL selection committee.

To gain some insight into the RPL process and the *actual* effects of the RPL policy on Sadia, and following Latour's 'first source of uncertainty', I explained to Sadia the research I was involved in, and asked her to produce a narrative account of her perceptions of RPL before she presented her portfolio to the committee. She readily agreed.

Her narrative included sections of the presentation she had prepared for the RPL selection committee and an account of her experiences in the formalised setting of the university classroom. In an attempt to stay true to an ANT account and to illuminate the effects of the RPL policy on Sadia, her narrative pieces below have remained unedited apart from some minor formatting (such as numbering the paragraphs to facilitate navigation) and changing the names of key actors for purposes of anonymity.

(1) The RPL process was explained as an 'aside' in a meeting we [Sadia and other RPL candidates] had with Shakira, Jackey and Lisa [UCT staff involved in the RPL assessment].[3] The main focus of that discussion was on a pedagogical process that develops the humane. As educators together we expressed our frustration in teaching within a constraining mainstream. It was so 'refreshing' to listen to these practitioners sharing sentiments about holistic teaching albeit in academia. I marvelled at their sincerity and compassion for their learners. I kinda felt at home ... it was this feeling of belonging and empathy about practice that drove me to write about me in the RPL and where I fit into the *bigger* scheme of things. (emphasis in original)

(2) Strangely enough, the actual reasoning behind the RPL as access to masters was furthest on my mind. At that stage I felt so good to simply just claim a space and make myself heard. It was liberating to speak my mind and vent all those bottled up feelings stored while teaching 'across the way'.[4] It was an extension of a soul-searching comment. I recall

telling Shakira 'I do not want to create waves,' and she responded, 'You have to create waves to get to the shore.'

(3) When Lisa presented us with an outline of the RPL profile, it was hardly daunting. I suppose I could have rendered a systematic scientific account of why I wanted to pursue the adult ed masters and plot my CV in chronological detail, but the meeting had premised a different way of knowing, and I saw the RPL as empowering me.

(4) Quite honestly, I did not regard the RPL [presentation] as an assessment of my writing ability. My presentation would bear testimony to the fact that it was hardly about writing; it was simply projecting the multiple faces of my community into a domain that had suppressed and darkened its rich colour before.

The RPL policy document states that agents can harness RPL, 'for access', 'for exemption', 'for advanced standing' and 'for lateral movement' (UCT, 2004: 6). Although agents such as Shakira, Jackey and Lisa harnessed RPL to facilitate access to the academy, Sadia mentions that she did not focus on the RPL process as ensuring 'access' to the master's programme (paragraph 2). Indeed, she notes that she 'did not regard the RPL as an assessment of writing ability' and that her RPL portfolio presentation 'was hardly about writing' (paragraph 4). In other words, she did not perceive the RPL process as a vehicle for demonstrating her level of proficiency in terms of the academy's literacy practices. Although she knew that the purpose of the RPL process was to offer access to the academy, Sadia chose to offer an alternative definition for the process, namely RPL as affirming 'a different way of knowing' (paragraph 3). This represents a form of risk taking that is intentional and not incidental. Therefore, in paragraph 4, Sadia mentions that she saw the RPL process as an opportunity to project 'the multiple faces of [her] community into a domain that had suppressed and darkened its rich colour before'. Thus, Sadia saw the RPL process as valuing the links between her and her community by allowing these networks to be presented and highlighted, and by affirming that knowing and knowledge production can be collective and communal rather than individual and insular.

In the above extract, words such as 'frustration' and 'constraining mainstream' are closely associated with traditional forms of teaching and knowing; while phrases such as 'pedagogical process that develops the humane', 'about me' and 'where I fit into the *bigger* scheme of things' (paragraph 1); 'claim a space', 'make myself heard', 'liberating to speak my mind', 'vent all those bottled up feelings' and 'an extension of a soul searching comment about UCT' (paragraph 2); and 'as empowering me' (paragraph 3) are closely associated with Sadia's alternative definition of RPL.

Sadia's narrative reveals a strong link between her definition of RPL as 'a different way of knowing' and the 'multiple faces' of her community. To broaden our understanding of this link, the following extract from her narrative illustrates how she went about compiling her RPL portfolio:

(5) I always found succour in creative outlets [such as the poems and drawings included in her portfolio] – having my thoughts rain down on paper for only me was a way of making sense of things near and far. I found it difficult to talk about what it is I see, whether it is the loose thread in old (she's 80-some-odd years), widowed, childless Aunty Tiem's scarf that dangles ominously on her face – a thread that defines her fanatically groomed existence and now seems oddly out of place, and there is no one to tuck that thread or cut it away for her as she toddles sadly in her high heels; or the child at my door who says he's homeless and I shove a coin in his hand and I watch it close like I watch the door of a stuffed cupboard while shoving the contents hoping it will stay and not fall out, all the while knowing that the closed cupboard hides a tangled mess.

(6) It's everyday life observations that was written about, and I felt whole bringing all the pieces from different strains of life together, most notably me as part of others and vice versa. It was my comfort zone away from other ways of writing – the cold distanced writing of school, then university and then teaching. I felt removed from myself in these clinically constrained settings, and I was scared of what it was doing to me ... so I always found myself running, and well, ran straight into RPL.

(7) Amazed I found the 'laboratory' of learning, this scientific, calculating giant amenable to my being. I could talk about me and the people who matter to me, and someone was listening. I wasn't simply drumming on the walls of UCT, and listening to the institution's selfless echo like I did before; I now heard myself and the voiceless masses.

In paragraph 5, Sadia mentions that she 'always found succour in creative outlets', and reveals that compiling her RPL portfolio allowed her to bring 'all the pieces from different strains of life together'; most notably, 'me as part of others and vice versa'. It seems that the RPL portfolio mirrored the literacy and literacy practices associated with 'creative outlets' and not the literacies associated with formal institutions, which she describes as 'clinically constrained settings' (paragraph 6). Instead of 'listening to the institution's selfless echo', she could now hear herself and 'the voiceless masses' (paragraph 7) who had played a role in her prior learning when she compiled her RPL portfolio.

'It Was Hardly about Writing' 229

In the extracts below, in which Sadia drew from the notes she made for her presentation to the RPL committee, we can see how Sadia animates the 'voiceless masses' in her presentation. These extracts provide another glimpse of Sadia's alternative definition of RPL (mentioned earlier), and the strong link this has with her community.

(8) So having taught at all these levels, I have realised one thing: 'Everyone's desire to have a voice' – so important to move from the traditional old-fashioned classroom-based approach to a more interactive environment.

(9) I call this image [of a teacher standing in front of a blackboard] the State of Emergency. It shows the outdated blackboard approach. So the state of emergency is not reserved for the turbulent 1980s when the physical state of emergency was declared, we all have our personal self-imposed states of emergency, notably, me: forsaking my education in 1985 was not an option and my parents enforced a state of emergency on me. I still feel like a sell-out to this day.[5]

(10) So now the issue is to nurture my passion for the community's upliftment, and ultimately find peace within myself and others. Others being the adults who have the opportunity to feel whole and more empowered through education. Here, I think of those adults in my very colourful neighbourhood where I grew up – a microcosmic reflection of broader society. I think of posh Aunty Dela around our corner, who dreamt of the better life shown in her glossy mags, never allowing her two daughters to associate with the neighbours.

(11) All in all, I marvelled at these people ... my people, who I feel deserve recognition in the classroom simply for their experience of life. We, as training facilitators have to decide how are we going to formalise their education. How emotionally committed are we? I am aiming towards this and to be a passionate adult educator where I am able to water the beautiful rose that had already blossomed, there with its fresh dewdrop. I simply want to make it glisten ... so we have all of our people cheering in our Madiba's 'land of the sun'.[6]

In paragraph 8, Sadia reflects on all her experiences as a teacher, her realisation of 'everyone's desire to have a voice', and the need for educators to transform their classrooms from teacher-centred to more interactive or student-centred spaces. What becomes clear is Sadia's admiration for her community and the strong link between her and her community. In paragraph 11 she states 'I marvelled at these people ... my people who I feel deserve recognition in the classroom simply for their experience of life.' She mentions that her ultimate aim is 'to find peace within [her]self and others', and that this peace is tied to her community. The peace that Sadia is speaking about here has a link to her own definition of RPL and her alternative problematisation, namely, how to 'to formalise their [her community's] education'.

Although Sadia's presentation was about formalising her prior learning so that she could gain access to a master's degree, her main concern, and the challenge she presented to the RPL committee, was how she, and the education sector more broadly, could formally recognise the knowledge that exists in her community, and in many communities like hers that have been denied access to good schooling and further education.

By comparing her community to a 'beautiful rose that had already blossomed', Sadia seems to suggest that her community has reached a point of development that does not require the interventions of people who perceive it as deficient in any respect. This philosophy is captured in the words 'I simply want to make it glisten' (paragraph 11). The pronoun 'it' and the word 'glisten' in the paragraph refer to her community's 'different way of knowing' (paragraph 3), and to the recognition she believes the university must give to her community for this knowledge.

In the following extract, which is in stark contrast to Sadia's experiences discussed above, she related some of her experiences while completing the coursework for her master's programme.

(12) I volunteer to present a summary of some theory – I think Schon on 'reflection learning'. Armed with colour transparencies, I venture to present a schematic overview of theory, including my critique of it. But it was ultimately all couched in academic 'fanfare'. Throughout the course, I struggled to find the real people (whose experience I hailed) amidst authors haranguing us with their jargon-riddled treatises about learning – we questioned, are these real people talking about real situations, do they practice what they preach or are they behind closed doors, armchair bound dictating empowering strategies? We reeled at the irony of us as adult educators committing the 'crime' we detest, that is educating to educate – spawning the reified 'us' and 'them', and in fact widening the 'social divide', the 'discourse chasm', the 'ideological rift' or whatever 'conceptualisations' we seek in order to craft an academically credible piece. Heavily loaded words beset with diverse multicultural meanings were bandied about at whim, and I marvelled at how adept we became at looking for the 'tacit', when we were in fact weighing the 'tacit' down and pushing it into obscurity.[7] I found myself looking around the room and between the pages for Aunty Bee skilfully tossing the koeksisters in coconut, Abu for his deep-set frown when we fidgeted

in the 'gadat' prayer, Aunty Kay's 'Sadia's laundry' appliquéd in fine even print on the hand-sewn bright orange bag which fitted snugly behind my door ... and oh so many other faces, sounds and fragrances squashed under a dense mass of formal works, and I felt I was being suffocated along with those loved ones I flaunted with great abandon in the RPL.

Interestingly, Sadia makes use of metaphors associated with mystery, struggle, oppression and criminal activity to describe her experience of the coursework she completed during the master's programme. These include 'armed', 'jargon-riddled treatises', 'dictating', 'committing the crime', 'heavily loaded words', 'weighing the tacit down', 'obscurity', 'squashed' and 'being suffocated'. These metaphors reflect a different perception of the academy from that which is evident in paragraph 7 where Sadia claimed that RPL allowed her and the 'voiceless masses' to own a space in the academy. In contrast to the RPL process, Sadia perceives the pedagogy employed in the academy's mainstream classrooms as aiming to weaken the links between her and her community. The reference to 'educating to educate' (paragraph 12) seems to refer to an approach to education that is detached from the community and devoid of an emotional commitment to changing the landscape of education as mentioned in paragraph 11.

To the Writers of Story Four

A key issue that emerges from the stories discussed in this chapter is that attempts at social ordering through writing and the production of texts often produce unpredictable effects. By juxtaposing parallel trajectories of attempts at translating actors as contained in Story Two and Story Three, we see a symmetrical account of the actual effects of these attempts. The production of UCT's RPL policy as a form of social ordering to ensure alternative access to the academy produced a 'risk-taking text' because its effects were unpredictable as could be seen in Saida's narrative pieces. One of the unpredictable effects of the policy was that Sadia attempted to translate the policy to produce an alternative problematisation to that offered by the policy writers. Although the policy writers could not be expected to predict the esoteric ways in which actors such as Sadia might harness the policy, her contestation offers us a glimpse of the complexities embodied by actors (human or non-human), and reveals some of the 'tangled mess' hidden behind the 'closed cupboard door' or inside a human being as a 'black box' of complexity (Law, 1994).

In Story Three, we also saw that the RPL process allowed Sadia to successfully translate other literacies (described as 'creative outlets' in paragraph 5) from outside the academy, and for these to enter the academy momentarily via her portfolio and during her RPL presentation. Giving Sadia access to the master's programme through RPL meant that the University also inadvertently gave access to the networks of 'artful arrangements of bits and pieces' that define the black box we have come to know as Sadia. The display of other literacies or other 'artful arrangements of bits and pieces' during the RPL process in itself contests the formal classroom and its associated literacy practices as described by Sadia (paragraph 12).

Story Three and the literacies that found their way into the RPL process reflect Latour's (2005) first source of uncertainty, namely that there are no clearly identifiable homogenous groups of people. What literacies RPL candidates will bring and present to the academy we cannot say, and we cannot also say for certain how they will expect the academy to give recognition to these literacies in a meaningful way. However, as Story Three has shown, there was an expectation that the academy would change in relation to practices of the RPL process. In Story Three, the RPL process seems to be a moment in which the heterogeneity of actors and the literacies they embody are temporarily unmasked and displayed on the academy's doorstep. If this moment is carried beyond the threshold of the academy, and into its many spaces, it may offer us – the possible writers of Story Four – a myriad of possibilities to transform and to order the academy's literacy landscape, and in doing so allow a hybrid of different literacies to emerge.

Contestations and uncertainties seem to inform the storyline of all the stories told in this chapter. Moreover, as Bosman warns in his short story, the complexities embodied in contestations are cautionary in nature because they signal moments in which the 'well-known and clearly recognised pattern' is betrayed. Not only will moments of betrayal disrupt the academy's attempts to translate students and their literacy practices, but they will also disrupt students' attempts at translating the academy for the network they hope to establish by entering postgraduate studies via the recognition of their experiences or of prior learning.

It seems that the question we are left with is: what do we do with these moments when translation fails and contestations are unmasked? Perhaps, a cursory answer is that the time has come for us to see contestations, disruptions and failures in translation as moments of freedom. They construct a space where the 'tangled mess' can fall under the spell of 'what could be' and escape (even momentarily) the stick of 'what ought to be' (as shown in paragraph 12 of Sadia's narrative) when dealing with the prior learning that adults carry with them into the academy.

The RPL process seems to embody this freedom; it appears to free up the academy's space by allowing contestations and other forms of literacy to be displayed and valued. The RPL process is a moment filled with the witchery of risk taking and it, therefore, has the potential to transform the classrooms of the academy into unpredictable, yet, magical spaces.

Notes

(1) I use the term 'literacies' instead of 'literacy' to signal the theoretical and empirical position which suggests that there are many different forms of reading and writing. The term 'literacy practices' refers to everyday practices associated with different forms of reading and writing in particular social contexts. See Barton (1994) for a more detailed explanation of these terms.
(2) In ANT, translation is the process whereby actors endeavour to delineate, fashion and stabilise social networks for long enough to establish themselves as participants and to achieve some kind of social ordering.
(3) Lecturers involved in the RPL assessment.
(4) Here Sadia is referring to some teaching she had done in another faculty at the university.
(5) The South African government, under the National Party, declared a 'state of emergency' in 1985 after students and civilians took to the streets to protest against apartheid and its education system. The state of emergency gave police and the army carte blanche to suppress the uprisings and curb the freedom of movement and association of all citizens. Although many school students decided to boycott classes, many others were forced to resume their schooling due to parental pressure. Some of these students, like Sadia, saw themselves as betraying the anti-apartheid movement.
(6) 'Land of the sun' is a phrase taken from the lyrics of a song that Sadia used to begin her RPL presentation.
(7) Sadia is referring to theories of tacit knowledge that she encountered during her coursework.

References

Barton, D. (1994) *Literacy: An Introduction to the Ecology of Written Language*. Oxford: Blackwell.
Bosman, H.C. (1948/2004) Old Transvaal Story. In C. MacKenzie (ed.) *Transitions: Half a Century of South African Short Stories*. Cape Town: Francolin.
Clarke, J. (2002) A new kind of symmetry: Actor-network theories and the new literacy studies. *Studies in the Education of Adults* 34 (2), 107–122.
Kendall, G. and Wickham, G. (2003) *Using Foucault's Methods*. London: Sage.
Latour, B. (2005) *Reassembling the Social: An Introduction to Actor-Network-Theory*. Oxford: Oxford University Press.
Law, J. (1994) *Organizing Modernity*. Oxford and Cambridge, MA: Blackwell.
UCT (University of Cape Town) (2004) Policy on Recognition of Prior Learning. Approved PC 09 2004 (Item 3), accessed 8 September 2008. www.uct.ac.za/downloads/uct.ac.za/about/policies/rec_prior_learning.pdf

Part 5

Peripheral Vision: Reflections from North and South

10 Resonances, Resistances and Relations: Reflecting on the Politics of Risk in Academic Knowledge Making

Theresa Lillis

> *It's always risky to offer reflective comments on the works and words of others particularly when, as with this book, they are forged out of long conversations[1] only snatches of which I have overheard (in brief face-to-face chat, in emails, in updates on the progress of the project). Risks of misrepresenting what (I think) writers have meant, of claiming too much space for my voice, of too comfortably occupying an authoritative position that the editors have gifted me. But as this book shows, writing is always a risky business, not least because, as Mapfumo Clement Chihota and Lucia Thesen state in Chapter 5, 'as we write, we always hover on the edge of commitment'.*

Resonances ...

There are many resonances with my own experiences, understandings, concerns and struggles in the pages of this book relating to aspects of identity that it is relatively comfortable to talk about here – as student, teacher, supervisor, writer, researcher, worker in higher education. I welcome **the timely critique of the negative institutional framing of risk** in contemporary academia, a framing which is increasingly shaping the working lives of scholars across the world. Recently, I (as one of a group of people having some responsibility for supporting research in our faculty) was required to act not as a mentor, friend, colleague but as a 'risk owner', called on to own the factors that might prevent the institution from meeting certain targets, such as targets for securing external funding, and to be held account for any failure to do so. And what is most worrying, from my parochial UK position just now, is that this shift towards 'risk management' is not simply an additional discourse to contend with (there are always many). It is dangerously close to pushing other recently hard-won discourses, around access, inclusion and participation, to the margins of UK higher education so that, within a very short period of time these potentially more transformative discourses feel dangerously close to being spat out, as an obsession with risk gets swallowed up. Risk, as Lucia Thesen (drawing on Caplan, 2000) points out in the Introduction, is overwhelmingly used in the centre as a reductive force, a *'hegemonic tool to discipline and regulate'* (Caplan, 2000: 14). In this book, the editors and their co-authors set out to challenge this stance, re-examining the actual and potential uses of risk as a resource for inclusion, engagement, inspiration, moral sustenance, play and transformation. Critiquing current framings and re-considering the possibilities of risk is the task that the writers of this book have set for themselves and in doing so they offer us ways of reimagining risk as a productive resource for academic knowledge making.

One clear example of the institutional negative framing of risk around student writing is in the link between **risk, student writing and plagiarism.** This is signalled in Moragh Paxton's account in Chapter 6 of Serena's supervisors' concerns that plagiarism was one of a *'a number of problems* [that] *put her at risk of not completing the dissertation'* (p. 12) and resonates with my experience of how concerns with plagiarism (often facilitated/determined by the availability of IT software) seem to have become the acceptable replacement for a discourse of deficit. Plagiarism is the contemporary indicator of 'risky' or 'at-risk' students: risky to the institution (standards, retention, completion) and risky to students themselves (if 'caught' they can be failed or thrown off a course). This current obsession with policing the ownership of the stuff of meaning making – mainly verbal language – is challenged strongly in Moragh Paxton's focus on more fundamental meaning-making questions, namely the need to value 'first hand experience' of health workers in the academic and scientific world of the health sciences. It is also challenged by Aditi Hunma and Emmanuel Sibomana's discussion of the development of voice in postgraduate writing and how concern with plagiarism can obscure what is actually going on (writers' struggle for legitimacy), particularly where students are writing across different contexts of production and uptake and where students 'who are considered competent academic writers in one context may be seen as incompetent in another' (p. 21).

Indeed **Voice** is the core notion in this book, figuring in every chapter to explore questions about how scholars enact agency by using the stuff available to them – genres, languages, registers, accents – to make knowledge and, in adopting a fundamentally Bakhtinian take on language, authors illustrate and emphasise how this stuff is always forged from existing words, histories, values, positions and tastes. Many voices and their geographies, histories and language(s)(ing) fill the pages of the book, (re) presented in different ways; as postgraduate students, writers, publishing scholars, adult learners, health workers, teachers, supervisors, authors, editors, gatekeepers, reviewers, political activists, community workers, from South Africa, Cape Town, London, the United States, Rwanda, Mauritius, Africa, Australia, using English(es), Cape Town dialect, French, isiXhosa.

And across the pages of this book is an implicit (and gentle in most chapters) and explicit (and fiercer in the chapter by Kate Cadman) call for a rethinking of whose voices are getting heard in contemporary academia. Voices(ing) that authors seek to make stronger in academia are brought to readers as active agents not least through the emphasis on **the lived experience of risk taking as a productive force for engaging in teaching, learning writing and knowledge production.** Participants in knowledge-making grapple with small and large decisions about where to take positive risks towards breaching academia's walls. We see this risk-taking in writers' striving for opportunities for making and valuing connections between previous/other/current experience and academia, as explored in chapters by Linda Cooper, Somikazi Deyi, Aditi Hunma and Emmanuel Sibomana; in scholars' use of specific theoretical tools, Actor Network Theory and 'translation', to make visible writers' efforts towards agency in the chapter by Moeain Arend; in desires by supervisors, teachers and writing circle facilitators to enable productive risk taking around meaning making, as in the chapters by Mapfumo Clement Chihota and Lucia Thesen and by Mary Scott; in a journal editor's desires to use his power to open rather than close the gates of entry into a high status academic journal, matched by the struggle an author faces about whether or not and under what conditions (and with what potential consequences) to step through such an opening, as in the chapter by Suresh Canagarajah and Ena Lee.

All of these discussions and accounts are richly unique and at the same time have specific echoes for me, of my own experiences and some of my understanding about others' experiences, of the troubling nature of participation in academia. Comments by Jerry in Chapter 1 who, whilst from a different place and time, remind me of the words of student writers and scholars I have worked with and researched. They remind me of Mary who, talking of hating the rigid conventions of what counts as appropriate academic language, said *'It makes me sick ... I don't think it's important at all* (laughs)..... *It's like trying to segregate, you know, you've got like a boundary that sets, you know, you apart from other people'* (in Lillis, 2001: 83). The account by Ena reminds me of scholars' experiences of the double and treble binds of writing for publication from outside the Anglophone centre, of being both pleased and uneasy with reviews which show interest in their work: pleased at recognition, whilst knowing that there are only certain conditions under which their contribution is (mis)recognised; for example, the Hungarian scholar who appreciated the help of an editor, whilst also stating that *'Saying something from Central Europe which is new is not good, not allowed. Of course it's absolutely their perspective to see Central Europeans as, I don't know, a tribe trying to do something scientific'* (Lillis & Curry, 2006: 107). And more personally, I share the worries of the postgraduate supervisor, evident in chapters by Linda Cooper and Kate Cadman, who's not sure whether what she is doing is right or good and is concerned about what is lost as much as what is gained in the countless redrafting she demands of writers' texts; and the fear of being misrecognised in my own writing, when trying to break from the rigidity of academic genres (as in Lillis, 2011), – a need emphasised by Moragh Paxton – fears that for me connect with the concerns and decisions discussed by Somikazi Deyi in Chapter 2 about using a semiotic resource often positioned as 'non-academic'.

And the chapters in the book carry these concerns, debates and desires in words on the page but also in the physical being and presence of the authors and participants. Mapfumo Clement Chihota and Lucia Thesen, drawing on Pelias (2005), argue that both the experience recounted and the recognition in the words of others (as by readers of this book) are felt in the body (Pelias, 2005: 3). Therefore, from the chapters, we both understand and feel the pleasure and excitement of Suresh Canagarajah delighted at being editor of a prestigious journal and having the power to transform practices; the palpable anger of Kate Cadman at the power swayed by the globally dominant 'epistemologically white' academy (p. 41); the complex pleasure of Somikazi Deyi signalled in the very title of her chapter 'a lovely imposition'. The range of emotions of lived academia in the pages of the book remind me of how common and powerful they are, all the more so for being backgrounded in the rational(isation) of the daily routines of the work that we do.

Resistances ...

Resonances are relatively comfortable. They signal connections with familiar knowledges, feelings and understandings and enable me/us to recognise me/ourselves in others and, we anticipate, others in me/us. There is a sense in which through such resonances we feel pleased to know each other, indeed, happy that we do know each other. We keep the familiar familiar (rather than the critical and unsettling ethnographic effort towards making the familiar strange). But this book is not about staying in comforting/able spaces and in taking risk seriously, it throws out a challenge to open up different futures, spaces and relations around academic knowledge making globally. The book speaks from the global south, speaking back to the centre's claim to know, to understand, challenging in particular the centre's positioning of what it means to be a scholar from the south, the periphery, an 'international' student and scholar. The chapters demand that centre-based scholars and academia resist easy claims to universal 'Enlightenment' positions on what counts as knowledge, and what counts as the valid means of the production of such knowledge, putting the spotlight instead on who gets to claim knowledge (where and how and with what material and semiotic resources), and with what consequences.

And here as a reader, I have to face the uncomfortable fact that I am positioned by the writers and chapters in this book as an outsider, a scholar from the privileged global north, located physically in western academia. At a rational level I know this. Of course I do. I am an academic located in the 'centre', the global north, with far greater material resources than most of the world, with the 'right' symbolic resources given contemporary academia's thrall to English, and the greater right to be heard. I know too well that it's much harder for scholars from outside the centre to have their voices recognised, often being taken up as either exotic or as parochial, with both being acts of profound misrecognition. I know this most strongly from research exploring scholars' experiences of writing from outside the Anglophone centre and all they have taught me (for some indication, see Lillis & Curry, 2010). I have learnt about local and global regimes of academic production and evaluation; about (contemporary) ideologies around English and valuable knowledge; about dealing with condescension hardly bothered to be dressed up as Enlightenment thinking (Reviewer: *Please could they outline why Madrid was chosen as the place of study in the first place, and why indeed Spain might be a useful comparison with other previous work?* Lillis & Curry, 2010: 142); about scholars' resistance ('we are not poor little Eastern Europeans') including scholars' laughter in the face of ridiculous challenges from junior 'centre' scholars – *how could a group of Portuguese scholars know Bernstein, an Anglophone centre theorist, better than UK based scholars?* (Answer – Easy. By working with the theorist and through such theory, reconfiguring it in light of very local concerns.) I know that the centre/periphery is real from the very obvious statistics on income and output which largely indicate that General Expenditure on Research and Development (GERD) maps (unsurprisingly) quite closely against a country's or region's global share of highly valued (*read* – ISI) world science journal article output: US, GERD = 31%, global share of scientific output = 27%; GERD South Africa, GERD = .93, global share of scientific output = .30 (Lillis & Curry, 2013 for details; drawn from a number of sources including UNESCO Science Report, 2010).

And there we have it. I am a scholar in the global north, with all the material and symbolic privileges that this bestows, a living instantiation of 'divine discourse' (Cadman, 2003 and discussed with different emphases in the Introduction and Chapter 4).

But this positioning
is not easy.
It feels odd.

How is it possible that someone from a working-class background – from a poor council estate in England where you stood out as an oddity if you passed the 11 plus (state selection exam), if you stayed on at school (after 16), if you went on to university – can get positioned as privileged and somehow necessarily a torch bearer for western academia? No, I will resist this positioning. I will not be treated as privileged by privileged academics [*read* – middle class, and however class is configured, academia is predominantly a middle class social space] from any part of the world!

And ... anyway ...

Whose north? Is there only one? From my small world there are at least a few with quite specific and powerful sociohistorical meanings but I'll mention just one other ...

The north (of England)

'It's grim up north.' The reference to harsh conditions in the industrial north (industry of course fed by colonialism) – often also signalling gritty determination, often collapsing into another discourse on cultural deficiencies – lives on in Britain. As does reference to the 'North-South Divide,' marking the social, cultural and economic divide between north and south of England and at its height in Thatcher's Britain, where 'there's no such thing as society' was challenged by striking miners (up north) and played out by football fans (from down south) flashing money at football fans (from up north) to emphasise 'we have jobs and money and you don't'. And of course 'north' often worked/s as much as a signifier of working-class conditions, desires and cultures as a geographical descriptor.

Oh p-l-ease! Let's not hear about poor me, I hear the reader say, spare us the sob story of working class conditions in the rich global north ...

Relations ...

Why make these comments and risk an angry or frustrated uptake in readers? To illustrate simply that we carry with us places and spaces which are shot through with stratifications, hierarchies and hegemonies and that in attempts to engage in dialogue in the world we have to acknowledge these as well as working at deepening our understandings. So in resisting being positioned in one way by the writers in this book I must also accept such positioning and work at re-locating myself/ourselves (those of us in the global north) by engaging in discussions about the nature and consequences of contemporary academic knowledge exchange. (Re)locating my/ourselves into a global north in debates and dialogue about global knowledge production and exchange does not make the other norths go away. Rather, they point to specific decisions and responsibilities that challenge me to resist the (easy if you are in the global north) temptations to get on with the 'business-as usual' of northern/central/western academia. And the pages of this book offer resources for how the metropole(itan) university might begin to engage. These involve drawing on theories which foreground the relational nature of language and meaning making, notably through the work of Bakhtin and also Blommaert (2005) who focuses on voice as a question of uptake; theories which foreground the need to work with and through 'epistemological paradox' (Introduction) recognising the complex geohistorical nature of agency and resources for agency, drawing on George (2003), as for Mbembe (2002) and Mudimbe (1994), discussed by Lucia Thesen in the Introduction; theories which work with and challenge binaries of centre and periphery, developed in chapters by Aditi Hunma and Emmanuel Sibomana and Mary Scott, where the authors focus on the nature of the metropole(itan) and Afropolitan university and relations between these, as well as the complex ways in which peripheries exist and intersect within centres and centres within peripheries. This theoretical emphasis on the relational across the book is grounded in almost every page in actual relations between people. It seems to me that here is the core strength of the book: to reconfigure risk as a productive act of relationship around knowledge making. We are all implicated in this relationship. The invitation to take the risk of reconfiguring the global relationship around academic knowledge production, sharing and exchange is what the book offers to us all. It is up to each of us to take it up.

Note

(1) This notion is based on Maybin, J. (1994) Children's voices: Talk, knowledge and identity. In D. Graddol, J. Maybin and B. Stierer (eds) *Researching Language and Literacy in Social Context* (pp. 131–150). Clevedon: Multilingual Matters.

References

Blommaert, J. (2005) *Discourse: A Critical Introduction*. Cambridge: Cambridge University Press.
Cadman, K. (2003) Divine discourse: Plagiarism, hybridity and epistemological racism. In S. May, M. Franken and R. Barnard (eds) *LED 2003, 1st International Conference on Language, Education and Diversity: Refereed Proceedings and Keynotes*. Hamilton: University of Waikato Press. Online document: http://hdl.handle.net/2440/39833
Caplan, P. (ed.) (2000) *Risk Revisited*. London: Pluto Press.
George, O. (2003) *Relocating Agency: Modernity and African Letters*. New York: SUNY Press.
Lillis, T. (2001) *Student Writing: Access, Regulation, Desire*. London: Routledge.
Lillis, T. (2011) Legitimising dialogue as textual and ideological goal in academic writing for assessment and publication. *Arts and Humanities in Higher Education* 10 (4), 401–432.
Lillis, T.M. and Curry, M.J. (2006) Professional academic writing by multilingual scholars: interactions with literacy brokers in the production of English-medium texts. *Written Communication* 23 (1), 3–35.
Lillis, T. and Curry, M.J. (2010) *Academic Writing in a Global Context*. London: Routledge.
Lillis, T. and Curry, M.J. (2013) English, academic publishing and international development: Access and participation in the global knowledge economy. In E. Erling and P. Seargeant (eds) *English and International Development*. Bristol: Multilingual Matters.
Mbembe, A. (2002) African modes of self-writing. *Public Culture* 14 (1), 239–273.
Mudimbe, V.Y. (1994) *The Idea of Africa*. Bloomington, IN: Indiana University Press.
Pelias, R. (2005) Performative writing as scholarship: An apology, an argument, an anecdote. *Cultural Studies <=>Critical Methodologies* 5, 415–424.
UNESCO (2010) *Science Report. The Current Status of Science Around The World*. Available www.unesco.org (accessed November–December, 2010).

11 Both Dead and Alive: Schrödinger's Cat in the Contact Zone

Brenda Cooper

> *As an alternative to starkly drawn north/south or centre–periphery geographical and conceptual divides, the metaphor of a contact zone permeates this study*
> Introduction, this volume

The contact zone is a site of risk. And risk carries possibilities and perils. Both. *Risk in Academic Writing: Postgraduate Writers, Their Teachers and the Making of Knowledge* foregrounds the possibilities. It builds on the concept of 'risk' as a theoretical tool, which contributes to meaning-making in the field of postgraduate literacies. It does so within a postcolonial context, where student writers battle to find their voices. It does so not only with the conviction that this is a necessity, but also within the framework of alternative practices. Chapter after chapter in the foregoing book links the risk–challenge inherent in postgraduate writing to the obligation for the creation of enabling structures on the part of postgraduate teachers, who learn as they teach. Both.

Risk, then, is theory and also practice. It transforms theory and modifies practice. This is what makes this book so original and valuable. The postcolonial context in which it plays out is both universal and specific, both north and south. Apprentice academics everywhere struggle to don the magic of the academic cloak without becoming invisible. But in the contact zone, where the cloak is tailored in an Oxford or Harvard, the jeopardy is doubled. At the same time, here in this space, there are political possibilities for transformation, carried on the projection of each individual apprentice scholar's voice. What can all of this have to do with Erwin Schrödinger, a physicist, who in Austria in 1935 conducted a thought experiment that involved a cat?

I encountered Schrödinger's experiment in the fourth novel by M.G. Vassanji, titled *Amriika*, and published in 1999. The first, framing, part of the novel is titled 'SHRODINGER'S CAT' (Vassanji, 1999: 5). The novel's protagonist is an East African Asian postgraduate student called Ramji, who has travelled far from his home in Dar es Salaam to study physics at a university on the East Coast of the United States. Ramji's bewilderments and challenges are exemplary of those experienced by international students in foreign universities. Ramji thinks about his grandmother in Tanzania when he witnesses lunar astronauts on television in the United States and realises that America is light years away from her, and his previous life, given that she 'could have no idea as to what exactly was happening to him' (Vassanji, 1999: 39). Ramji has gone to another planet, one his grandmother calls Amriika for which the novel is named. The thought experiment with the cat speaks to him; it would speak to many of the students featured in this book. In the words of one of Ramji's professors:

> Imagine a cat inside a closed black box together with a contraption that, when turned on, has a 50% chance of giving off a radiation, which would trigger the release of a poison gas and kill the cat. We turn the contraption on through some remote means. After a given time – let us say half an hour – would you think the cat was alive or dead? What is the state of the cat? (Vassanji, 1999: 38)

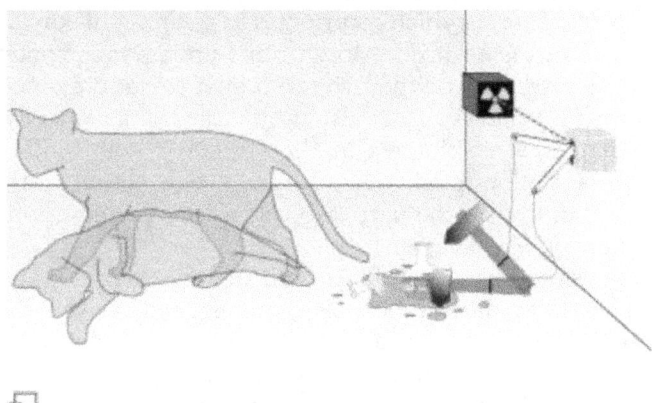

The image: www.en.wikipedia.org/wiki/File:Schrodingers_cat.svg (accessed April 2013)

Schrödinger's intriguing point is that until such time as scientists entangle themselves in the experiment by opening the box and finding a dead or an alive cat, the cat lives in a double dimension. Dead and alive. Both. Ramji identifies with the cat in a box, living in two dimensions. His concern is with the cat and what *it* might be thinking. While it seems that Schrödinger's question was 'when does the system stop existing as a mixture of states and become one or the other'? (Clark, 2011), the answer for the ex-physicist, MIT-trained Vassanji, is that traveling cats like himself, like Ramji, existing in the contact zone, do so perilously and simultaneously in more than one world and language. The mixture of states is their mode of being. Vassanji, whose forebears originally migrated to East Africa from India, was born in Kenya and grew up in Tanzania. He studied physics at MIT, gave up a career in science to become a writer and settled in Canada, where he has lived since 1978.

The contact zone which this book occupies, and to which Vassanji transported his postgraduate student, Ramji, is a mobile space where researchers and theories travel back and forth with greater and lesser success. It is a dangerous site where the plural is imperative in order for risk to find its catalysing function – postgraduate literacie*s*; Englishe*s*, continent*s* and dimension*s*. What the chapters of *Risk in Academic Writing* demonstrate is that within the rigid parameters of the singular, the risk to students like Ramji invariably metamorphoses into loss. Thesen is right to mourn a situation in which 'writing requires us to commit to *this* path, for *now*, and to leave other paths behind' (Introduction). And so, chapters in this book emphasise the plural instead of the one, narrow path; they play with the concept of hybridity, which is capacious (see especially Chapters 3 and 6 in this book). This refusal of the mono enables Scott to see the ghosts in the texts of her students and to bring them back to life. This she does through the transformation into poetry of the errors identified by the punitive academic writing norm. How apt that she ends her chapter with lines from T.S. Eliot including 'There is always another one walking beside you' (Scott in this book). Eliot may form part of the dominant European canon, but his insights are poignant and potent for Scott's context of 'foreign' students, whose lives and languages are erased. America drowns out Amriika and Ramji's beloved grandmother is banished, along with all her treasures.

What are these treasures? 'Aunty Bee skillfully tossing the koeksisters in coconut' perhaps? (Arend, in this book). And, more to the point of this book, how might Sadia, the postgraduate student with the koeksister-making aunty, or Arend, her academic mentor, make knowledge out of the skill of coconut tossing and of the stories of Sadia's aunty? This book answers this question in two intriguing ways. First, by finding *new ways of writing scholarly research*; second, by fashioning *new theoretical tools*.

Arend tells a tale of four stories out of which emerges *a new kind of academic writing*. Many of the foregoing chapters subvert the dominant genre of academic writing, whether we are referring to the exposure of the pipes and gutters of academic journal submission in Canagarajah and Lee's chapter (to which I will return) or in another conversation in Chapter 4, where Hunma and Sibomana compare experiences as international students from Mauritius and Rwanda, respectively. Then, there is Scott's 'narrowing of the conventional gap between academic writing and devices used in poetry' (Scott in this book). Similarly, Cadman begins her chapter with an apt prose/poetic epigraph taken from Ania Walwicz, which includes the line 'The University is going to enter into new modes of writing' (Cadman in this book). The chapter proceeds to take an auto-ethnographic approach with some misgivings, which are written into the chapter as an internal dialogue. In all of these chapters we have echoes, conversations and multiplicity in this promising, perilous space of the contact zone, where the stern, shrill and singular voice of scholarly authority is softened by a chorus and a choir.

This brings us back to the challenge of making theory from within the realities, needs and imperatives of the contact zone. Arend's evocative fourth story, is one to which we scholars, exploring alternatives on new ground, are invited to turn anecdote into knowledge. For example, Arend signals how to turn a koeksister into a non-human actor by way of his use of Bruno Latour's theory of the network of agents and voices. In other words, there are a myriad of possibilities to transform the academy's literacy landscape, and in doing so allow a 'hybrid of different literacies to emerge' (Arend in this book) but only if we fashion theoretical tools with which to do so. In this way, the material, experiential realities of Sadia's life may find a place in the scholarly archive, but only if they contribute to enabling a thousand and one other stories in different times and places to find voices in ongoing social, personal and political narratives. In Chapter 9 of the book, Arend answers Cooper's call in the first for a conversation between experiential and academic knowledge. *Risk in Academic Writing* is, in fact, driven by the urgency to make theory, to increase the stores of knowledge from, and useful to, southern contexts. This is one of the solutions to finding the more than one pathway into postgraduate writing that potentially liberates choruses of writing voices.

What this book makes clear is that the experiential dimension, which has to be theorised, occurs within the local, everyday context in which it is lived, by definition. Schrödinger was concerned that his experiment was counter-intuitive and illustrated what he saw as the problem of quantum mechanics applied to everyday objects, resulting in a contradiction with common sense. However, a cat has to be either dead or alive according to whose common sense? Whose everyday? Magic and science, faith and laboratory testing intermingle and motivate all of our lives, whether we live them out in Europe or Africa, but it is perhaps in the contact zone that this imperative to accommodate the plural becomes most urgent. To make theory out of this lived reality, Bruno Latour (2010) has had to coin a new word. The factish. Fact and fetish. Both. The factish obliterates the binary between fact and fetish and, more importantly, between Africa and Europe. This is so because while the cultural and political substance of our factishes may differ, human beings everywhere require that mix of belief and verifiable evidence in order to make meaning, and to pass through the rites of passage that enable us to become adults in a social world. The factish enables us, personhood as a whole, to *'pass'* (Latour, 2010: 23, emphasis in original), 'to live' (Latour, 2010: 28). It is *'the wisdom of the passage'* (Latour, 2010: 35, emphasis in original).

In this way, the concept of the factish becomes a theoretical tool. Mieke Bal's (2002) 'rough guide' to travelling concepts in the Humanities champions the malleability of the concept as a tool that enables conversations across fields and disciplines by establishing a common language (Bal, 2002: 22). The heavy weight of theory and the deadly academic burden of 'coverage' (Bal, 2002: 8) may be suspended in the interests of pushing knowledge boundaries. Bal points out that 'precisely because they travel between ordinary words and condensed theories, concepts can trigger and facilitate reflection and debate on all levels of methodology in the humanities' (Bal, 2002: 29). Made up words like 'factish' and ordinary words like 'risk' in *Risk in Academic Writing* push knowledge boundaries because they become theoretical. Theory making in the contact zone finds itself making up words like 'factish' or taking everyday words linked to local experience and endowing them with conceptual and methodological power. Risk, the Introduction demonstrates, has its own history of conceptual use, but it becomes thickened and theoretical in productive and political ways in this book.

This risk taking in making and voicing new knowledge from the South is what motivated Achille Mbembe (2002) to coin the term *'African Modes of Self-Writing'*. This does not assume an essential African self that writes; Mbembe writes with an intense awareness of Africa's heterogeneity and chequered, uneven history and futures. What he is calling for is boundary pushing within all of the modes and methods of creating knowledge, within our complex continent, which has to find its own styles and theories of expression. And in so doing, the many modes of African self-writing may impact on the planet and on humanity globally. Or as Geri Augusto (2007) puts it:

> African universities and the local knowledges they may critically interrogate and re-appropriate, articulating those with global sciences and

other knowledge systems where relevant, might keep humanity from foreclosing unknown future options. Who knows where the cures for tomorrow will come from, or the new construals of our planet's ecology as whole systems rather than reductionist parts ... or new ways to conceive of reconciliation, or to define the *human?* (Augusto, 2007: 204, emphasis in original)

Thesen and Cooper's collection contributes to this project of research and transformation. In fact, it is exemplary of this kind of knowledge-making from a southern perspective, knowledge that is also global and crosscutting; it is an African mode of self-writing. The book's position in the cross-currents of the contact zone declines binaries and polarities and refuses to fall into the trap of dead *or* alive. It understands that academic gatekeepers are not positioned on the one side of the border with postgraduate writers and their radical champions – the authors in this book – on the other. Cooper in the first chapter wisely recognises that experiential knowledge may, in fact, be a barrier to the acquisition of an academic writing voice; at the same time, she warns that the exclusion of experience may be to the great loss of our academic archive. The dilemmas posed by the necessary gatekeeping in academic writing are no more powerfully illustrated than in Chapter 3 in which Canagarajah confronts that he is a gatekeeper of sorts. It is a chapter that simultaneously reinforces the necessity for academic fields and traditions, which have to be built upon, and also fundamentally challenges these conventions. Canagarajah engages in conversation with Ena Lee, a novice researcher, whose paper ultimately could not achieve publication in a journal he edited, albeit that he was deeply committed to changing the process and outcome of submissions. The chapter reinforces the necessity of aspects of academic writing traditions in what it acknowledges was 'a failed encounter' where Lee's paper did not meet the requirements for academic publication. While this is the substance of the paper, its form of writing simultaneously interrogates those requirements through a conversational engagement with Lee, providing more than one viewpoint of the process.

Along these lines, in Chapter 6, Paxton acknowledges that 'what makes research-proposal writing particularly complex, is the dual and conflicting roles it carries as *both* gatekeeper and formative pedagogical tool' (Paxton in this book, my emphasis). This accounts for why Cadman in Chapter 7 feels 'caught in a web of insights that is likely to bring to the fore my conscious complicity in this violence, and lead me to an unproductive confusion' (Cadman in this book). Her confusion, however, may just be productive and even exemplary in the contact zone.

Historical, personal, scientific and magical dimensions in conversation throw up new concepts and tools, which make theory and produce knowledge. This characterises research in the north and research in the south. It is true of the writing of established researchers and of postgraduate writers. But risk looms particularly large in the context of this book, which is populated by postgraduate novices, on the move in the contact zone. And by their teachers, the foregoing authors, who help them metamorphose risk into challenge as they together wrestle with the turnpike to pull an opening just wide enough for a travelling cat to walk through into the lands of the living and also the dead. Both.

References

Augusto, G. (2007) Transforming knowledge, changing knowledge relations, and epistemic openness in the university in Africa. *Social Dynamics* 33 (1), 199–205.

Bal, M. (2002) *Travelling Concepts in the Humanities.* Toronto: University of Toronto Press.

Clark, A.D. (2011) *Physics in 5 Dimensions. Bye, Bye Big Bang.* Neunkirchen: Books on Demand.

Latour, B. (2010) *On the Modern Cult of the Factish Gods.* Durham, NC: Duke University Press.

Mbembe, A. (2002) African modes of self-writing. *Public Culture* 14 (1), 239–273.

Vassanji, M.G. (1999) *Amriika.* Toronto: McClelland & Stewart.

Index

Note: n refers to the notes.

academic English 2, 149, 170–171, 172, 196 n15
  see also grammar
academic knowledge 28–31, 241, 243
  see also experiential knowledge
academic literacies 5, 247
  of RPL students 219, 226, 228, 232–233, 233 n1, 248
academic writing 1, 167, 169
  extra-academic 189–192
  'how-to' guides 4, 6
  of international students 104–105, 108, 113–114, 123, 124
  new modes 45, 55, 168, 215, 247–248
  post-academic 179, 190
  pre-academic 179–180, 189
  scientific 159
access to higher education 2, 12–13, 17, 28, 29, 103, 105
  see also RPL
Activity Theory 30
actor network theory (ANT) 221–222
  and risk 219, 223, 224, 225, 227, 231, 233
adult learner theses 27–29, 31–32
  case studies 33–44, 45, 46
  see also experiential knowledge
African languages 48–51, 52–54, 55
African philosophy 186
African research 14–15, 111–112, 177, 186–187, 249–250
Afropolitanism 109–111, 112, 117, 124, 164 n4
Ahluwalia, P. 177
Aitchison, C. 4, 95, 133

Alexander, N. 49
Althusser, L. 170
Ammon, U. 180, 191
Anderson, L. 64
Ang, I. 62, 82
Angelil-Carter, S. 12
ANT *see* actor network theory (ANT)
Appadurai, A. 184, 194 n4, 208
archive *see* jussive knowledge archive; trace archive
Armstrong, N. 168
Arnoldi, J. 22 n2, 62, 91
Ashcroft, B. 171
assessment criteria 156, 173, 189, 191, 192, 203
'at-risk' students 12–13, 109, 118, 238
Atkinson, D. 91
Augusto, G. 249–250
autoethnography 59, 64, 166–167

Bakhtin, M. 5, 15, 43, 123, 143, 151
Bal, M. 249
Ball, S. 215
Barkhuizen, G. 90
Bartholomae, D. 207
Bartlett, A. 4, 7, 132
Barton, D. 233 n1
Bataille, G. 176
Battiste, M. 176
Bawarshi, A.S. 150
Bazerman, C. 150
Beardsley, M.C. 127
Beck, U. 8, 9, 10, 11
Belcher, D. 64, 95, 97 n5
Bell, J.S. 90

Index

Bell, R. 186
Bernstein, P.L. 8
Bhabha, H. 94, 126, 135, 171, 183, 194 n4
  see also 'third space'
Bhatia, V.K. 93
Bhatt, R.M. 191, 194 n3
Blommaert, J. 5, 31, 205, 208, 209
  mobility 149, 150–151, 159, 206, 214
  voice as 'uptake' 152, 243
Bosman, H.C. 219, 220, 223, 232
Boud, D. 2, 133, 134, 143
Bourdieu, P. 66, 118, 203
Bowker, G. 14, 17, 44, 49
Butler, P. 206

Cadman, K. 156, 164, 175, 177, 191
  autoethnography 167, 169
  'divine discourse' 2, 20, 114, 242
  pedagogic approaches 174, 182, 189, 190, 193
  writing conventions 4, 149
Canagarajah, S. 59, 87, 119
  academic writing 180, 195 n9
  publishing 5, 184–185
Caplan, P. 9–10, 238
Carroll, K.K. 186, 187–188
Casanave, C.P. 4, 10, 27–28, 45, 95, 96
Chang, H. 64
Chihota, C. 7, 137, 138, 237
citation counts 8, 12, 137
  see also referencing
Clark, A.D. 247
Clark, R. 151
Clarke, J. 222, 223
Collins, P.H. 186
Comaroff, J. 5, 8
Comaroff, J.L. 5, 8
communal knowledge 39, 41, 45, 191, 227, 229–231
Connell, R. 2, 14, 30, 151, 176, 195 n7
  southern knowledge 185, 186, 188
constructionist positions (social theory) 9
contact zone 2–3, 248, 249, 250
  international students 100, 109, 118, 126
  and risk 96, 245, 247
Cooper, B. 216
Cooper, L. 46 n10
Cope, B. 150

Cornell, D. 187, 188, 195 n12
critical thinking 189, 190, 195 n12
  of international students 103, 106, 115–116, 122, 125
Curry, M.J. 2, 5, 64, 240, 241
Curtis, M. 153
Cuthbert, D. 133

Daniels, H. 31, 42
De Certeau, M. 208
De Fina, A. 63
De Saussure, F. 148
deletions 1, 3, 32, 42–44, 52–54, 55
  see also voice
Denzin, N. 181
Derrida, J. 123
Diawara, M. 177
'divine discourse' 2, 20, 114, 123, 242
Dixon, K. 4
Douglas, M. 8, 9, 10, 143
Dudley-Evans, T. 97 n5
Duff, P. 95

Eagleton, T. 195 n4
'ecology of knowledges' 184–185, 194
Egziabher, T.B.G. 175, 194
Elbow, P. 133, 178
Eliot, T.S. 216, 217 n5, 247
Ellis, C. 64
emotions 43, 54, 132, 141–143, 240
Enders, J. 2
English *see* academic English
English, F. 215
English grammar 180, 183, 189, 190, 191, 206
enrolment (ANT) 222, 223, 225
epistemicide 175, 178
epistemology 175
  race-based 186
  racist 176, 177, 178
ethics approval 12, 155, 157
ethnography *see* autoethnography
ethnopoetics 20, 207, 208–209, 210, 215, 216
experiential knowledge
  as barrier 30, 32–33, 36, 250
  interaction with academic knowledge 28–31, 162, 225
  and voice 28, 32, 41–45

experiential knowledge *(Continued)*
experiential learning theories 29, 30
extra-academic writing 189–192

facilitators (writers' circles) 136, 137, 139–141, 143–144, 146
'factish' (Latour) 249
Fahey, J. 207
feminist theorists 30, 162, 170, 172
Fenwick, T. 29
fictocriticism 168, 179, 180
Flavell, H. 179, 193
Flowerdew, J. 64, 97 n5
Fowler, A. 164 n1
francophone students *see* Mauritian students; Rwandan students
Freire, P. 106, 113
Frow, J. 132

Gardiner, M.E. 43
gatekeeping 5, 12, 122, 124, 222, 250
  by research proposals 12, 155–156, 157, 163
Gee, J.P. 7, 114, 120, 121
Geertz, C. 63, 154, 169
genre 4, 146 n3, 148–152, 164 n1
Georgakopoulou, A. 63
George, O. 15, 243
ghost texts 206–207, 209–215, 216
Giddens, A. 8, 9
grammar 180, 183, 189, 190, 191, 206
Grossman, J. 28
Gunew, S. 170, 193
Gxilishe, S. 49

Hall, S. 170, 194 n4
Halliday, M.A.K. 150, 210
Hargreaves, A. 143
Hasan, R. 150
Haugh, M. 116, 124
Heath, S.B. 69
Hegel, W.G.F. 124
Herrington, A.J. 153
higher education *see* universities
Hofmeyr, I. 14–15
Hoggart, R. 170
Hooks, B. 177
Houndonji, P. 186
'how-to' guides 4, 6

Hu, M. 195 n14
hybrid discourses 59, 90–91, 94, 149, 164
  limitations 60–61, 62, 87–88
  and risk 91–92, 96
  and voice 80, 89, 91, 152–153, 190
  see also 'third space'
Hyland, K. 4
Hymes, D. 148, 152, 208, 210

identity *see* research identity
indigenous knowledge 173, 176–177
indigenous research methodology 186
Ingleton, C. 195 n13
interessement (ANT) 222, 223, 225
international students
  in contact zone 100, 109, 118, 126
  coping strategies 101, 104, 118–122, 126
  critical thinking 103, 106, 115–116, 122, 125
  lecturers' attitudes to 122
  research identity 116, 121, 124, 125, 126
  and risk 109, 122–123, 125
  writing skills 104–105, 108, 113–114, 123, 124
internationalisation policy 2, 104, 110, 111–112, 125
interpolation 171–172, 173, 176, 184, 187, 194 n3
introduction-methods-results-discussion (IMRD) 59, 60, 61
isiXhosa thesis
  administrative issues 48, 54–55
  supervisory feedback 50–54
  see also African languages
Ivanic, R. 123, 151, 152

Janks, H. 4, 150
Jansen, J.D. 155
Jones, C. 116
journal articles *see* research article (case study); research-article genre
jussive knowledge archive 14, 17, 44, 45

Kalantzis, M. 150
Kamler, B. 4, 163
Keim, W. 2
Kendall, G. 222, 224
Kenway, J. 207

Kidokoro, T. 195 n14
Kneebone, R. 159
knowledge *see* academic knowledge; communal knowledge; ecology of knowledges; experiential knowledge; indigenous knowledge; scientific knowledge
knowledge archive *see* jussive knowledge archive
Kraak, A. 111
Kress, G. 15, 150, 207, 208
Kubota, R. 68, 78, 89
Kutz, E. 115

Lakeoff, R.T. 171
language 5–6, 171
 see also academic English; African languages; grammar; linguistic resources
Language Policy for Higher Education (2002) 48, 55
Latour, B. 221, 222, 226, 249
laughter 137, 141, 143, 146
Law, J. 219, 221, 223, 224, 231
lecturers, attitude to students 122
Lee, A. 2, 4, 133, 134, 143
Lee, E. 66
Li, X. 4
Lillis, T. 64, 95, 154, 239, 240
 dominance of English 2, 5, 241
Ling, M.L. 195 n8
linguistic resources 118–119, 152, 159–160
literacy *see* academic literacies; academic writing; reading
Lorde, A. 172, 184
Luhmann, N. 8, 10, 11
Luke, A. 150
Lupton, D. 7, 8, 9, 92, 96
Lyng, S. 92
Lyons, S.R. 186

Mangena, F. 187
Marika, R. 195 n5
Martin, J. 150
Maryns, K. 152
Matsuda, P.K. 95
Maurais, J. 191
Mauritian students 100, 102–105

coping strategies 101, 104, 118–120, 121–122, 126
 see also international students; Rwandan students
Maybin, J. 22 n1, 244 n1
Mbembe, A. 14–15, 243, 249
Mbiti, J.S. 186
McCandless, E. 188, 195 n11
McGregor, L. 22 n4
McLellan, C. 111
McWilliam, E. 11–12
mediators *see* writing specialists
mentoring (research article) 62, 63–64, 84, 87, 93, 95
Mercer, G. 4, 7, 132
metropole-periphery divide 2, 30, 116–117, 175, 241–242
metropolitan academy *see* northern academy
Michelson, E. 28, 30, 162
Mihesua, D.A. 176, 177
mobilisation (ANT) 222, 223, 225
mobility 2
 of students 112, 203–204, 208, 209, 211, 216
 of texts 4–5, 151, 152
Montaigne, M. de 114
Moreton-Robinson, A. 176
Morphet, A. 36
Morrell, R. 187
mother tongue 48, 49, 50, 118, 119
Mthembu, T. 111–112
Mudimbe, V.Y. 15, 243
Mullen, C.A. 95
Muller, J. 29–30
multilingual language policy 17, 48, 50, 55
multilingual writers 59, 60, 62, 63, 65, 89
multimodal semiosis 207, 208
Murray, D. 133
Murray, R. 155
Myers, G. 211

Nakata, M. 176
narrative form 59, 64, 90, 166–167
 in adult learner thesis 39–40, 41, 42
 in research article 65, 69–71, 79, 80–81
 in research proposal 161–163
National Language Project (NLP) 50

north, as relative concept 151, 242–243
northern academy 195 n7
  challenges to 176–177, 179–180, 184–185, 192, 193–194, 241
  dominance of 2, 172–173, 174–178, 180
  research methodology 187–188
  see also southern academy
'nou base' 101, 104, 118–120, 121–122, 126
novice researchers 1, 100, 126
  and risk 92, 93, 95, 123, 169
  voice 62, 63, 89, 94
Nuttall, S. 22 n4
Nyamnjoh, F. 12

O'Brien, M. 195 n5
Odora-Hoppers, C. 177
oral genres 41, 42, 208–209
other 2, 14, 116, 124, 126, 170
  and risk 9, 11, 13, 15, 92

Pahl, K. 116
Parker, B. 186
Parker, R. 133
Patanakan, M. 195 n14
Paxton, M. 150
pedagogy *see* writing pedagogy
peer-based writing groups 133–134
  see also writers' circles
Pelias, R. 133, 240
Pennycook, A. 12, 192
performative writing 19, 88, 133, 146
peripheral vision 13–15
periphery-metropole divide 2, 30, 116–117, 175, 241–242
plagiarism 12, 116, 183, 191, 238
poetry 208, 216, 226, 247, 248
Pollock, D. 133
Porsanger, J. 176
Portelli, A. 41
post-academic writing 179, 190
'postgraduate condition' 7, 13, 137–139, 141–142
power relations 3, 13, 29, 124–125, 179
Pratt, M.L. 3, 59, 60, 62, 96, 100
pre-academic writing 179–180, 189
Preece, J. 175, 188
Price, Max (UCT) 109–110, 127 n3
problematisation (ANT) 222, 223, 224, 225, 231

productive risk 12, 123, 146, 224, 238, 239
'proxy persons' 101, 120–121
publishing 5, 61, 88, 89–90, 94–95, 184–185
Punch, K. 155

race-based epistemology 186
racist epistemology 176, 177, 178
Ralphs, A. 28
Ramanathan, V. 91
Ravelli, L.J. 4
reading 15, 127, 189–190, 203
realist position (social theory) 9
recognition of prior learning *see* RPL
reductive risk 11–12, 13, 123, 237–238
refereeing (research article) 67–68, 76–77, 97 n5
  author's responses 74–75, 76, 82, 85–86, 89, 92–93
  reviewers' comments 72–74, 79, 83–84
referencing 120, 159, 160, 183, 191
Reiff, M.J. 150
research article (case study)
  author's voice 66, 75, 80, 83, 88
  mentoring 62, 63–64, 84, 87, 93, 95
  narrative form 65, 69–71, 79, 80–81
  supervisory feedback 66, 67, 82
  see also refereeing
research-article genre 59
  conventions 60, 65, 88, 90
  publishing 61, 89–90, 94–95
  see also hybrid discourses
research identity 4, 133, 139, 151, 153
  of international students 116, 121, 124, 125, 126
research methodology
  African 186
  indigenous 186
  northern 187–188
  southern 188–189, 190–191
research proposals
  case studies 154–155, 156–163
  gatekeeping function 12, 155–156, 157, 163
  value of hybridity 149, 152–153
Rigney, L.I. 176, 177, 186
risk 15–16, 249
  in actor network theory 219, 223, 224, 225, 227, 231, 233

in contact zone 96, 245, 247
in hybrid discourses 91–92, 96
international students 109, 122–123, 125
novice researchers 92, 93, 95, 123, 169
and other 9, 11, 13, 15, 92
as productive 12, 123, 146, 224, 238, 239
as reductive 11–12, 13, 123, 237–238
social theory perspectives 7, 8–11
risk management 3, 8, 11–12, 113, 238
see also 'at-risk' students
risk-talk 10, 92
Rose, M. 114
Rouhani, S. 111
Rowsell, J. 116
Royal Society 5
RPL 28, 29, 219, 224–233
Rwandan students 101, 105–108, 114, 120–121
see also international students; Mauritian students
Rwomire, A. 12

Santos, B.S. 175, 185, 195 n7
Scheurich, J.J. 172, 176, 178, 189
Schrödinger, E. 245–246, 247, 248
Schroeder, C. 4
scientific knowledge 8, 9, 175
see also academic knowledge
scientific writing 159
Scott, M. 5, 95, 217 n2, 217 n4
Seale, C. 190
self-representation 168, 179, 191, 196 n15
Sengupta, S. 166
Serpell, R. 188
Sheridan, D. 116
Shohat, E. 87
Sitas, A. 177
Smith, L.T. 176, 186
Smitherman, G. 91
social ordering (ANT) 219, 221–223, 224, 231
social theory 7, 8–11, 30, 151
south 2, 151
southern academy 241
knowledge production 186–187, 250
research methodology 188–189, 190–191
writing pedagogy 192–194
see also northern academy
spirituality 187–188
Spivak, G.C. 194 n4
St. Pierre, E. 170
Standard English *see* academic English
Starfield, S. 4
Steinberg, C. 143
Steinhauer, E. 176, 186
student mobility 112, 203–204, 208, 209, 211, 216
students *see* 'at-risk' students; international students; Mauritian students; Rwandan students
supervisor-student relationship 122, 132, 140–141
see also writing specialists
supervisory feedback
adult learner theses 31, 32, 34, 35, 43–44
isiXhosa thesis 50–54
research article 66, 67, 82
research proposal 156–161, 162, 163
Swales, J. 4, 59, 90, 91, 150
Swart, S. 187

Tardy, C.M. 95
Tennenhouse, L. 168
TESOL Quarterly (TQ) 61–62, 68–69, 71, 74, 90, 97 n2
text mobility 4–5, 151, 152
thesis format 55, 192, 196 n16
see also adult learner theses; isiXhosa thesis
'third space' 19, 61, 173, 176, 189
Bhabha 126, 135, 171
Thomson, P. 4, 163
Tikley, L. 175, 186
Todd, L. 112
trace archive 14, 17, 44, 45, 49
translation (ANT) 222–223, 224, 225, 231, 232, 233 n2
triangulation 181

ubuntu 186–187, 188, 195 n12
UCT 117
internationalisation policy 104, 110, 112
RPL policy 219, 224–233

Umulliko 176
universities
  citation counts 8, 12, 137
  ethics approval 12, 155, 157
  risk management 8, 11–12, 113, 238
  see also UCT; Wits University
Usher, R. 2

Van Marle, K. 187, 188
Vassanji, M.G. 246, 247
ventriloquation 41, 46 n9
Vera-Sanso, P. 10
Vithal, R. 155
voice 3, 15, 21 n1, 238–239
  as dialogue 6, 123–124, 151
  in experiential knowledge 28, 32, 41–45
  in hybrid discourses 80, 89, 91, 152–153, 190
  impact of genre 148–149, 151
  and linguistic resources 152, 159–160
  of novice researchers 62, 63, 89, 94
  see also deletions
Vygotsky, L. 30, 36, 49

Walwicz, A. 166, 168, 192
Warrior, R. 176, 177
Wei, Z. 63
Wenger, E. 126
Wertch, J.V. 42, 152
Wickham, G. 222, 224
Wilkinson, I. 91, 92

Williams, B.T. 61
Williams, G. 150
Williams, R. 170–171, 215
Wilson, A.C. 177
Wilson, S. 187
Wimsatt, W.K. 127
Wits University 112, 114, 117
writer's block 135, 142
writers' circles 6–7, 134–137, 146 n3
  emotional spaces 141–143
  facilitators 136, 137, 139–141, 143–144, 146
  as rehearsal space 131, 132, 145–146
writing *see* academic writing; ghost texts; hybrid discourses
writing courses/workshops 104–105, 121, 132, 204–205
writing groups 133–134
writing pedagogy 3, 133–134, 192–194, 215–216
writing specialists 152–153, 179
  in student-supervisor relationship 149, 150, 156, 157, 164

Xhosa thesis *see* isiXhosa thesis

Young, M. 22 n1, 29
Young, M.D. 176, 189

Zamel, V. 60, 114
Zhou, Y. 195 n14
Zinn, J.O. 8, 10

For Product Safety Concerns and Information please contact our EU Authorised Representative:

Easy Access System Europe

Mustamäe tee 50

10621 Tallinn

Estonia

gpsr.requests@easproject.com

www.ingramcontent.com/pod-product-compliance
Lightning Source LLC
Chambersburg PA
CBHW070557300426
44113CB00010B/1288